Blackstone's
Police Q&A

Crime
2023

Twenty-first edition

Paul Connor

UNIVERSITY PRESS

Great Clarendon Street, Oxford, OX2 6DP,
United Kingdom

Oxford University Press is a department of the University of Oxford.
It furthers the University's objective of excellence in research, scholarship,
and education by publishing worldwide. Oxford is a registered trade mark of
Oxford University Press in the UK and in certain other countries

First published in 2022

Public sector information reproduced under Open Government Licence v3.0
(http://www.nationalarchives.gov.uk/doc/open-government-licence/open-government-licence.htm)

Published in the United States of America by Oxford University Press
198 Madison Avenue, New York, NY 10016, United States of America

British Library Cataloguing in Publication Data
Data available

ISBN 978–0–19–286996–8

DOI: 10.1093/law/9780192869968.001.0001

Printed and bound by
CPI Group (UK) Ltd, Croydon, CR0 4YY

Contents

Introduction

There are several purposes for which multiple-choice questions (MCQs) are very useful. The first is in producing a reliable, valid and fair test of knowledge and understanding across a wide range of subject matter. Another is an aid to study, preparation and revision for such examinations and tests. The differences in objective mean that there are differences in the approach that MCQ writers take to creating MCQs. Whereas the design of fully validated MCQs to be used in high-stakes examinations which will effectively determine who passes and who fails has very strict guidelines as to construction, content and style, less stringent rules may be applied to MCQs that are being used for study and revision. For that reason, there may be MCQs that are appropriate in the latter setting which would not be used in the former. In developing the MCQs for this book, the fundamental rules of MCQ design have been followed but the MCQs do not (indeed, they cannot) mirror the level of psychometric rigour that is—and has to be—adopted by the type of examining bodies referred to previously.

These MCQs are designed to reinforce your knowledge and understanding, to highlight any gaps or weaknesses in that knowledge and understanding; and to help focus your revision of the relevant topics.

Good luck!

Blackstone's Police Q&As—Special Features

References to Blackstone's Police Manuals

Every answer is followed by a paragraph reference to Blackstone's Police Manuals. This means that once you have attempted a question and looked at an answer, the Manual can immediately be referred to for help and clarification.

Unique numbers for each question

Each question and answer has the same unique number. This should ensure that there is no confusion as to which question is linked to which answer. For example, Question 2.1 is linked to Answer 2.1.

Checklists

The checklists are designed to help you keep track of your progress when answering the multiple-choice questions. If you fill in the checklist after attempting a question, you will be able to check how many you got right on the first attempt and will know immediately which questions need to be revisited a second time. Please visit www. blackstonespoliceservice.com and click through to the Blackstone's Police Q&As 2023 page. You will then find electronic versions of the checklists to download and print out. Email any queries or comments on the book to: police@oup.com.

Acknowledgements

The publisher and the author wish to thank Huw Smart and John Watson for their contributions to previous editions of this book.

1 | *Mens Rea* (State of Mind)

QUESTIONS

Question 1.1

PC DUXFORD is concerned about the issues regarding intoxication and how this might impact on her investigation of offences and questions she asks in any subsequent interviews. She approaches her supervisor, PS GILLINGHAM, and asks for some advice on the matter.

In relation to the issues surrounding intoxication, which of the comments below would represent the correct advice to give to PC DUXFORD by PS GILLINGHAM?

A Voluntary intoxication can be raised in answer to a charge of an offence of specific intent but not basic intent; involuntary intoxication can be raised in answer to a charge of both specific and basic intent.

B Voluntary intoxication can be raised in answer to a charge of an offence of basic intent but not specific intent; involuntary intoxication can be raised in answer to a charge of both specific and basic intent.

C Voluntary intoxication can be raised in answer to a charge of an offence of specific intent but not basic intent; involuntary intoxication can be raised in answer to a charge of basic intent but not specific intent.

D Voluntary intoxication can be raised in answer to a charge of an offence of both specific and basic intent; involuntary intoxication can be raised in answer to a charge of specific intent but not basic intent.

Question 1.2

PARKER was responsible for and supervising a group of children during a school trip which involved canoeing activities on a river. One of the children drowned and PARKER is being interviewed regarding the incident. It has been suggested that

PARKER could potentially be held responsible for the death of the child and convicted of an offence of manslaughter by gross negligence.

Which of the following comments is correct in relation to the 'negligence' element of this offence?

A PARKER would have to be shown to have acted recklessly in order to establish negligence.

B PARKER would have to be shown to realise that his behaviour was not that of a responsible person.

C PARKER would have to be shown to be at fault or to blame for the death of the child and to have acted in a way that runs contrary to the expectations of the reasonable person.

D PARKER would have to be shown to have brought about the death of the child unintentionally but in a way that could be described as careless or dangerous by an ordinary person.

Question 1.3

PC BOX has arrested FULLER for an offence of handling stolen goods (contrary to s. 22 of the Theft Act 1968). The officer is preparing to interview FULLER regarding the offence and is considering her questions regarding the 'points to prove' to establish if FULLER has committed the offence—this includes the term 'knowing'.

Which of the following would amount to 'knowing' goods were stolen?

A One knows something is stolen only if one is absolutely sure that it is so.

B One knows something is stolen if one is absolutely sure that it is so or feels virtually certain it is.

C One knows something is stolen if one is absolutely sure that it is so or almost certain it is.

D One knows something is stolen if one is absolutely sure that it is so or convinced it is.

Question 1.4

MANNIGER has been arrested on suspicion of committing criminal damage (contrary to s. 1(1) of the Criminal Damage Act 1971). It is alleged that MANNIGER threw a stone at a greenhouse and the stone smashed one of the windows causing £200 worth of damage. PC DUFFY is the officer in the case and is considering what questions to ask in interview to establish if MANNIGER was 'reckless' regarding the damage.

What will PC DUFFY have to establish to show that MANNIGER was 'reckless'?

A That he foresaw the consequences of his actions as being possible or probable but nevertheless went on to take the risk.

B That he ought to have foreseen a risk prior to going on to take it.

C That he took a risk the consequences of which would have been obvious to any reasonable bystander.

D That he took a risk that a person with the same characteristics as MANNIGER would have realised was unreasonable to take in the circumstances.

Question 1.5

AZIZ has a grudge against SMITH (his neighbour) and intends seeking revenge against him. He intends to frighten SMITH and pours paraffin through his letter box and sets fire to it; he is aware that the house is occupied at the time he does this. The blaze he starts spreads and a child in the house dies from smoke inhalation caused by the fire. AZIZ has been charged with an offence of manslaughter by unlawful act and is being tried in Crown Court regarding the offence.

Considering the law regarding the concept of 'intention', which of the following is correct?

A As it was a natural and probable consequence that a person could be killed by the behaviour, the court may infer that AZIZ intended the death of the child.

B The court, i.e. the jury, should consider whether a reasonable person would have foreseen the consequences of AZIZ's actions—if that 'reasonable person' would have done so, they may infer that AZIZ intended the consequences.

C Whether or not a defendant intended a particular consequence will be a question of law to be decided, in this case, by a judge.

D If AZIZ foresaw the probability of the death of a person then that can be put before the jury and they may infer an intention from it (the foresight).

Question 1.6

CRANSHAW and GUBBIN work for a large insurance company. CRANSHAW supervises GUBBIN but the two do not get on at all, resulting in several heated disagreements. GUBBIN wants to punish CRANSHAW and knows that CRANSHAW has her lunch in a nearby pub each day. He has a chat with POLLOCK (his friend) and encourages

1. *Mens Rea* (State of Mind)

POLLOCK to assault CRANSHAW in the pub as a favour to him. POLLOCK agrees and GUBBIN provides a description of CRANSHAW to POLLOCK. POLLOCK goes into the pub, sees CRANSHAW and punches her in the face causing her injury. POLLOCK aims another punch at CRANSHAW who ducks out of the way causing POLLOCK to strike and injure BUTTON who is an innocent bystander. On his way out of the pub, POLLOCK sees EDGE who he has had personal disagreements with and he attacks EDGE causing EDGE serious injury.

Considering the liability of GUBBIN and the doctrine of transferred *mens rea*, which of the following comments is correct?

A GUBBIN would be liable for the assault injuries to CRANSHAW alone.

B GUBBIN would be liable for the assault injuries to CRANSHAW and BUTTON but not for the assault injuries sustained by EDGE.

C GUBBIN would be liable for the assault injuries to CRANSHAW and EDGE but not for the assault injuries sustained by BUTTON.

D GUBBIN would be liable for the assault injuries sustained by CRANSHAW, BUTTON and EDGE.

ANSWERS

Answer 1.1

Answer **A** — There is no general defence of intoxication. If there were, a high proportion of criminal behaviour would clearly go unpunished. What intoxication does is to potentially remove the necessary *mens rea* required for a defendant to commit an offence. Intoxication can be divided into two categories: voluntary intoxication (you got yourself in that condition) and involuntary intoxication (you are not responsible for getting in that condition). The distinction between the two types of intoxication is important when considering whether the offence the defendant is alleged to have committed is one of 'specific' or 'basic' intent.

Where an offence is a specific intent offence, e.g. murder or theft, a defendant who was voluntarily intoxicated at the time the offence was committed may be able to show that he/she was so intoxicated that he/she was incapable of forming the *mens rea* required for the offence. An individual who is voluntarily intoxicated *would not* be able to say this if accused of an offence of basic intent as the courts have accepted that a defendant is still capable of forming basic intent even when completely inebriated (*DPP* v *Majewski* [1977] AC 443).

Where the offence is a basic intent offence, e.g. a s. 47 assault, a defendant who was involuntarily intoxicated (perhaps because his/her drink had been spiked) at the time the offence was committed may be able to say that he/she lacked the *mens rea* for that basic intent offence.

Therefore, voluntary intoxication can be raised in answer to a charge of an offence of specific intent but not basic intent; involuntary intoxication can be raised in answer to a charge of both specific and basic intent. You might have to look at the answers carefully, but this is option A; answers B, C and D are therefore incorrect.

Crime, paras 1.1.2.1 to 1.1.2.2

Answer 1.2

Answer **C** — Negligence is generally concerned with the defendant's compliance with the standards of reasonableness of ordinary people. The concept of negligence focuses on the consequences of the defendant's conduct rather than demanding proof of a particular state of mind at the time and ascribes some notion of 'fault' or 'blame' to the defendant who must be shown to have acted in a way that runs contrary to the expectations of the reasonable person (correct answer C). There is no 'subjective' element associated with negligence (ruling out answers A and B). There

5

is no requirement, in order to establish 'negligence', that the defendant has behaved unintentionally but in a way that could be described as careless or dangerous by an ordinary person (answer D is incorrect).

Crime, para. 1.1.9

Answer 1.3

Answer **B** — The term 'knowing' is relevant to several offences such as s. 22 of the Theft Act 1968 (handling stolen goods).

One knows something if one is absolutely sure that it is so.

Since it is difficult to be absolutely sure of anything, it has to be accepted that a person who feels 'virtually certain' about something can equally be regarded as 'knowing' it (see *R* v *Dunne* (1998) 162 JP 399); the term is virtually certain, answers A, C and D are therefore incorrect.

Crime, para. 1.1.7

Answer 1.4

Answer **A** — Recklessness has been set out by the courts in *R* v *G and R* [2003] UKHL 50: the approach taken to the interpretation of the word 'reckless' is that it will be 'subjective'.

The requirements of subjective recklessness can be found in the case of *R* v *Cunningham* [1957] 2 QB 396 and are satisfied in situations where the defendant foresees the consequences of his/her actions as being probable or even possible. The fact that the consequences ought to have been foreseen by the defendant will not be enough so answer B is incorrect. As recklessness is subjective, what would be obvious to a reasonable bystander or a person with the same characteristics as MANNIGER would be immaterial (answers C and D are incorrect).

Crime, para. 1.1.3

Answer 1.5

Answer **D** — Section 8 of the Criminal Justice Act 1967 states:

A court or jury, in determining whether a person has committed an offence,—
(a) shall not be bound in law to infer that he intended or foresaw a result of his actions by reason only of its being a natural and probable consequence of those actions; but

(b) shall decide whether he did intend or foresee that result by reference to all the evidence, drawing such inferences from the evidence as appear proper in the circumstances.

The fact that the result was a natural and probable consequence is, by itself, not enough to infer intent (making answer A incorrect). There is a body of case law around the area of 'probability', culminating in two cases in the House of Lords (*R v Moloney* [1985] AC 905 and *R v Hancock* [1986] AC 455). Following those cases, it is settled that foresight of the probability of a consequence does not amount to an intention to bring that consequence about, *but may be evidence of it*. So you cannot claim that a defendant *intended* a consequence of his/her behaviour simply because it was virtually certain to occur. What you can do is to put evidence of the defendant's foresight of that probability before a court, which may infer an intention from it (correct answer D). Answer B suggests that this involves a 'reasonable person' rather than the defendant—this is incorrect. Answer C is incorrect as whether or not a defendant intended a particular consequence will be a question of fact left to the jury (or magistrate(s) where appropriate).

Crime, para. 1.1.2

Answer 1.6

Answer **B** — The issue of transferred *mens rea* can be important in relation to the liability of accessories (in this question POLLOCK is the principal and GUBBIN is the accessory (by counselling the assault)). If POLLOCK's intentions are to be extended to GUBBIN, it must be shown that those intentions were either contemplated and accepted by GUBBIN at the time of the offence, or that they were 'transferred'. There is an excellent example of this in the *Investigators' Manual* which follows the story-line of this question.

Example

A person (X) encourages another (Y) to assault Z. Y decides to attack a different person instead. X will not be liable for that assault because it was not contemplated or agreed by X. If, however, in trying to assault Z, Y happens to injure a third person inadvertently, then 'transferred *mens rea*' would result in X being liable for those injuries even though X had no wish for that person to be so injured.

So GUBBIN would not be liable for the assault injuries to EDGE (making answers C and D incorrect). GUBBIN would be liable for the assault injuries to CRANSHAW and BUTTON (correct answer B) making answer A incorrect.

Crime, para. 1.1.11

2 *Actus Reus* (Criminal Conduct)

QUESTIONS

Question 2.1

WEST worked for a major retail company on the night shift. The company has a variety of unisex facilities in one of their buildings including changing and toilet facilities. One evening, the night shift manager walks in on WEST whilst she is using the unisex facilities and changing and is standing in her underwear. The manager walks over to her and takes his penis out, inviting WEST to put it in her mouth, he then grabs her bra strap. The manager is charged with sexual touching (contrary to s. 3 of the Sexual Offences Act 2003).

What, if any, is the company's corporate liability in relation to the activity of its manager?

A It would be liable as a principal offender as WEST is effectively its representative on night shift.

B It would be liable as a principal offender as the company introduced unisex facilities, thus increasing the risk of this type of activity.

C It would not be liable at all for the actions of its employee in these circumstances as this offence is triable either way (rather than summary only).

D It could be liable as an accessory for aiding and abetting the activity should relevant evidence exist.

Question 2.2

OWEN is a hitchhiker who has been picked up by FITCHET who is driving his car along a busy dual carriageway. During the course of the journey, FITCHET makes several sexual comments towards OWEN who becomes very uneasy about FITCHET and asks to be let out of the car. At this, FITCHET grabs hold of OWEN's right breast and shouts that he is going to rape her. OWEN is petrified and, to escape the attack, she opens the door of the car (which is travelling at approximately 50 mph) and jumps out into the road. OWEN hits the surface of the road and breaks both of her legs.

Would FITCHET be liable for the serious injury to OWEN?

A No, as OWEN's actions in jumping out of the car would be considered to be an intervening act.

B Yes, as the response of a victim can never amount to an intervening act.

C No, because OWEN made the choice to jump out of the car entirely of her own volition.

D Yes, as the actions of OWEN are those which might be reasonably expected from any victim in such a situation.

Question 2.3

DAY and his girlfriend agreed to take care of his sister who had been diagnosed with anorexia. The sister was initially able to look after herself; gradually, however, her condition deteriorated until she became bedridden. She needed medical help but none was summoned and she eventually died in squalor, covered in bed sores and filth. DAY and his girlfriend were jointly charged with manslaughter due to their failure to act to prevent the sister's death.

Which of the following is correct?

A Only DAY will be guilty (it was his sister who died and a duty of care can only exist between blood relatives).

B Both will be guilty; they both assumed a duty of responsibility and had failed to carry out that duty.

C Neither will be guilty as at the time they assumed responsibility the sister was able to look after herself.

D Neither will be guilty as the disease she was suffering from was self-induced.

Question 2.4

MULLER intends to commit a burglary at a local electrical goods shop. He does not have much in the way of experience as a burglar so telephones BERGSTROM (who MULLER was told was an expert burglar) and asks for his advice about how he should carry out the burglary. BERGSTROM tells MULLER to commit the offence at 4 am and provides MULLER with precise information about how to disable the alarm system in the shop. MULLER listens to the advice and does exactly as BERGSTROM told him. After disabling the shop alarm system, he breaks in at 4 am and steals a large quantity of high-value electrical goods.

Is BERGSTROM liable as an accessory to the burglary carried out by MULLER?

A No, as BERGSTROM was not physically present at the scene when the burglary took place.

B Yes, BERGSTROM has aided the commission of the burglary offence.

C No, as BERGSTROM was approached for advice by MULLER rather than inciting or encouraging MULLER to commit the offence.

D Yes, BERGSTROM has counselled the burglary offence.

Question 2.5

TIMKINS wishes to take revenge on someone who owes him a lot of money but will not pay it back. He approaches HURLEY who he knows supplies imitation firearms and asks for a handgun. HURLEY supplies what he believes to be an inactive weapon that has had the firing mechanism removed. TIMKINS approaches the male who owes him money, his intention is to put the gun to his head and pull the trigger believing it will not go off; however, HURLEY has given him a 'live' gun by mistake and TIMKINS fatally wounds the man who owed him money. HURLEY is later charged with an offence of murder.

Is HURLEY an accessory to the offence of murder?

A No, he did not intend to help TIMKINS commit a murder.

B No, as he only intended to supply an imitation firearm.

C Yes, he is reckless when he supplies a 'live' weapon, even by accident.

D Yes, he is an accessory as he knowingly supplied the weapon, whatever the circumstances of the death.

Question 2.6

RODDICK commits an armed robbery and is pursued by armed police officers. RODDICK grabs a woman at a bus stop and uses her as a human shield and starts shooting at the police officers; they return fire and accidentally kill the woman RODDICK was using as a human shield. RODDICK is unhurt, but as he has used all his ammunition he surrenders to the officers. He is charged with manslaughter of the woman he used as a human shield.

Considering the issues in relation to 'intervening acts', which of the following is correct?

A RODDICK cannot be guilty of manslaughter as the officers' actions in returning fire were 'voluntary' therefore an intervening act.

B RODDICK cannot be guilty of manslaughter as the officers' actions in returning fire were 'deliberate' therefore an intervening act.

C RODDICK will be guilty of manslaughter as the woman's death was a natural and foreseeable result of his behaviour.

D RODDICK will be guilty of manslaughter but only if the officers' actions in returning fire were reasonable.

Question 2.7

DONOVAN is part of a gang that always carry weapons. Some of the gang are together one night when they are attacked by a rival gang. During the fight, one of the rival gang is stabbed and dies. DONOVAN did not have a knife himself that night and did not inflict the fatal wound nor does he know who did, although he knows that his gang friends regularly carry knives and often used them in fights.

Is DONOVAN guilty of murder as part of a joint enterprise?

A Yes, as he is aware that his friends often carry knives.

B Yes, as he is aware that his friends often carry knives and may use them.

C No, as DONOVAN himself did not have a knife that night.

D No, as there was not an agreement prior to the incident that a knife might be used.

Question 2.8

CONDRON was walking through the park one day when he saw two males involved in a bare-knuckle fight. As a boxing fan, he recognises that these are two trained boxers and he thinks it is a good fight. Indeed, he encourages one male more than the other. The male he was encouraging then punches the other breaking his jaw; at this point, the police arrive and arrests are made.

Which of the following is correct in relation to CONDRON's liability as an accessory to the assault (the broken jaw)?

A He will be liable as he encourages the male who commits the assault.

B He will be liable as he did nothing to prevent the assault taking place.

C He will not be liable as mere words of encouragement are not enough to be an accessory.

D He would not be guilty unless the fighters state that his actions encouraged them to fight.

Question 2.9

TALLOW is a drug dealer and regularly supplies DONALDSON with heroin. TALLOW visits DONALDSON at her home address and sells her £200 worth of heroin before leaving. Several hours after TALLOW has left, DONALDSON prepares the heroin for injection, applies a tourniquet to her arm and injects all of the heroin. She dies several minutes later of an overdose.

With regard to the chain of causation and intervening acts, which of the following comments is correct?

A TALLOW supplied DONALDSON with the heroin and is therefore the direct cause of her death and would be liable for her murder.

B DONALDSON exercised her free will and brought about her own death by injecting the heroin; TALLOW is not liable for her death.

C Although TALLOW is not the direct cause of DONALDSON's death, the fact that he supplied her with the heroin makes him guilty of her manslaughter.

D Even if TALLOW actually prepared the heroin and injected DONALDSON with it, bringing about her death, he would not commit an offence.

Question 2.10

GOLD stabs KHAN in the leg, almost severing the femoral artery. KHAN is rushed to hospital and his life can be saved by blood transfusion. KHAN refuses as he is paranoid that the blood he will be given will contain the HIV virus. This is an unreasonable belief due to the screening process transfusion blood has to go through. In fact, KHAN does not die of blood loss as the hospital staff work a small miracle without giving him a blood transfusion; however, he contracts multiple antibiotic-resistant staphylococcus aureus (MRSA) and dies as a result of that disease.

How culpable is GOLD for the death of KHAN?

A He is fully culpable as the stab wound was the first injury KHAN received.

B He is partly culpable as the stab wound was not the primary cause of death.

C He is not culpable at all as KHAN's blood loss did not cause his death.

D He is not culpable at all as there were two new intervening acts between his actions and KHAN's death.

Question 2.11

GUNNERSON is homeless and enters a shop during opening hours and hides in the storeroom as it has been below freezing all week at night. During the night, the heating is off in the storeroom. Being a former electrician, GUNNERSON rigs the heating system; however, in doing so he leaves several live wires bare. In the morning, he leaves the storeroom in the condition he made it. Later that day, an assistant electrocutes herself on a wire that GUNNERSON had made bare and is injured as a result.

Is GUNNERSON liable by omission for the assistant's injuries?

A Yes, as he was under an obligation to avert the danger he had caused.

B Yes, as he took it upon himself to assume responsibility for the electrical system in the storeroom.

C No, he was not under any statutory obligation to intervene before the assistant was injured.

D No, there was no proximity between him and the assistant at the time she was injured.

Question 2.12

McGHEE was a heavy cannabis user and, whilst under the influence of cannabis, he entered his neighbour's house and stabbed her causing grievous bodily harm. He is charged with the offence and wishes to use automatism as a 'defence', stating that he regularly blacked out after using cannabis.

In relation to this defence, which of the following is correct?

A The question is not whether the accused is acting intentionally or not but whether there is a complete destruction of control.

B The question is not whether the accused is acting intentionally or not but whether there is a complete destruction of voluntary control.

C The question is not whether the accused is acting consciously or not but whether there is a complete destruction of control.

D The question is not whether the accused is acting consciously or not but whether there is a complete destruction of voluntary control.

ANSWERS

Answer 2.1

Answer **D** — This question addresses the issues of corporate liability. Companies have been successfully prosecuted for offences involving strict liability (*Alphacell Ltd* v *Woodward* [1972] AC 824) as well as offences which require *mens rea* (*Tesco Supermarkets Ltd* v *Nattrass* [1972] AC 153).

Liability is not limited to summary offences and companies can be liable for the actions of some of their employees as accessories under certain circumstances (*R* v *Robert Millar (Contractors) Ltd* [1970] 2 QB 54), making answer C incorrect.

Clearly, there are some offences that would be conceptually impossible for a legal corporation to commit (e.g. some sexual offences) but, given that companies can be guilty as accessories, they may well be capable of aiding and abetting such offences even though they could not commit the offence as a principal; answers A and B are therefore incorrect.

Crime, para. 1.2.9

Answer 2.2

Answer **D** — Actions by the victim will sometimes be significant in the chain of causation such as where a victim of a sexual assault was injured when jumping from her assailant's car (*R* v *Roberts* (1971) 56 Cr App R 95). Where such actions take place, the victim's behaviour *will not be regarded as introducing a new intervening act* (making answer A incorrect). If the victim's actions are those which might reasonably be anticipated from any victim in such a situation, there will be no new and intervening act and the defendant will be responsible for the consequences flowing from them (correct answer D). The chain of causation can be broken if the victim's actions are done entirely of his/her own volition but, whilst OWEN made the choice to jump out of the car, this was not a choice she made without cause—she did it to escape being raped by FITCHET and that is not an action born out of a free and informed choice to behave in that way, making answer C incorrect. Answer B is incorrect as where the actions of a victim are done entirely of his/her own volition or those actions are, in the words of Stuart-Smith LJ, 'daft' (*R* v *Williams* [1992] 1 WLR 380), they will amount to a new intervening act and the defendant cannot be held responsible for them.

Crime, para. 1.2.7

Answer 2.3

Answer **B** — Criminal conduct is most often associated with actions: damaging or stealing property, injuring or deceiving others, but occasionally liability is brought about by a failure to act.

Most of the occasions where failure or omission will attract liability are where a duty to act has been created. Such a duty can arise from a number of circumstances, a summary of the main ones being:

D Dangerous situation created by the defendant. For example, in *R* v *Miller* [1983] 2 AC 161 the defendant was 'sleeping rough' and entered a building and fell asleep on a mattress while smoking a cigarette. When he awoke, he saw the mattress was smouldering but instead of calling for help or doing anything about the smouldering mattress, he simply moved into another room in the building and fell asleep. The mattress caught fire and the fire spread to the rest of the building. The defendant was convicted of arson, not for starting the fire but for failing to do anything about it.

U Under statute, contract or a person's public 'office'. Examples would include:
  - Statute—a driver who is involved in a damage or injury accident fails to stop at the scene of the accident (s. 170 of the Road Traffic Act 1988), a driver who fails to cooperate with a preliminary test procedure (s. 6(6) of the Road Traffic Act 1988) or a person who does not disclose information in relation to terrorism (s. 19 of the Terrorism Act 2000).
  - Contract—a crossing keeper omitted to close the gates (a job that was part of his contractual obligations) at a level crossing and a person was subsequently killed by a passing train (*R* v *Pittwood* (1902) 19 TLR 37).
  - Public office—whilst on duty, a police officer stood aside and watched as a man was beaten to death outside a nightclub. The officer then left the scene without calling for assistance or summoning an ambulance. For this, the officer was convicted of the common law offence of misconduct in a public office (*R* v *Dytham* [1979] QB 722).

T Taken it upon him/herself—the defendant voluntarily undertakes to care for another who is unable to care for him/herself as a result of age, illness or infirmity and then fails to care for that person. For example, in *R* v *Stone* [1977] QB 354 the defendant accepted a duty to care for her partner's mentally ill sister who subsequently died from neglect.

Y Young person—in circumstances where the defendant is in a parental relationship with a child or a young person, i.e. an obligation exists for the parent to look after the health and welfare of the child and he/she does not do so.

In this scenario, both DAY and his girlfriend had taken his sister into their home, they had assumed a duty of care for her and had been grossly negligent in the performance of that duty. The fact that she was DAY's sister was merely incidental to this; answer A is therefore incorrect. The actual reason why the person needed care is irrelevant, it is the duty imposed that is important, and the condition of the person when they first assume that duty is also of no relevance; answers C and D are therefore incorrect.

Crime, para. 1.2.5

Answer 2.4

Answer **D** — An accessory does not have to be physically present at the scene of an offence to be liable for it. This is the case when you consider the activities of a person who aids or abets an offence but not when a person counsels or procures an offence (making answer A incorrect). Being an accessory can take many forms and, whilst inciting, encouraging or instigating an offence is 'abetting', a person can aid, counsel or procure an offence as an accessory—this involves a number of other activities and makes answer C incorrect. To 'aid' an offence requires the presence of the accessory at the scene of the offence, making answer B incorrect. Answer D is correct as BERGSTROM has advised MULLER about how to commit the burglary offence.

Crime, paras 1.2.8, 1.2.8.1

Answer 2.5

Answer **A** — Generally, the state of mind (*mens rea*) which is needed to convict an accessory is: 'proof of intention to aid as well as of knowledge of the circumstances' (*National Coal Board* v *Gamble* [1959] 1 QB 11 at p. 20). The minimum state of mind required of an accessory to an offence is set out in *Johnson* v *Youden* [1950] 1 KB 544. In that case, the court held that before anyone can be convicted of aiding and abetting an offence, he/she must at least know the essential matters that constitute that offence.

There must also be a further mental element, namely an intention to aid the principal. Whether there was such an intention to aid the principal is a question of fact to be decided in the particular circumstances of each case.

Although HURLEY knowingly supplied a weapon, he does not fit the criteria of:

- intention to aid;
- knowledge of the circumstances;

as they relate to the death; therefore he cannot have aided and abetted it as he did not envisage a death occurring; answers B, C and D are therefore incorrect.

Crime, para. 1.2.8.1

Answer 2.6

Answer **C** — A defendant will not be regarded as having caused the consequence for which he/she stands accused if there was a new intervening act sufficient to break the chain of causation between his/her original action and the consequence in question, in this case the death of the woman. The causal link can be broken by a new intervening act provided that the 'new' act is 'free, deliberate and informed' (*R v Latif* [1996] 1 WLR 104). Were the officers' actions 'free, deliberate and informed'? For that to be the case, the officers would have had to have shot the woman deliberately and not whilst trying to take reasonable measures for self-preservation and in the performance of their legal duty to apprehend RODDICK; answers A and B are therefore incorrect.

Even if the police officers were at fault, their conduct was not free, deliberate and informed. RODDICK created a situation in which the woman's life was inevitably endangered, and what happened was a natural and foreseeable consequence of that behaviour; answer D is therefore incorrect.

Crime, para. 1.2.7

Answer 2.7

Answer **B** — The main features that will determine DONOVAN's liability as an accessory in a joint enterprise will be:

- the nature and extent of the agreed offence;
- whether the accessory knew the principal had a knife;
- whether a different knife was used;
- whether the knife was used differently than agreed.

The House of Lords has held that where one party (D) to a joint enterprise to commit an offence foresees as a real possibility that another party (E) may, in the course of it, do an act, with the requisite *mens rea*, constituting another offence (and E does so), D is liable for that offence. This is the case even if D has not expressly or tacitly agreed to that offence, and even though he expressly forbids it.

DONOVAN is aware that knives are being carried *and* that they may be used; answer A is therefore incorrect. That makes him an accessory even though there was no agreement and he did not agree to a knife being used; answers C and D are therefore incorrect.

Crime, para. 1.2.8.2

Answer 2.8

Answer **D** — There are two ways of attracting criminal liability for an offence: either as a principal or an accessory.

A principal offender is one whose conduct has met all the requirements of the particular offence. An accessory is someone who helped in or brought about the commission of the offence. If an accessory 'aids, abets, counsels or procures' the commission of an offence, he/she will be treated by a court in the same way as a principal offender for an indictable offence (Accessories and Abettors Act 1861, s. 8) or for a summary offence (Magistrates' Courts Act 1980, s. 44). The expression 'aid, abet, counsel and procure' is generally used in its entirety when charging a defendant, without separating out the particular element that applies. Generally speaking, the expressions mean as follows:

- aiding = giving help, support or assistance;
- abetting = inciting, instigating or encouraging.

Each of these would usually involve the presence of the secondary party at the scene (unless, for example, part of some prearranged plan):

- counselling = advising or instructing;
- procuring = bringing about.

These activities would generally be expected to take place before the commission of the offence.

Presence at the scene of a crime can be capable of constituting encouragement if the accused is present in pursuance of a prior agreement with the principal, but if the accused is only accidentally present then he must know that his/her presence is actually encouraging the principals, and they must be so encouraged to carry on; answers A and C are therefore incorrect. However, neither mere presence at the scene of a crime nor a failure to prevent an offence will generally give rise to liability (*R v Coney* (1882) 8 QBD 534); answer B is therefore incorrect.

Crime, para. 1.2.8

Answer 2.9

Answer **B** — If a drug dealer supplies drugs to another person who then kills him/herself by overdose, the dealer cannot, without more, be said to have caused the death. Death would have been brought about by the deliberate exercise of free will by the user, making answers A and C incorrect. Answer D is incorrect as the Court of Appeal has accepted that, under certain circumstances, where a person buys a controlled drug from another and immediately injects it, resulting in his/her death, the supplier can attract liability for the person's death.

Crime, para. 1.2.7

Answer 2.10

Answer **A** — A defendant will not be regarded as having caused the consequence for which it is sought to make him/her liable if there was a *novus actus interveniens* (or new intervening act) sufficient to break the chain of causation between his/her original action and the consequence in question.

The chain of causation can be broken only where the effect of the intervening act is so overwhelming that any initial injuries are relegated to the status of mere historical background. So what caused KHAN's death? The answer is the stab wound because 'but for' it KHAN would not have been in hospital to contract MRSA. The fact that he did not die of blood loss caused by the wound is irrelevant; answer C is therefore incorrect. No matter how many intervening acts there have been, the chain of causation in this case is unbroken; answer D is therefore incorrect.

GOLD is fully culpable not partly culpable if you apply the 'but for' test; answer B is therefore incorrect.

Crime, paras 1.2.6, 1.2.7

Answer 2.11

Answer **A** — Most criminal offences require the defendant to carry out some positive act before liability can be imposed. There can ordinarily be no liability for failure (or omission) to act, unless the law specifically imposes such a duty upon a particular person. The general rule is illustrated by the example of when A sees B drowning and is able to save him by holding out his hand. A abstains from doing so in order that B may be drowned, and B is drowned. A has committed no offence.

Although A may have failed to save B, he did no positive act to cause B's death.

GUNNERSON certainly committed an act that led to the injuries, but how liable is he? Most of the occasions where failure or omission will attract liability are where a *duty to act* has been created. Such a duty can arise from a number of circumstances. The main ones can be summarised as being:

D Dangerous situation created by the defendant. For example, in *R v Miller* [1983] 2 AC 161 the defendant was 'sleeping rough' and entered a building and fell asleep on a mattress while smoking a cigarette. When he awoke, he saw the mattress was smouldering but instead of calling for help or doing anything about the smouldering mattress, he simply moved into another room in the building and fell asleep. The mattress caught fire and the fire spread to the rest of the building. The defendant was convicted of arson, not for starting the fire but for failing to do anything about it.

U Under statute, contract or a person's public 'office'. Examples would include:
   * Statute—a driver who is involved in a damage or injury accident fails to stop at the scene of the accident (s. 170 of the Road Traffic Act 1988), a driver who fails to cooperate with a preliminary test procedure (s. 6(6) of the Road Traffic Act 1988) or a person who does not disclose information in relation to terrorism (s. 19 of the Terrorism Act 2000).
   * Contract—a crossing keeper omitted to close the gates (a job that was part of his contractual obligations) at a level crossing and a person was subsequently killed by a passing train (*R v Pittwood* (1902) 19 TLR 37).
   * Public office—whilst on duty, a police officer stood aside and watched as a man was beaten to death outside a nightclub. The officer then left the scene, without calling for assistance or summoning an ambulance. For this, the officer was convicted of the common law offence of misconduct in a public office (*R v Dytham* [1979] QB 722).

T Taken it upon him/herself—the defendant voluntarily undertakes to care for another who is unable to care for him/herself as a result of age, illness or infirmity and then fails to care for that person. For example, in *R v Stone* [1977] QB 354 the defendant accepted a duty to care for her partner's mentally ill sister who subsequently died from neglect.

Y Young person—in circumstances where the defendant is in a parental relationship with a child or a young person, i.e. an obligation exists for the parent to look after the health and welfare of the child and he/she does not do so.

One of those occasions is the duty to avert a danger of one's own making. If a person creates a dangerous situation through his/her own fault, he/she may be under a duty to take reasonable steps to avert that danger, and may therefore incur criminal liability for failing to do so.

GUNNERSON had not 'assumed' responsibility for the electrical system, which still remains the shop's responsibility; answer B is therefore incorrect. Although he has no statutory duty, as can be seen the almost moral duty he holds does not release him from his liability; answer C is therefore incorrect. Proximity to the victim may be compelling in a duty to protect someone from danger, but it is not a prerequisite; answer D is therefore incorrect.

Crime, para. 1.2.5

Answer 2.12

Answer **D** — Strictly speaking, automatism is not a 'defence'; it is an absence of a fundamental requirement for any criminal offence, namely the 'criminal conduct' (*actus reus*). Therefore if defendants have total loss of control over their actions, they cannot be held liable for those actions and, provided the loss of control is total, there may be grounds to claim a defence of automatism.

This view was confirmed in *R v Coley* [2013] EWCA Crim 223, where it was said that the question is not whether the accused is acting consciously or not but whether there is a 'complete destruction of voluntary control'. As it is conscious acts and not intention, answers A and B are therefore incorrect. It is voluntary control not control; answer C is therefore incorrect.

Crime, para. 1.2.3

3 | Incomplete Offences

QUESTIONS

Question 3.1

PALMER is a paedophile who wants to carry out a sexual assault against his next-door neighbour's 11-year-old child. He plans to kidnap her when she is playing in a nearby park and take her to his lock-up garage where the assault will be committed. PALMER's problem is that he only has one arm and does not think he will be able to restrain the child. He approaches SCHOLEY (who PALMER thinks would be interested in these types of offence if asked to join in) and asks him to help out in the kidnap and sexual assault. PALMER believes that his request will encourage SCHOLEY to commit the offences and if he says 'Yes' the two men will commit the offences. SCHOLEY is utterly horrified by PALMER's suggestion and refuses to have anything to do with PALMER's plan.

With regard to offences under ss. 44 to 46 of the Serious Crime Act 2007 (encouraging or assisting crime), which of the following comments is correct?

A An offence has not been committed as PALMER's encouragement did not have the effect that he desired (that SCHOLEY would join the venture).

B To prove encouragement, PALMER would need to approach SCHOLEY or another person on a second occasion.

C PALMER has not committed an offence as he would need to intend that his act will encourage or assist the commission of an offence (he only believes that it will).

D PALMER has committed the offence in these circumstances.

Question 3.2

GREAVES and MALK market a device that can be used to falsify readings of gas and electricity meters and they install it in houses of customers. The device itself does not allow the customers to have entirely free gas or electricity; it simply allows them to have more than the meter reads. Neither GREAVES nor MALK install a device in their houses.

Would this constitute an offence of conspiracy to defraud (contrary to common law)?

A Yes, provided there is intent to defraud a victim.

B Yes, provided an offence is committed, intent is irrelevant.

C No, as neither GREAVES nor MALK install a device in their houses.

D No, as there is no attempt to obtain entirely free gas or electricity.

Question 3.3

KHAN is standing in a local election but realises he probably won't have enough votes and is likely to lose. His campaign assistants are AWAD and SHORT. The three decide to rig the election by asking people if they intend to use their postal or proxy vote. If they do not, they offer to collect the postal ballot paperwork for 'official records'. In fact, they used the collected votes to vote for KHAN, who still did not win the election.

Which of the following is correct in relation to the offence of conspiracy to defraud contrary to common law?

A This offence is not committed as no one has lost a 'proprietary right'; they voluntarily handed over their votes.

B This offence is not committed as KHAN did not win the election.

C Only KHAN as he was the beneficiary of the conspiracy.

D All three are guilty of this offence.

Question 3.4

GIVENS and HUNTER set out to put copies of brand new films online for subscribers to view instead of going to the cinema to see the new releases. They do not have a licence from the film companies to do so and the quality of the films is very poor, certainly not worth the money subscribers will pay to view them. They intend to make a profit from showing these films.

In these circumstances, which of the following is correct in relation to an offence under common law of conspiracy to defraud?

A They have committed this offence in relation to the film companies.

B They have committed this offence in relation to the subscribers.

C They have committed this offence in relation to the film companies and the subscribers.
D They have not committed this offence as no one has been deprived of something; the subscribers see the film and the film companies still show it in the cinema.

Question 3.5

PEEBLES has a vendetta against a pub owner who barred him due to rowdy behaviour. He meets with an ex-army colleague and PEEBLES suggests that they seek revenge on the pub owner. PEEBLES encourages his friend to help him set fire to the pub and states that it would be even better if the landlord was inside and died in the fire. The friend does not mind the arson but is against the murder offence and agrees to help only if the landlord is not there at the time; however, he later changes his mind about helping PEEBLES and reports the conversation to the police.

In relation to s. 46 of the Serious Crime Act 2007 (encouraging or assisting offences believing one or more will be committed) with regard to the murder offence, what are the implications of PEEBLES's actions?

A PEEBLES would commit this offence if it could be proved that he believes at the time that a homicide offence will be committed.
B PEEBLES would commit this offence if it could be proved that he believes at the time that an offence would be committed, no belief needed as to which offence.
C PEEBLES would only commit this offence in relation to the arson as that is all his friend agreed to.
D PEEBLES would not commit this offence as his friend did not actually commit any offence that he was encouraged to do by PEEBLES.

Question 3.6

WAREHAM is aware that his friend HEWISH is planning to carry out a burglary on a bank and wants to help if he can. WAREHAM's wife works at the bank and tells WAREHAM that the alarm will be off from 4 am until 5 am for essential maintenance; she is aware of the plan but doesn't believe that anybody would be stupid enough to try to break into a bank. WAREHAM tells HEWISH about the alarm and he breaks into the bank, although he is arrested on the way out having been captured on CCTV.

Who, if anybody, has committed an offence of encouraging or assisting an offence contrary to s. 45 of the Serious Crime Act 2007?

A WAREHAM only.
B Both WAREHAM and his wife.
C The wife only.
D Neither WAREHAM nor his wife.

Question 3.7

ALEXANDER wishes to kidnap and sexually assault a child. To do so, he obtains a length of rope, some masking tape and a large knife. He enters the grounds of the school and hides in a lavatory in the school, waiting for a child to come into the lavatory. However, ALEXANDER was seen entering the school and the police were called. ALEXANDER is found by police officers trespassing in the lavatory block of the school.

At what point, if any, does ALEXANDER commit the offence of attempted kidnap?
A At no point does he commit this offence.
B When he takes possession of the rope, masking tape and the knife.
C When he enters the school boundary.
D When he enters the school lavatory.

Question 3.8

MAKINGS has attempted to commit criminal damage. If the attempt had been successful, the value of the damage would have been about £50.

Given the value, making the substantive offence triable summary only, which of the following is correct?
A MAKINGS could be charged with an attempt as all offences can be attempted.
B MAKINGS could be charged with an attempt as the substantive offence is summary only by statutory limit.
C MAKINGS cannot be charged as no summary only offence can be attempted.
D MAKINGS cannot be charged as the substantive offence is summary only by statutory limit.

Question 3.9

McEVOY is due to be a contestant on a 'live' general knowledge TV show. When McEVOY takes part in the show, his wife will be watching at home. Before the show begins, husband and wife devise a plan so that when McEVOY is asked a question by the host of the show, McEVOY's wife will send him a text message via his mobile phone that will contain the correct answer. If all goes according to plan, the two will win up to £50,000.

Does this amount to a statutory conspiracy (contrary to s. 1 of the Criminal Law Act 1977)?

A Yes, the two have agreed on a course of conduct that will amount to the commission of an offence.

B No, McEVOY cannot commit statutory conspiracy if the only other party to the agreement is his wife.

C No, for there to be a conspiracy there must be an agreement with at least three people involved.

D Yes, unless the plan is later abandoned by the two.

Question 3.10

BOW, GREENE and BURGESS agree to be drug dealers for SCIMITER who is happy to supply them with drugs. They collaborate to ensure that the drugs SCIMITER supplies to them are then further supplied to drug users. They each select a particular area of the town they live in to be their 'turf'; that is, the area for which they will be the main supplier of drugs. At the moment, though, no actual drugs have been supplied to them by SCIMITER.

Are any of these persons guilty of statutory conspiracy to supply controlled drugs contrary to s. 1 of the Criminal Law Act 1977?

A All four are guilty, as each of them is aware of the overall common purpose to which they all attach themselves.

B BOW, GREENE and BURGESS are guilty as they are the ones with the joint agreement.

C SCIMITER only is guilty, as although there is a joint agreement only he will actually supply the drugs that are subject to the agreement.

D None of them are guilty as the intended recipients of the drugs to be supplied were the conspirators themselves.

Question 3.11

PRETTY wishes to kill his wife who will not grant him a divorce, and looks for a contract killer. The police, however, are aware of his plan and send an undercover officer to meet him and pose as a contract killer. PRETTY and the undercover officer posing as a contract killer agree that for £2,000 the officer will shoot and kill PRETTY's wife. Naturally, the officer has no intention of committing the murder.

In relation to conspiracy, which of the following is true?

A As an agreement has been reached to carry out an offence, this is a statutory conspiracy.

B As an agreement has been reached to carry out an offence, this is a common law conspiracy.

C As the officer will not carry out the murder, the offence of conspiracy is not made out.

D Although the officer will not carry out the murder, PRETTY is still guilty of conspiracy.

Question 3.12

Police officers are carrying out an undercover operation involving drug supply. BEATTIE mistakes one of the undercover officers for a drug supplier and approaches him and asks if he can supply heroin to him. The officer agrees to such supply in order to preserve his cover. Other officers arrest BEATTIE for encouraging or assisting in the commission of an offence. He denies this and argues that the officer could not have been encouraged to commit an offence as the police have defences to drug possession; he also argues that it was impossible for the officer to supply heroin.

Given that this is an undercover police operation, which of the following is correct?

A This could be seen as entrapment as the officer agrees to supply the drugs.

B The fact BEATTIE approached an undercover police officer means the officer cannot have committed an offence.

C The fact that the officer could not actually supply drugs means BEATTIE cannot commit an offence.

D BEATTIE can commit the offence as it would be possible for the officer to supply the drugs.

ANSWERS

Answer 3.1

Answer **D** — The offence under s. 46 of the Act is committed when a person does an act (the request by PALMER to SCHOLEY) capable of encouraging or assisting the commission of one or more of a number of offences (kidnap and sexual assault) and he/she *believes* that one or more of those offences will be committed and that his/her act will encourage or assist in the commission of one or more of them. One conversation is ample, making answer B incorrect. Only a *belief* is required (not intention—that is under s. 44 of the Act and makes answer C incorrect). Answer A is incorrect as the offence can be committed regardless of whether the encouragement or assistance has the effect the defendant intended or believed it would have.

Crime, para. 1.3.2

Answer 3.2

Answer **A** — Common law conspiracy to defraud involves:

> ... an agreement by two or more [persons] by dishonesty to deprive a person of something which is his or to which he is or would or might be entitled [or] an agreement by two or more by dishonesty to injure some proprietary right [of the victim] ...

(*Scott* v *Metropolitan Police Commissioner* [1975] AC 819: *Crime,* para. 1.3.3.2).

Intent to defraud a victim must be shown (*R* v *Hollinshead* [1985] AC 975); answer B is therefore incorrect.

There is no requirement to prove that the end result would amount to the commission of an offence, simply that it would result in depriving a person of something under the specified conditions or in injuring his/her proprietary right; answers C and D are therefore incorrect.

Crime, para. 1.3.3.2

Answer 3.3

Answer **D** — The common law offence of conspiracy is defined in the leading case of *Scott* v *Metropolitan Police Commissioner* [1975] AC 819, where Viscount Dilhorne said:

> ... an agreement by two or more [persons] by dishonesty to deprive a person of something which is his or to which he is or would be or might be entitled [or] an agreement

by two or more by dishonesty to injure some proprietary right of his suffices to constitute the offence ...

... it suffices if there is a dishonest agreement to expose the proposed victim to some form of economic risk or disadvantage to which he would not otherwise be exposed.

Although the requirement for an agreement between at least two people is the same (answer C is therefore incorrect), this offence is broader than statutory conspiracy. There is no requirement to prove that the end result would amount to the commission of an offence, simply that it would result in depriving a person of something under the specified conditions or in injuring his/her proprietary right. The people who handed over the postal vote ballot slips lost their right to vote for who they wanted as KHAN used their votes for himself. The fact that he didn't win the election is irrelevant; answers A and B are therefore incorrect (*R* v *Hussain* [2005] EWCA Crim 1866).

Crime, para. 1.3.3.2

Answer 3.4

Answer **A** — Conspiracy to defraud involves:

... an agreement by two or more [persons] by dishonesty to deprive a person of something which is his or to which he is or would or might be entitled [or] an agreement by two or more by dishonesty to injure some proprietary right [of the victim] ...

There are two principal variants of this offence, although these are not mutually exclusive. The first is defined in the leading case of *Scott* v *Metropolitan Police Commissioner* [1975] AC 819. There may or may not be an intent to deceive in such cases, and there may or may not be an intent to cause economic or financial loss to the proposed victim or victims, but it suffices if there is a dishonest agreement to expose the proposed victim to some form of economic risk or disadvantage to which he/she would not otherwise be exposed. Subscribers may see the film, the quality is irrelevant and their entitlement is met by seeing the film; answers B and C are therefore incorrect. The *film* company, however, has been deprived of funds as the subscribers have not paid it to view its product; answer D is therefore incorrect.

You must show intent to defraud a victim (*R* v *Hollinshead* [1985] AC 975).

You must also show that a defendant was dishonest as set out in *Barlow Clowes* and *Royal Brunei Airlines* (*Barlow Clowes International (in liq)* v *Eurotrust International Ltd* [2006] 1 All ER 333 and *Royal Brunei Airlines Sdn Bhd* v *Tan* [1995] 3 All ER 97).

Crime, para. 1.3.3.2

Answer 3.5

Answer **B** — The Serious Crime Act 2007, s. 46 states:

(1) A person commits an offence if—
  (a) he does an act capable of encouraging or assisting the commission of one or more of a number of offences: and
  (b) he believes—
    (i) that one or more of those offences will be committed (but has no belief as to which); and
    (ii) that his act will encourage or assist the commission of one or more of them.
(2) It is immaterial for the purposes of subsection (1)(b)(ii) whether the person has any belief as to which offence will be encouraged or assisted.

The offence is made out as soon as an act is done to encourage or assist in the committing of an offence; its actual completion is irrelevant, therefore answer D is incorrect. In addition, it is the person doing the encouraging who commits the offence, the agreement of the other person is again not necessary; answer C is therefore incorrect.

The essence is that one or more offences are encouraged, but the defendant need not believe that one specific offence will be committed; answer A is therefore incorrect.

Crime, para. 1.3.2

Answer 3.6

Answer **A** — Section 45 of the Serious Crime Act 2007 states:

Encouraging or assisting an offence believing it will be committed

(1) A person commits an offence if—
  (a) he does an act capable of encouraging or assisting the commission of an offence; and
  (b) he believes—
    (i) that the offence will be committed; and
    (ii) that his act will encourage or assist its commission.

So there are three elements that have to be fulfilled and we will examine those in relation to both WAREHAM and his wife.

- There is an act capable of encouraging or assisting the commission of an offence.
  - Telling the burglar that the alarm is off is obviously such an act, both WAREHAM and his wife are culpable here.
- The person must believe the offence will be committed.

- Only WAREHAM is culpable as he was keen to help his friend.
- The person must believe that his act will encourage or assist the commission of an offence.
  - Only WAREHAM is culpable as only he wishes to encourage or assist in the offence.

All three elements must be present for the offence to be committed, so only WAREHAM commits this offence; answers B, C and D are therefore incorrect.

Crime, para. 1.3.2

Answer 3.7

Answer **A** — Section 1(1) of the Criminal Attempts Act 1981 requires the accused to have committed an act which is 'more than merely preparatory' to the offence attempted. Where trial is on indictment, it is for the judge to determine whether there is evidence on which a jury could properly find that the accused's actions did go beyond mere preparation, but it is then for the jury to decide that question as one of fact; there is no specific formula used by the courts in interpreting this requirement.

Courts have accepted an approach of questioning whether the defendant had 'embarked on the crime proper' (*R* v *Gullefer* [1990] 1 WLR 1063) but there is no requirement for him/her to have passed a point of no return leading to the commission of the substantive offence. However, he/she must have passed the more than merely preparatory stage, which at this point he has not; answers B, C and D are therefore incorrect.

Crime, para. 1.3.4

Answer 3.8

Answer **B** — The Criminal Attempts Act 1981, s. 1 deals with attempts to commit substantive offences. If the attempted offence is triable summarily only, it cannot be an offence under s. 1; answer A is therefore incorrect. However, if the only reason the substantive offence is triable summarily only is because of a statutory limit imposed in some cases (e.g. criminal damage to property of a low value), the offence can be attempted; answers C and D are therefore incorrect.

Crime, para. 1.3.4

Answer 3.9

Answer **B** — Although there has been an agreement that if carried out in accordance with the conspirators' intentions will involve the commission of an offence, the offence of statutory conspiracy is not made out. This is because a defendant cannot be convicted of statutory conspiracy if the *only* other party to the agreement is his/her spouse, a child/children under 10 years of age or the intended victim.

Crime, para. 1.3.3.1

Answer 3.10

Answer **A** — Section 1 of the Criminal Law Act 1977 states:

(1) Subject to the following provisions of this part of this Act, if a person agrees with any other person or persons that a course of conduct will be pursued which, if the agreement is carried out in accordance with their intentions, either—
   (a) will necessarily amount to or involve the commission of any offence or offences by one or more of the parties to the agreement; or
   (b) would do so but for the existence of facts which render the commission of the offence or any of the offences impossible, he is guilty of conspiracy to commit the offence or offences in question.

For there to be a conspiracy, there must be an agreement. Therefore there must be at least two people involved. Each conspirator must be aware of the overall common purpose to which they all attach themselves. If one conspirator enters into separate agreements with different people, each agreement is a separate conspiracy (*R v Griffiths* [1966] 1 QB 589).

A person can be convicted of conspiracy even if the other conspirators are unknown (as to the effect of the acquittal of one party to a conspiracy on the other parties, see s. 5(8) of the Criminal Law Act 1977).

However, a defendant cannot be convicted of a statutory conspiracy if the only other party to the agreement is:

- his/her spouse (or civil partner);
- a person under 10 years of age;
- the intended victim.

(Criminal Law Act 1977, s. 2(2).)

In this scenario, SCIMITER has conspired to supply drugs to his co-conspirators. Although they further conspire for the onward supply of the drugs, they are all guilty of conspiring to supply drugs.

Crime, para. 1.3.3.1

Answer 3.11

Answer **C** — As the officer clearly will frustrate the agreement, answers A and D are incorrect. This was considered by the House of Lords in *Yip Chieu-Chung* v *The Queen* [1995] 1 AC 111, where N, the appellant's only fellow conspirator in a plan to smuggle heroin out of Hong Kong, was an undercover agent working with the knowledge of the authorities. The House of Lords held that if N's purpose had been to prevent the heroin being smuggled, no indictable conspiracy would have existed. Their Lordships said:

> The crime of conspiracy requires an agreement between two or more persons to commit an unlawful act with the intention of carrying it out. It is the intention to carry out the crime that constitutes the necessary *mens rea* for the offence ... [A]n undercover agent who has no intention of committing the crime lacks the necessary *mens rea* to be a conspirator.

Conspiracy requires an agreement which will amount to or involve the commission of an offence. Where no such offence is likely, the offence is not made out. Common law conspiracy involves conspiracy to defraud only and therefore B is incorrect.

Crime, para. 1.3.3.1

Answer 3.12

Answer **D** — One of the arguments that is often raised by defendants who are caught by undercover officers is that they were induced or pressurised into committing the offence by the officers and that, as a result, either they should not be prosecuted or the evidence of the officer(s) should be excluded. This is mostly true where the approach is made by the officers to the suspect. And it is in this area only that entrapment is likely to occur; where the suspect approaches the officer, the officer cannot 'entrap' someone who voluntarily looks to commit an offence; answer A is therefore incorrect.

What of the situation where, rather than approaching others, an undercover police officer is approached to take part in a proposed offence? There are several types of situation where this may occur.

In relation to this activity, there is no need for the person encouraged to have any intention of going on to commit the offence. The Divisional Court has held that there is no requirement for 'parity of *mens rea*' between the parties (*DPP* v *Armstrong* [2000] Crim LR 379). In that case, the defendant had approached an undercover police officer asking him to supply child pornography. At his trial, the defendant argued that as the officer in reality had no intention of supplying the pornography, there was no offence of incitement (now encouraging/assisting an offence). On appeal by the prosecutor, the Divisional Court held that incitement, like conspiracies and attempts, was an ancillary offence where criminal liability was attributed to the defendant where the full offence had not been committed. Consequently, the intent of the person incited was irrelevant. The court also held that the issue of impossibility did not arise in circumstances such as Armstrong's because it had been 'possible' for the officer to supply the material; answers B and C are therefore incorrect.

Crime, para. 1.3.2

4 | General Defences

QUESTIONS

Question 4.1

COOK is in debt to a drug dealer and when two persons wearing suits arrive at his door he believes them to be people sent by the drug dealer to injure him. COOK decides to push past the people at the door and in doing so one of the people falls backwards and suffers a head injury. The people were in fact employees of the local council who had come to speak to COOK about a planning application he had recently made.

If COOK were to claim he was acting in self-defence due to mistaken belief, which of the following is correct?

A That the degree of force used was reasonable (this will be decided by reference to the circumstances as COOK believed them to be).

B That the degree of force used was proportionate (this will be decided by the court and by reference to the circumstances as they actually were).

C That the degree of force used was no more than necessary (this will be decided by reference to the circumstances as a reasonable person sharing the same characteristics as COOK would believe them to be).

D That the degree of force used was minimal (this is an objective decision decided by the magistrates or jury as the case may be).

Question 4.2

DCs CROSS and BACKHOUSE are investigating an offence of causing grievous bodily harm. EMERY (the person allegedly responsible for the offence) is a householder who used force on BIRD who broke into EMERY's house. The officers make a number of comments in relation to the use of force by EMERY.

Considering the law under s. 76 of the Criminal Justice and Immigration Act 2008, which of the comments below is correct?

A DC CROSS states that if EMERY used force merely in order to protect his property then the use of force would always be unacceptable.

B DC BACKHOUSE states that the use of disproportionate force can, in 'house-holder' cases, be justified in certain circumstances.

C DC CROSS states that EMERY could use force against BIRD but only for the purpose of self-defence or in defence of another.

D DC BACKHOUSE states that, in 'householder' cases, the use of grossly disproportionate force can be justified.

Question 4.3

UPTON approaches ALI (who does not know UPTON) and tells him that unless he kills PINTER immediately, his wife and child will be killed. UPTON produces a gun and several photographs of ALI's family and tells him that he has been observed for some time. UPTON gives ALI the gun and PINTER's details and, believing that UPTON will kill his wife and child, ALI goes to PINTER's house and kills him. ALI is arrested at the scene and states that the only reason he committed the offence was because he was placed under duress.

Would ALI be able to use this defence?

A No, as the defence is not available in respect of an offence of murder.

B Yes, as the threat drove ALI to commit the offence.

C No, as the threat of harm must be made solely to the person who goes on to commit the relevant offence.

D Yes, as the offence was carried out immediately after the threat was made.

Question 4.4

GLOVER and his wife plan to kill his wife's mother to benefit from the terms of her will. GLOVER is a pharmacist and supplies poison to his wife who administers it; however, the dose he supplied is not enough and his mother-in-law does not die. When questioned by the police, he states that his wife threatened to kill him if he did not supply the poison.

Will GLOVER be able to use duress as a defence to a charge of attempted murder?

A Yes, provided he supplied the poison fearing death if he did not.

B Yes, provided he supplied the poison fearing death or serious injury if he did not.

C No, as GLOVER is a secondary offender (he aided the offence), the defence of duress is not available.

D No, as duress is not a defence that can be used in answer to a charge of attempted murder.

Question 4.5

PARKER is a member of a gang of thieves who specialise in pickpocket thefts. The leader of the gang is GREEN who tells the gang who to target when they are out on the streets. While the gang are on the streets, GREEN sees KENWORTHY (who is not part of the gang) stealing from several pedestrians. GREEN is outraged by what he sees as an 'invasion of his turf' and tells PARKER that he needs to prove his loyalty to the gang by stabbing KENWORTHY and he gives PARKER a knife. PARKER does not want to stab KENWORTHY and says so to GREEN, who responds, 'Stab him or I'll break your little girl's arm tomorrow when she leaves school!' GREEN has a history of violent behaviour and PARKER genuinely believes he will seriously injure his child if he does not do as GREEN has said. He stabs KENWORTHY who is seriously injured as a result. PARKER is arrested and charged with an offence of s. 18 wounding (under the Offences Against the Person Act 1861).

Considering the general defence of duress, which of the following comments is correct?

A PARKER could not use the defence as it is only available to a charge of murder or attempted murder.

B PARKER could not use the defence as the serious physical injury that was threatened was threatened to his child rather than to PARKER himself.

C PARKER could not use the defence as it is only available when the person concerned is threatened with death.

D PARKER could not use the defence because he would have an opportunity to neutralise the effect of the threat.

Question 4.6

MULLALLY has suffered from domestic violence for several months and one evening she is subjected to significant threats. She fears violence from her husband and grabs the car keys to escape, fearing she will be killed or seriously injured. She has been drinking heavily all evening. As she drives out of her driveway, the police arrive having been called by neighbours; they try to stop her leaving but she drives off. She is stopped by other officers about a mile away and fails the breath test. At court she claims the defence of duress of circumstances and claims that she knew the police were there but that they would have been unable to help her and that running away was her only option.

In relation to the defence of duress of circumstances, which of the following is correct?

A The defence will succeed as MULLALLY drove because she genuinely believed that if she did not do so death or serious injury to herself would result.

B The defence will succeed as MULLALLY drove because she genuinely believed, even if mistakenly, that if she did not do so death or serious injury to herself would result.

C The defence may not succeed as a sober reasonable person sharing the same characteristics would have stopped, knowing that the police had arrived to deal with the situation.

D The defence may not succeed as MULLALLY had the opportunity to neutralise the effects of the threat by stopping for the police officers who had attended her house.

Question 4.7

Constable CROWLEY is on the tactical firearms unit and has been called to a hostage situation. Unfortunately, the incident ends when Constable CROWLEY fatally shoots RUSSELL, who was the assailant.

In relation to the lawfulness of CROWLEY's use of lethal force, what test will be applied?

A That he had an honestly held belief that it was necessary.

B That such force was reasonable in the circumstances.

C That such force was no more than absolutely necessary.

D That such force was necessary to protect the life of another.

Question 4.8

MARONEY was arrested and has been charged with an offence of assaulting a police officer who arrested her. The officer was in plain clothes at the time of the incident. MARONEY wishes to contest the matter stating that she did not know he was a police officer and had made a genuine mistake.

In relation to the defence of mistake, which of the following is correct?

A The defence applies where there was a genuine and honest belief that was reasonably held.

B The defence applies where there was a reasonable and honest belief.

C The defence applies where there was a genuine and reasonable belief that was honestly held.

D The defence applies where there was a genuine and honest belief.

Question 4.9

KIRK, who is 65 years old, wakes up one night and finds someone in his lounge. Fearing he is about to be burgled, he takes a golf club and hits the stranger on the head with it, fracturing his skull. Unfortunately, the stranger is his daughter's new boyfriend who was sleepwalking. KIRK believed the force was necessary as he is an older man and the younger male was well over 6ft in height. He has also never met this boyfriend before.

Could KIRK use the defence of reasonable force for purposes of self-defence under s. 76 of the Criminal Justice and Immigration Act 2008?

A Yes, as it applies to defence of property and he reasonably believed it was necessary force.

B Yes, as it applies to defence of property and, although it was a mistaken belief, it was a reasonable mistake to make.

C No, this defence does not apply to defence of property, only defence of self or another.

D No, as the amount of force used was disproportionate to the amount of force necessary in the defence of property.

Question 4.10

GARSIDE was found in possession of a shotgun and on the way to commit a burglary. When he was arrested and interviewed, however, he stated that his wife was being held captive by an armed gang who threatened to kill her if he did not commit the burglary. He also stated that it was his idea and not the gang's that he should take the shotgun; his intention was to use it to resist arrest and he felt his wife's life was in danger.

Considering that GARSIDE has committed an offence contrary to s. 18 of the Firearms Act 1968 (carrying a firearm or imitation firearm with intent to resist arrest), will he be able to claim the defence of duress?

A Yes, but only if he can show that the intention to resist arrest was as a result of duress.

B Yes, in these circumstances duress is available as a defence, as this was the reason he took the shotgun.

C No, duress is not available as he was only asked to carry out a burglary, the firearms offence was his idea.

D No, the defence of duress is not available if the threat is made against a third party, unless the third party is present at the time of the offence.

Question 4.11

PC SULLIVAN visits a house owned by KHAN to arrest KHAN for an offence of theft which occurred two weeks ago in a shopping centre near KHAN's house. KHAN answers the door to the officer who asks KHAN's name. When KHAN responds, PC SULLIVAN places his hand on KHAN's shoulder and arrests him on suspicion of theft and also tells KHAN where and when the offence took place. KHAN is outraged as he knows that he is innocent as he only returned from a three-month holiday in India two days ago. A struggle develops during which KHAN assaults PC SULLIVAN. KHAN is never charged with the theft but he is charged with an offence of assault with intent to resist arrest (contrary to s. 38 of the Offences Against the Person Act 1861). He pleads 'not guilty' and the case goes to trial. KHAN states that PC SULLIVAN had no right to arrest him as he was innocent of the theft and the arrest was therefore unlawful.

Considering the law in relation to the defence of mistake, which of the following comments is correct?

A There are no circumstances where a genuine or honest mistake could provide a defence to an offence of assault with intent to resist arrest.

B KHAN had made a mistake of law (believing the officer had no power of arrest in the circumstances) which could form the basis for a defence of mistake to the charge of assault with intent to resist arrest.

C KHAN had formed the genuine but mistaken opinion that the arrest was unlawful which means he could use the defence of mistake in answer to the charge of assault with intent to resist arrest.

D Belief in one's own innocence, however genuine or honestly held, cannot afford a defence to a charge of assault with intent to resist arrest.

Question 4.12

NORSTER had driven his stepson to work although he was disqualified from driving. He claimed that he had done this because his wife had threatened to commit suicide unless he did so, as the boy was in danger of losing his job if he was late. The wife had suicidal tendencies and a doctor had told NORSTER that it was likely that she would carry out any threat to take her own life. In fact, the wife had no intention of killing herself that night; it was just her way of ensuring that her son was not late for work.

In these circumstances, would the defence of duress of circumstances be likely to succeed?

A Yes, as NORSTER had reasonable grounds to suppose his wife's threat was real due to the doctor's report.

B Yes, because NORSTER had an honestly held belief that his wife may carry out her threat.

C No, because there was no actual threat to NORSTER's life.

D No, because the threat made by the wife was not in fact true.

Question 4.13

ROSS works as a clerk for a large car sales firm. She is examining a number of expenses claims (required for accounting purposes) that have been submitted by FINLAY (a supervisor at the car sales firm). ROSS discovers a significant number of irregularities suggesting that expenses amounting to £3,000 are false and she confronts FINLAY regarding the irregularities. FINLAY admits that the expenses are false but threatens ROSS to the effect that if she does anything about the false claims he will make sure she loses her job, and he tells ROSS to falsify the expenses claims so that they appear genuine. FINLAY has a great deal of influence at the firm and ROSS honestly believes he could get her sacked. ROSS fears that this loss of income will have a dramatic impact on her standard of living and she falsifies the expenses for FINLAY.

Would ROSS be able to claim that she was acting under duress of circumstances in relation to any offences that she commits by falsifying the expenses claims?

A No, as she did not have cause to fear that she would suffer death or serious injury if she did not do as FINLAY demanded.

B Yes, as the defence is available in answer to any charge except for treason.

C No, as duress of circumstances is only a defence to a charge of murder or attempted murder.

D Yes, because she honestly believed that she would be sacked if she did not do as FINLAY demanded.

ANSWERS

Answer 4.1

Answer **A** — Section 3(1) of the Criminal Law Act 1967 provides that:

> A person may use such force as is reasonable in the circumstances in the prevention of crime, or in effecting or assisting in the lawful arrest of offenders or suspected offenders or of persons unlawfully at large.

Clarification of the law is provided by s. 76 of the Criminal Justice and Immigration Act 2008 which expands on the common law of self-defence and the defences provided by s. 3(1) of the Criminal Law Act 1967, which relate to the use of force in the prevention of crime or making an arrest.

The question whether the degree of force used by the defendant was reasonable in the circumstances is to be decided by reference to the circumstances as the defendant believed them to be (s. 76(3)). This makes answers B, C and D incorrect.

Crime, para. 1.4.5.3

Answer 4.2

Answer **B** — There are circumstances where the use of force against a person or property will be permissible. This aspect of criminal law is dealt with by s. 76 of the Criminal Justice and Immigration Act 2008. The law can be formulated along the following lines.

A person may use such force as is reasonable in the circumstances as he believes them to be for the purpose of:

(a) self-defence; or
(b) defence of another; or
(c) defence of property; or
(d) prevention of crime; or
(e) lawful arrest.

So there are a variety of circumstances where the use of force may be permissible, making answer C incorrect. This includes the use of force to protect property, making answer A incorrect.

Section 43 of the Crime and Courts Act 2013 amends s. 76 of the Criminal Justice and Immigration Act 2008 so that the use of *disproportionate* force can be regarded as reasonable in the circumstances as the accused believed them to be when house-holders are acting to protect themselves or others from trespassers in their homes (self-defence). The use of *grossly* disproportionate force would still not be permitted, making answer D incorrect.

Crime, paras 1.4.5.2 to 1.4.5.4

Answer 4.3

Answer **A** — The defence of duress is not available in respect of an offence of murder (*R* v *Howe* [1987] AC 417). Answer C is incorrect as the threat can be made to 'loved ones'. Answer B is incorrect as although the threat drove ALI to commit the offence, this is just one of the requirements and answer A supersedes this. Answer D is not correct as the requirement relating to time (imminently) relates to the threatened injury to the defendant or his/her 'loved ones'.

Crime, para. 1.4.3

Answer 4.4

Answer **D** — Where a person is threatened with death or serious physical injury un-less he/she carries out a criminal act, he/she may use the defence of duress. Note that this includes a threat of serious injury, not just death, therefore answer A is incorrect (*R* v *Graham* [1982] 1 WLR 294). However, the defence is not available in respect of an offence of murder (see *R* v *Howe* [1987] AC 417) or attempted murder (*R* v *Gotts* [1992] 2 AC 412); answer B is therefore incorrect. This applies to either a principal or secondary offender but only in relation to attempted murder not any offence; answer C is therefore incorrect.

Crime, para. 1.4.3

Answer 4.5

Answer **D** — Where a person is threatened with death or *serious physical injury* unless he/she carries out a criminal act, he/she may have a defence of duress (*R* v *Graham* [1982] 1 WLR 294). This means that answer C is incorrect. It would seem that the threat need not be made solely to the person who goes on to commit the relevant offence; there are authorities to suggest that threats of death/serious harm to loved ones may allow a defence of duress, meaning that answer B is incorrect. The de-fence is not available in respect of an offence of murder (*R* v *Howe* [1987] AC 417) or attempted murder (*R* v *Gotts* [1992] 2 AC 412), as a principal or secondary offender. It is, however, available in *other offences* even in offences of strict liability, meaning that answer A is incorrect.

Duress is not available as a defence if it is proved that the defendant failed to take advantage of an opportunity to neutralise the effects of the threat (perhaps by escaping from it), which a reasonable person of a similar sort to the defendant would have taken in the same position. An example of this approach is the case of *R* v *Heath* [2000] Crim LR 109, where the defendant alleged that he had been pressurised into transporting drugs. Because the defendant had more than one safe avenue of escape (going to the police which he did not do because he was scared and because he was a drug addict, and going to his parents in Scotland which he did not do because he did not want them to know about the position he was in) the defence failed. Whether a defendant could be expected to take such an opportunity of rendering the threat ineffective, e.g. by seeking police protection, will be a matter for the jury. Therefore, a defendant who is ordered to steal from a shop in 24 hours' time or suffer a serious physical injury for failing to do so might be unable to utilise the defence as a jury may consider that the defendant had ample opportunity to take evasive action and avoid the threat.

Crime, para. 1.4.3

Answer 4.6

Answer **C** — The defence of duress of circumstances relates to times when circumstances leave the defendant no real alternative but to commit an offence. This type of duress should be distinguished from the defence of 'duress' where there is a threat made to the defendant compelling them to commit an offence; with duress of circumstances, there is no such threat being made. Answer D relates to 'duress' where there is an opportunity to neutralise the threat which means that the defence cannot be used and for that reason answer D is incorrect. In this question, the defendant drove away as she felt she had no real alternative.

In determining whether or not the defence of 'duress of circumstances' is available, the court held that the jury must ask two questions in relation to the defendant:

- Were they (or might they have been) impelled to act as they did because, as a result of what they reasonably believed, they had good cause to fear they would suffer death or serious injury if they did not do so?
- If so, would a sober person of reasonable firmness and sharing the same characteristics, have responded to the situation in the way that they did?

The answer to both questions must be yes; if not, the defence fails. In the circumstances of this question, answers A and B state that the defence will succeed and this is not the case; answers A and B are therefore incorrect. The fact is that the 'circumstances' changed when the police arrived and that there was an alternative to driving.

Crime, para. 1.4.4

Answer 4.7

Answer **C** — The law in relation to 'self-defence' was clarified by s. 76 of the Criminal Justice and Immigration Act 2008. Section 76 deals with the practical application of these areas of law using elements of case law to illustrate how the defence operates. It does not change the test that allows the use of reasonable force.

Where such a defence is raised in relation to taking someone's life, the provisions of Art. 2 of the European Convention on Human Rights will apply. The requirements of Art. 2 are more stringent than under s. 3(1) of the Criminal Law Act 1967 and s. 76 of the Criminal Justice and Immigration Act 2008. Under Art. 2, the test will be whether the force used was no more than absolutely necessary and lethal force will be 'absolutely necessary' only if it is strictly proportionate to the legitimate purpose being pursued. In order to meet those criteria, regard will be had to:

- the nature of the aim being pursued;
- the inherent dangers to life and limb from the situation;
- the degree of risk to life presented by the amount of force employed.

The only circumstances in which lethal force might be permissible here are where the defendant was acting:

- in defence of any person from unlawful violence;
- in order to effect a lawful arrest or to prevent the escape of a person lawfully detained;
- in action lawfully taken for the purpose of quelling a riot or insurrection.

It is important to note that the taking of life in order to prevent crime is not mentioned in Art. 2.

So the test is 'no more than absolutely necessary'; answers A, B and D are therefore incorrect.

Crime, para. 1.4.5.3

Answer 4.8

Answer **D** — There are occasions where a defendant makes a mistake about some circumstance or consequence, but claims that a defendant 'made a mistake' or did something 'inadvertently' will only be an effective defence if they negate the *mens rea* for that offence. Therefore, if someone picks up another person's shopping at a supermarket till or wanders out of a shop with something they have yet to pay for, their mistake or inadvertence, in each case, might negative any *mens rea* of 'dishonesty'. As the requirement for the *mens rea* in such a case is subjective, then the defendant's mistake or inadvertence will be judged subjectively. The same will generally be true for offences requiring subjective recklessness. It does not matter whether the mistake was 'reasonable' (*DPP* v *Morgan* [1976] AC 182); answers A, B and C are therefore incorrect. The appropriate test is whether the defendant's mistaken belief was an honest and genuine one. There are occasions where a genuine mistake on the part of the defendant may amount to a defence.

In *R* v *Lee* [2000] Crim LR 991, a case arising from an assault on two arresting police officers, the Court of Appeal reviewed the law in this area, reaffirming the following points:

- A genuine or honest mistake could provide a defence to many criminal offences requiring a particular state of mind, including assault with intent to resist arrest (*R* v *Brightling* [1991] Crim LR 364).
- A defence of mistake had to involve a mistake of fact, not a mistake of law (see later).
- People under arrest are not entitled to form their own view as to the lawfulness of that arrest. They have a duty to comply with the police and hear the details of the charge against them (*R* v *Bentley* (1850) 4 Cox CC 406).
- Belief in one's own innocence, however genuine or honestly held, cannot afford a defence to a charge of assault with intent to resist arrest under s. 38 of the Offences Against the Person Act 1861.

A defendant attempted to argue that his honest and reasonable mistake as to the *facts* of his arrest (as opposed to the law) after he was lawfully arrested for a public order offence was different from the decision in *Lee*. The Divisional Court did not agree with him (see *Hewitt* v *DPP* [2002] EWHC 2801 (Admin)).

Crime, para. 1.4.2

Answer 4.9

Answer **B** — Section 76 of the Criminal Justice and Immigration Act 2008 added a gloss to s. 3(1) of the Criminal Law Act 1967 and states reasonable force may be used in the prevention of crime. Therefore, if a person is acting in order to prevent a crime against his/her property, force can be used to protect property; answer C is therefore incorrect. However, whether such force is reasonable or not will be subject to the requirements of s. 76 of the Criminal Justice and Immigration Act 2008.

In deciding whether or not the degree of force used was reasonable in the circumstances, s. 76(7) requires certain considerations to be taken into account:

- that a person acting for a legitimate purpose (the purposes of the defences to which s. 76 applies) may not be able to weigh to a nicety the exact measure of any necessary action; and
- that evidence of a person's having only done what the person honestly and instinctively thought was necessary for a legitimate purpose constitutes strong evidence that only reasonable action was taken by that person for that purpose.

This does not mention force being necessary, only that it was done in circumstances such that the person using that force believed it was necessary; answer A is therefore incorrect.

This does not prevent other matters from being taken into account where they are relevant in deciding whether the degree of force used was reasonable in the circumstances. Section 76 retains a single test for self-defence and the prevention of crime (or the making of an arrest) which can be applied in each of these contexts. The law has been developed in line with case law regarding self-defence and the use of force, most notably the case of *Palmer* v *The Queen* [1971] AC 814. The defence will be available to a person if he/she honestly believed it was necessary to use force and if the degree of force used was not disproportionate in the circumstances as he/she viewed them. The section reaffirms that a person who uses force is to be judged on the basis of the circumstances as he/she perceived them, that in the heat of the moment he/she will not be expected to have judged exactly what action was called for and that a degree of latitude may be given to a person who only did what he/she honestly and instinctively thought was necessary. A defendant is entitled to have his/her actions judged on the basis of his/her view of the facts as he/she honestly believed them to be. This does not therefore define what force will be proportionate; answer D is therefore incorrect.

Crime, para. 1.4.5.3

Answer 4.10

Answer **A** — The offence under s. 18 of the Firearms Act 1968 states:

(1) It is an offence for a person to have with him a firearm or imitation firearm with intent to commit an indictable offence, or to resist arrest or prevent the arrest of another, in either case while he has a firearm or imitation firearm with him.

It is important to note that the offence asked of GARSIDE is different from the offence he stands accused of; this does not mean *per se* that he cannot use the defence of duress. However, where applicable intent is a fundamental element of an offence; the accused must show that he/she had, or could only have formed, that intent by reason of that duress. Without showing that the only compelling factor in the formation of the relevant intent is duress, then the defence will fail (*R* v *Fisher* [2004] EWCA Crim 1190); answer C is therefore incorrect. Note the relevant intent here is that of resisting arrest, not possession of the shotgun; therefore answer B is incorrect.

The question is whether the threat has to be directed at the accused or whether threats to third parties, especially close relatives, can suffice. There seems to be consensus amongst legal commentators on this point and certainly in principle threats to third parties should be capable of constituting duress. Even the bravest person may be prepared to risk his/her own neck whilst baulking at subjecting his/her loved ones to serious peril. Indeed, there is authority recognising threats to the accused's common law wife, and in *R* v *Ortiz* (1986) 83 Cr App R 173 threats to the accused's wife or family appear to have been considered to be sufficient; answer D is therefore incorrect.

Crime, para. 1.4.3

Answer 4.11

Answer **D** — In *R* v *Lee* [2001] 1 Cr App R 19, a case arising from an assault on two arresting police officers, the Court of Appeal reviewed the law in this area, reaffirming the following points:

- A genuine or honest mistake *could* provide a defence to many criminal offences requiring a particular state of mind, including assault with intent to resist arrest (*R* v *Brightling* [1991] Crim LR 364). This makes answer A incorrect.
- A defence of mistake had to involve a mistake of fact, not a mistake of law. Generally, it is no defence to claim a mistake as to the law because all people are presumed to know the law once it is made (making answer B incorrect).

- People under arrest are not entitled to form their own view as to the lawfulness of that arrest. They have a duty to comply with the police and hear the details of the charge against them (*R* v *Bentley* (1850) 4 Cox CC 406). This makes answer C incorrect.
- Belief in one's own innocence, however genuine or honestly held, cannot afford a defence to a charge of assault with intent to resist arrest under s. 38 of the Offences Against the Person Act 1861 (correct answer D).

Crime, para. 1.4.2

Answer 4.12

Answer **B** — In *R* v *Martin* [1989] 1 All ER 652, Simon Brown J stated that the principles of duress of circumstances may be summarised as:

- First, English law does in extreme circumstances recognise a defence of necessity. It can arise from objective dangers threatening the accused or others in which case it is conveniently called 'duress of circumstances'.
- Secondly, the defence is available only if, from an objective standpoint, the accused can be said to be acting reasonably and proportionately in order to avoid a threat of death or serious injury.
- Thirdly, assuming the defence to be open to the accused on his account of the facts, the issue should be left to the jury, who should be directed to determine these two questions:
  - (1) Was the accused, or may he have been, impelled to act as he did because as a result of what he reasonably believed to be the situation he had good cause to fear that otherwise death or serious injury would result?
  - (2) If so, may a sober person of reasonable firmness, sharing the characteristics of the accused, have responded to that situation by acting as the accused acted?

If the answer to both these questions was yes, then the jury would acquit: the defence of necessity would have been established. Further, the court in *Martin* was willing to contemplate the defence succeeding where an unqualified or disqualified driver took control of a car to get a person who had suffered a heart attack to hospital.

The important aspect to this defence, then, is that it will only avail the defendant as long as he/she is acting under compulsion of the prevailing circumstances when committing the offence. It appears that the defendant need only hold an *honest* belief that those circumstances exist without necessarily having *reasonable grounds* for that belief (see *DPP* v *Rogers* [1998] Crim LR 202) and there is no need for the threat to be 'real'. In other words, there is no need for the doctor's report. Provided the defendant honestly believed his wife's threat (whether it was true or not), the defence could succeed; answers A and D are therefore incorrect.

The threat also does not have to be directed against the person who commits the unlawful act; answer C is therefore incorrect.

Crime, para. 1.4.4

Answer 4.13

Answer **A** — The defence is not available to offences of murder, attempted murder or treason and offences under the Misuse of Drugs Act 1971—the defence is available against any other charge (including hijacking, *R v Abdul-Hussain* [1999] Crim LR 570), making answers B and C incorrect. Answer D is incorrect as the defence of 'duress of circumstances' (necessity) is only available when the crime is committed in order to avoid death or serious injury—here ROSS is not committing the crime to avoid that outcome (ROSS is the victim of blackmail, of course, but you are not being questioned on that offence or the possible outcomes that these circumstances would have in reality—the question is asking about duress of circumstances and nothing else).

Crime, para. 1.4.4

5 | Homicide

QUESTIONS

Question 5.1

Constable MEREDITH is dealing with an incident where a person in a care home suffered neglect to the extent that they died. The officer is wondering whether an offence under s. 5 of the Domestic Violence, Crime and Victims Act 2004 (causing or allowing a child or vulnerable adult to die or suffer serious physical harm) has been committed.

In relation to this, which of the following is correct?

A Yes, provided there is evidence that the victim died as a result of the unlawful act.

B Yes, provided the victim suffered from a physical or mental disability and died as a result of the unlawful act.

C No, as the offence only applies to households and care homes are unlikely to be households.

D No, this offence only applies to domestic situations where there is a relationship between the suspect and the victim.

Question 5.2

HOPKINS had many convictions for domestic violence against his wife. One evening, HOPKINS attacks his wife who 'snaps' and grabs hold of a knife and stabs him through the heart instantly killing him. HOPKINS states that she did intend to cause serious injury to her husband when she stabbed him. She is charged with murder.

In relation to 'loss of control' as defined by s. 54 of the Coroners and Justice Act 2009, which of the following is correct?

A She could use this defence provided her loss of control was sudden.

B She could use this defence provided someone of her age may have acted the same way in the same circumstances.

C She could not use this defence as it was a calculated act as she intended to stab him.

D She could not use this defence as it applies to manslaughter offences only.

Question 5.3

DE JONG is depressed and is contemplating suicide and confides in a friend, DEERING, of his wish to do so. DEERING decides to help his friend and goes to a drug dealer he knows and asks for a supply of very strong opiates. DEERING then gives DE JONG the drugs and leaves to allow him to commit suicide. DE JONG, however, changes his mind and does not take the drugs. In any case, the drug dealer has duped DEERING as the 'opiates' he supplied were in fact vitamin tablets.

Has DEERING committed an offence of encouraging or assisting suicide contrary to s. 2 of the Suicide Act 1961 as amended?

A Yes, as he has taken action that could assist or encourage another to commit suicide.

B Yes, as he has taken action that could assist or encourage another to commit suicide and the act was intended to so do.

C No, as DE JONG did not commit or attempt to commit suicide.

D No, as the actions could not have assisted or encouraged suicide as the pills could not have caused the death of DE JONG.

Question 5.4

IVY and his wife had been to the local pub where they had been drinking heavily and arguing. IVY returned to their house where he chopped wood with an axe and drank more lager. His wife was still in the public house drinking. When she returned to the house, she picked up the axe and said she was going to put it in his head. In fear that this would happen, he took the axe from her and struck her seven or eight times with the axe, killing her, and is charged with murder. IVY wishes to use 'loss of control' as a defence to the charge of murder.

For the purposes of this defence (loss of control), which of the following is correct in relation to what the defence would be based on?

A That a reasonable person with a normal degree of tolerance and self-restraint, and in the same circumstances, might have reacted in the same way as IVY.

B That a reasonable person with a normal degree of tolerance and self-restraint, and in the same circumstances, might have reacted in the same or in a similar way to IVY.

C That a person of IVY's sex and age with a normal degree of tolerance and self-restraint, and in the circumstances, might have reacted in the same way as IVY.

D That a person of IVY's sex and age with a normal degree of tolerance and self-restraint, and in the same circumstances, might have reacted in the same or in a similar way to IVY.

Question 5.5

LONGHURST is outside a pub and gets into an altercation with several people outside that public house. He assaults two of them and the landlord comes out and assaults LONGHURST. Very angry at this, LONGHURST picks up a brick and throws it through the pub window; it hits a customer on the head and the customer dies of his injuries. LONGHURST is arrested and claims he was intoxicated through drink and drugs and that this affected his judgement.

In relation to any homicide offences committed by LONGHURST, which of the following is correct?

A LONGHURST is guilty of murder in these circumstances as he was reckless in his actions.

B LONGHURST is guilty of manslaughter in these circumstances as he committed an inherently unlawful act.

C LONGHURST is not guilty of manslaughter by an unlawful act as he had no intention to injure the deceased and was intoxicated at the time.

D LONGHURST is not guilty of any homicide offence in these circumstances as the unlawful act was directed at property not a person.

Question 5.6

BROTHERTON and his cousin hold extreme political views and are concerned about the influence that Europe is having on UK policy. BROTHERTON decides to telephone his cousin and propose that his cousin goes to France to murder the president of France. He telephones his cousin but there is no reply to the call. BROTHERTON waits for 30 minutes and then calls his cousin again; this time his cousin answers and BROTHERTON makes his proposal. BROTHERTON is serious about his proposal but his cousin thinks it is a joke.

Would BROTHERTON commit an offence of solicitation to murder (contrary to s. 4 of the Offences Against the Person Act 1861) in these circumstances?

A Yes, but only when BROTHERTON's cousin answers the telephone and hears what BROTHERTON has to say.

B Yes, the offence is committed when BROTHERTON makes the initial but un-answered call to his cousin.

C No, as the cousin was not in any way encouraged to commit murder.

D No, as the intended victim was not a British subject and in fact is outside the UK.

Question 5.7

MALONE owned a taxi firm which was failing financially. MALONE owned the building which contained the firm's office and decided to set fire to the building to claim from the insurance company. MALONE enlisted the help of a friend, LARIMY, who had no connection with the company, and one evening they went to the building with cans of petrol and matches. MALONE spread the petrol around the in-side of the premises and lit a fire, while LARIMY stood near the door as the lookout. Unfortunately, when the petrol ignited there was an explosion which killed LARIMY and injured MALONE.

In relation to MALONE's liability for the offence of involuntary manslaughter, which of the following statements is correct?

A MALONE would be guilty of manslaughter by unlawful act in these circumstances as arson is an unlawful act.

B MALONE would be guilty of manslaughter by gross negligence in these circum-stances; he owns the property but was reckless as to the result of his actions.

C MALONE would not be guilty of either offence as he owns the building and did not commit an unlawful act and his actions were not grossly negligent.

D MALONE would not be guilty of either offence as he owns the building and did not commit an unlawful act and his actions were not grossly negligent as LARIMY was not an employee.

Question 5.8

SHIPLEY has been charged with an offence of murder and is due to appear in court. SHIPLEY intends pleading not guilty to murder and will ask the court to ac-cept a plea of guilty to the offence of manslaughter on the grounds of diminished responsibility.

Which of the following is correct, in respect of the 'impairment of responsibility' that SHIPLEY must have suffered, in order to succeed with this approach?

A The mental impairment suffered must have been substantial and must also have been the sole cause of SHIPLEY's actions in committing the manslaughter.

B The mental impairment must have been substantial and it must be shown that it contributed in some way to SHIPLEY's actions in committing the manslaughter.

C The mental impairment need not be substantial, provided it contributed in some way to SHIPLEY's actions in committing the manslaughter.

D The mental impairment need not be substantial, provided it can be shown that it was the sole cause of SHIPLEY's actions in committing the manslaughter.

Question 5.9

TILLY was aged 5 years and was on the at-risk register for previous assaults on her by members of her family. She lived at home with her mother, and whilst her mother's boyfriend was a frequent visitor, he did not live there. TILLY's mother was aware that her boyfriend was violent particularly when drunk and had assaulted TILLY previously. One night after he returned home drunk from the pub, the boyfriend was fed up with TILLY's crying and went up and shook her violently. TILLY died from injuries received from that shaking activity.

Who could be charged with an offence contrary to s. 5 of the Domestic Violence, Crime and Victims Act 2004 (causing or allowing a child or vulnerable adult to die or suffer serious physical harm)?

A Only TILLY's mother.

B TILLY's mother provided it could be established that she foresaw the attack on TILLY.

C Only the boyfriend.

D Both TILLY's mother and her boyfriend.

Question 5.10

PIDGEON operates a website which encourages teenage girls to commit suicide. The intention is to promote suicide and that one or more of its readers will commit suicide. A member of the group did indeed attempt to commit suicide and left a note indicating that it was due to the influence of the material on the website run by PIDGEON; their suicide attempt was unsuccessful.

Which of the following is correct in relation to the offence of encouraging or assisting suicide (contrary to s. 2 of the Suicide Act 1961)?

A The offence is complete in these circumstances.

B For the offence to be complete, PIDGEON would have to have known personally the person who attempted to take their own life.

C The offence could never be complete as this offence cannot be committed by online activity.

D The offence could never be complete as the person did not actually commit suicide—only attempted it.

ANSWERS

Answer 5.1

Answer **C** — The Domestic Violence, Crime and Victims Act 2004, s. 5 states:

(1) A person ('D') is guilty of an offence if—
  (a) a child or vulnerable adult ('V') dies or suffers serious physical harm as a result of the unlawful act of a person who—
    (i)   was a member of the same household as V, and
    (ii) had frequent contact with him,
  (b) D was such a person at the time of that act,
  (c) at that time there was a significant risk of serious physical harm being caused to V by the unlawful act of such a person, and
  (d) either D was the person whose act caused the death or serious physical harm …

The offence applies only to a household and where the suspect shared that household; this is not the case with a care home; answers A and B are therefore incorrect.

It does not have to be a domestic situation as people will be a member of a particular household if they visit it so often and for such periods of time that it is reasonable to regard them as a member of it even if they do not actually live there (s. 5(4)(a)); answer D is therefore incorrect.

Crime, para. 1.5.5

Answer 5.2

Answer **B** — Section 54 of the Coroners and Justice Act 2009 sets out the criteria which need to be met in order for the partial defence of loss of self-control to be successful, those being:

- the defendant's acts and omissions resulted from a loss of self-control;
- the loss of self-control had a qualifying trigger; and
- a person of the defendant's sex and age with a normal degree of tolerance and self-restraint and in the circumstances of the defendant might have acted in the same or similar way to the defendant.

Section 54(2) states that the loss of control need not be sudden—answer A is therefore incorrect.

A qualifying trigger is defined as:

- The defendant's fear of serious violence from the victim against the defendant or another identified person.
- A thing or things done or said (or both) which constituted circumstances of an extremely grave character and caused the defendant to have a justifiable sense of being seriously wronged.
- A combination of the previous two factors.

This will apply even where a 'calculated' act takes place; answer C is therefore incorrect. The defence applies only to murder charges, not manslaughter; answer D is therefore incorrect.

Crime, para. 1.5.3.2

Answer 5.3

Answer **B** — Section 2 of the Suicide Act 1961 (as amended) states:

(1) A person ('D') commits an offence if—
 (a) D does an act capable of encouraging or assisting the suicide or attempted suicide of another person, and
 (b) D's act was intended to encourage or assist suicide or an attempt at suicide.
(1A) The person referred to in subsection (1)(a) need not be a specific person (or class of persons) known to, or identified by, D.
(1B) D may commit an offence under this section whether or not a suicide, or an attempt at suicide, occurs.

So that act has to be done, and done with the intention of assisting/encouraging suicide; answer A is therefore incorrect.

This offence is an alternative verdict on a charge of murder/manslaughter (Suicide Act 1961, s. 2(2) as amended). The person committing the offence need not know, or even be able to identify, the other person. So, for example, the author of a website promoting suicide who intends that one of more of his/her readers will commit suicide is guilty of an offence, even though he/she may never know the identity of those who access the website. The offence applies whether or not a person commits or attempts suicide; answer C is therefore incorrect.

Section 2A of the Suicide Act 1961 (as amended) states:

(1) If D arranges for a person ('D2') to do an act that is capable of encouraging or assisting the suicide or attempted suicide of another person and D2 does that act, D is also to be treated for the purposes of this Act as having done it.

(2) Where the facts are such that an act is not capable of encouraging or assisting suicide or attempted suicide, for the purposes of this Act it is to be treated as so capable if the act would have been so capable had the facts been as D believed them to be at the time of the act or had subsequent events happened in the manner D believed they would happen (or both).

(3) A reference in this Act to a person ('P') doing an act that is capable of encouraging the suicide or attempted suicide of another person includes a reference to P doing so by threatening another person or otherwise putting pressure on another person to commit or attempt suicide.

Section 2A(1) describes a liability when a defendant arranges for another to encourage or assist suicide so that responsibility cannot be avoided by using a third party as a conduit to commit the offence. Note that that third party must actually do the 'act', i.e. they must encourage or assist the suicide.

Section 2A(2) has the effect that an act can be capable of encouraging or assisting suicide even if the circumstances are such that it was impossible for the act to actually encourage or assist suicide. An act is therefore treated as capable of encouraging and assisting suicide if it would have been so capable had the facts been as the defendant believed them to be at the time of the act (e.g. if pills provided with the intention that they will assist a person to commit suicide are thought to be lethal but are in fact harmless), or had subsequent events happened as the defendant believed they would (e.g. if lethal pills which were sent to a person with the intention that the person would use them to commit or attempt to commit suicide get lost in the post), or both; answer D is therefore incorrect.

Crime, paras 1.5.6, 1.5.6.1

Answer 5.4

Answer **D** — Section 54 of the Coroners and Justice Act 2009 states:

(1) Where a person ('D') kills or is a party to the killing of another ('V'), D is not to be convicted of murder if—

   (a) D's acts and omissions in doing or being a party to the killing resulted from D's loss of self-control,

   (b) the loss of self-control had a qualifying trigger, and

   (c) a person of D's sex and age, with a normal degree of tolerance and self-restraint and in the circumstances of D, might have reacted in the same or in a similar way to D . . .

Section 54 sets out the criteria which need to be met in order for the partial defence of loss of self-control to be successful, those being:

- the defendant's conduct resulted from a loss of self-control;
- the loss of self-control had a qualifying trigger; and
- a person of the defendant's sex and age with an ordinary level of tolerance and self-restraint and in the circumstances of the defendant might have acted in the same or similar way to the defendant.

There is no 'reasonable person' element so answers A and B are therefore incorrect. The similar person also acted in the same or similar way, not just the same; answer C is therefore incorrect.

Crime, para. 1.5.3.2

Answer 5.5

Answer **B** — In order to prove manslaughter by an unlawful act, you must prove:

An unlawful act by the defendant, that is, an act which constitutes a criminal offence in its own right, irrespective of the fact that it ultimately results in someone's death.

The act must be inherently unlawful; however, it need not be directed or aimed at anyone and can include acts committed against or towards property such as criminal damage or arson (*R* v *Goodfellow* (1986) 83 Cr App R 23); answer D is therefore incorrect.

Intention to injure is irrelevant and intoxication is no defence to a crime of basic intent; answer C is therefore incorrect.

Murder, however, does require a specific *mens rea* to kill or seriously injure which is not present here; answer A is therefore incorrect.

Crime, para. 1.5.4.1

Answer 5.6

Answer **A** — Section 4 of the Offences Against the Person Act 1861 states:

Whosoever shall solicit, encourage, persuade or endeavour to persuade, or shall propose to any person, to murder any other person, whether he be a subject of Her Majesty or not, and whether he be within the Queen's dominions or not, shall be guilty of [an offence].

The proposed victim may be outside the UK and it does not matter whether or not the person is in fact encouraged to commit murder; answers C and D are therefore incorrect. Answer B is incorrect as the offence is not complete until someone is in receipt of the solicitation.

Crime, para. 1.5.7

Answer 5.7

Answer **A** — In order to prove manslaughter by an unlawful act, you must prove:

- an unlawful act by the defendant, i.e. an act which is unlawful in itself, irrespective of the fact that it ultimately results in someone's death. The act must be inherently unlawful;
- that the act involved a risk of bodily harm. That risk will be judged objectively, i.e. would the risk be apparent to a reasonable and sober person watching the act.

Clearly, setting fire to a building using accelerants carries a risk and as the building is leased and arson does not have the protection that simple damage to your own property has, the act is unlawful; answers C and D are therefore incorrect.

A charge of manslaughter may be brought where a person, by an instance of gross negligence, has brought about the death of another. The ingredients of this offence were reviewed and restated by the Court of Appeal and essentially consist of death resulting from a negligent breach of a duty of care owed by the defendant to the victim in circumstances so reprehensible as to amount to gross negligence (*R* v *Misra and Srivastava* [2004] EWCA Crim 2375). There is no duty of care owed to the victim and therefore answers B and D are incorrect.

Crime, paras 1.5.4.1, 1.5.4.2

Answer 5.8

Answer **B** — The Homicide Act 1957, s. 2 states:

(1) A person ('D') who kills or is a party to a killing of another is not to be convicted of murder if D was suffering from an abnormality of mental functioning which—
   (a) arose from a recognised medical condition,
   (b) substantially impaired D's ability to do one or more of the things mentioned in subsection (1A), and
   (c) provides an explanation for D's acts and omissions in doing or being party to the killing.

Whether the 'impairment of mental responsibility' is 'substantial' or not will be a question of fact for the jury to decide. Minor lapses of lucidity will not be enough. Answers C and D are therefore incorrect.

In the case of *R* v *Dietschmann* [2003] 1 AC 1209, the House of Lords accepted that a mental abnormality caused by a grief reaction to the recent death of an aunt with whom the defendant had had a physical relationship could suffice. In that case, their Lordships went on to hold that there is no requirement to show that the 'abnormality of mind' was the sole cause of the defendant's acts in committing the killing. Answers A and D are therefore incorrect.

Crime, para. 1.5.3.1

Answer 5.9

Answer **D** — Section 5 of the Domestic Violence, Crime and Victims Act 2004 states:

(1) A person ('D') is guilty of an offence if—
   (a) a child or vulnerable adult ('V') dies or suffers serious physical harm as a result of the unlawful act of a person who—
      (i) was a member of the same household as V, and
      (ii) had frequent contact with him,
   (b) D was such a person at the time of that act,
   (c) at that time there was a significant risk of serious physical harm being caused to V by the unlawful act of such a person, and
   (d) either D was the person whose act caused the death or serious physical harm or—
      (i) D was, or ought to have been, aware of the risk mentioned in paragraph (c),
      (ii) D failed to take such steps as he could reasonably have been expected to take to protect V from the risk, and
      (iii) the act occurred in circumstances of the kind that D foresaw or ought to have foreseen.

You will need to answer 'yes' to all the following questions for the offence to be made out.

- Was the victim a child or vulnerable adult? Yes.
- Was the defendant a member of the same household? For these purposes, a person will be a member of a particular household if he/she visits it so often and for such periods of time that it is reasonable to regard him/her as a member of it, even if he/she does not actually live there, so yes.
- Was there a significant risk of serious physical harm being caused to the victim by the unlawful act of such a person? Yes.
- Was the defendant the person who caused the victim's death? Yes.
- Was the defendant also—although not the person who caused the death—a member of the household? Yes.
  - If yes, were they aware of that risk? Yes.
  - Did they fail to take steps to protect the victim from that risk? Yes.
  - Did the act occur where it was foreseen or ought to have been foreseen? Yes.

As can be seen by all the yes answers, the offence is made out for both the mother and the boyfriend, the mother being culpable even in circumstances where she ought to have foreseen the attack; answers A, B and C are therefore incorrect.

Crime, para. 1.5.5

Answer 5.10

Answer **A** — The Suicide Act 1961, s. 2 states:

(1) A person ('D') commits an offence if—
    (a) D does an act capable of encouraging or assisting the suicide or attempted suicide of another person, and
    (b) D's act was intended to encourage or assist suicide or an attempt at suicide ...

The person committing the offence need not know, or even be able to identify, the other person. For example, the author of a website promoting suicide who intends that one of more of its readers will commit suicide is guilty of an offence, even though the author may never know the identity of those who access the website. The offence applies whether or not a person commits or attempts suicide; answers B, C and D are therefore incorrect.

Crime, para. 1.5.6

QUESTIONS

Question 6.1

TURVEY has just lost his job and is finding money hard to come by. RANDELL feels sorry for TURVEY and gives him a packet of ten cigarettes that also contains a small amount of cocaine. TURVEY knows nothing about the cocaine inside the packet of cigarettes. Several hours later, TURVEY is stopped by PC MAIR, who discovers the cocaine inside the cigarette packet.

Which of the following statements is correct with regard to TURVEY?

A Provided TURVEY has physical control of the cigarettes and knows of their presence, he has 'possession' of the drug.

B The only requirement for 'possession' is that TURVEY had the drug in his physical control.

C To show that TURVEY has 'possession' of the drug, you must show that he actually knew that what he possessed was cocaine.

D TURVEY cannot be in 'possession' of the cocaine because he does not know of its existence.

Question 6.2

HINDS has a bottle of vitamin tablets in her handbag. Unknown to her, her son had put three Ecstasy tablets in the bottle that morning. Before leaving the house, HINDS checks that she has the bottle containing the tablets in her handbag.

Which of the following is correct?

A HINDS is in possession of a controlled drug, but would have a defence to the offence under s. 28 of the Misuse of Drugs Act 1971 in these circumstances.

B HINDS is in possession of a controlled drug but would have a defence under s. 5 of the Misuse of Drugs Act 1971 in these circumstances.

C HINDS is not in possession of a controlled drug as she did not put the tablets in the bottle.

D HINDS is not in possession of a controlled drug as she has no knowledge of what the tablets are.

Question 6.3

FISCHER is a member of the National Crime Agency. She has been involved in an undercover operation in relation to drug trafficking. SMITH is a major drug dealer and has asked FISCHER to help in the supply of cocaine. FISCHER has provisionally agreed to this to maintain her cover. In fact, FISCHER has no intention of illegally supplying drugs, and SMITH is later arrested for incitement to supply a controlled drug (contrary to s. 19 of the Misuse of Drugs Act 1971).

Has SMITH committed the offence in this situation?

A Yes, the offence is complete when SMITH asks FISCHER to supply the drugs.

B No, as FISCHER has no intention of supplying the drugs.

C Yes, but only if FISCHER actually supplied the drugs.

D No, as the offence of incitement does not apply to the offence of supplying a controlled drug.

Question 6.4

MORRISON is a self-employed chemist and her partner, OLDMAN, confessed to her that he was addicted to heroin (a Class A drug); MORRISON is not registered as a drug addict. MORRISON was shocked by the news but agreed to help OLDMAN break his addiction and suggested that she unofficially obtains some methadone (a substitute for heroin) in order to do so. MORRISON took some methadone from the storeroom of her chemist shop and gave it to OLDMAN.

With regard to MORRISON's actions in taking and possessing the methadone from the storeroom of the chemist shop and the offence of possessing a con-trolled drug (under s. 5(2) of the Misuse of Drugs Act 1971 only), which of the following is correct?

A MORRISON is in unlawful possession of the methadone and has no defence under the Misuse of Drugs Act 1971.

B MORRISON is in unlawful possession of the methadone but has a defence under the Misuse of Drugs Act 1971.

C MORRISON is in lawful possession of the methadone as she had lawful possession due to her occupation; her intent is irrelevant.

D MORRISON is in lawful possession of the methadone as it is not a controlled drug, being only a Class A substitute.

Question 6.5

CORCORAN (who is 20 years old) is sitting outside a school in his car and decides to smoke some cannabis (a Class B drug). As it is 11 am and classes are taking place at the school, a number of school pupils and several members of staff at the school see what is going on. Staff alert the police and PC WHITE is sent to the incident. Before the officer arrives, SHAW (who is 17 years old and a friend of CORCORAN's) walks past CORCORAN and the two start a conversation. After several minutes, CORCORAN finishes smoking the cannabis and just then PC WHITE arrives in a marked police vehicle. As the officer arrives, CORCORAN panics and hands SHAW a large bag of cannabis saying, 'I want to smoke this later so look after it for me and I'll pay you £20'. SHAW knows that he is being handed cannabis and agrees and walks away and watches as PC WHITE searches CORCORAN and his car. Finding nothing, the officer leaves. SHAW walks back to CORCORAN and returns the cannabis to him. CORCORAN gives £20 to SHAW and drives off.

Considering the offence of supplying a controlled drug (contrary to s. 4(3) of the Misuse of Drugs Act 1971) and the law in relation to that offence, which of the following comments is correct?

A CORCORAN and SHAW are guilty of the offence. Because of the time and place of the offence, the court will be required to consider 'aggravating' factors (under s. 4A of the Act) in relation to CORCORAN only.

B CORCORAN and SHAW are guilty of the offence. Because of the time and place of the offence, the court will be required to consider 'aggravating' factors (under s. 4A of the Act) in relation to both men.

C Only CORCORAN is guilty of the offence. Because of the time and place of the offence, the court will be required to consider 'aggravating' factors (under s. 4A of the Act) in relation to it.

D Only SHAW is guilty of the offence. As he is under 18 years of age, the court will not consider the offence 'aggravated' (under s. 4A of the Act).

Question 6.6

An undercover police officer conducted several telephone conversations with PRIOR who was suspected of supplying heroin. PRIOR stated that although he had none with him at the times of the phone calls, he would be happy to supply in the future. In fact, PRIOR never did supply any drugs to the officer as he was arrested before that could happen. In relation to the offence under s. 4(3)(a) of the Misuse of Drugs Act 1971, offering to supply a controlled drug, PRIOR argues that he is not guilty of that offence as he is not really making a genuine offer to supply as the purchaser was an undercover police officer.

In relation to this, which of the following is correct?

A PRIOR will be guilty as an offence was committed whether or not the offer was genuine.

B PRIOR will be guilty of that offence, provided the prosecution shows that he actually had the ability to supply the drugs.

C PRIOR will not be guilty of that offence as he did not actually have heroin at the time he made the offer.

D PRIOR will not be guilty of that offence as it was not a 'real' offer as the police officer could not accept the actual drugs.

Question 6.7

FLANDERS used his knowledge of chemistry to help his friends and provide them with drugs. He has drug-making equipment in the basement of his house which he uses to make crack from cocaine in order that it can be vaporised and inhaled by his friends. A warrant under s. 23 of the Misuse of Drugs Act 1971 is executed at FLANDERS's home address and the police recover the drugs and the drug-making equipment.

Considering only the offence of production of a controlled drug (contrary to s. 4(2) of the Misuse of Drugs Act 1971), which of the following comments is correct?

A FLANDERS is guilty of this offence merely by being in possession of the equipment from which the drug is produced.

B FLANDERS is guilty of this offence even though he is only producing one drug from another.

C FLANDERS is not guilty of this offence as he is not producing a controlled drug, he is only transforming one to another.

D FLANDERS is not guilty of this offence as essentially crack and cocaine are the same drug and FLANDERS did not 'produce' the cocaine.

Question 6.8

ARCHER is short of money and is approached by ZIEGLER who offers ARCHER £300 per week if ARCHER will permit ZIEGLER to use ARCHER's house as a base to produce cannabis; ARCHER agrees. ZIEGLER sets up a hydroponic growing system to aid the cultivation of the cannabis plants in ARCHER's house and four months later the plants have fully grown. ZIEGLER harvests the plants and, in order to maximise his profits, he adds a variety of bulking agents (such as lead and ketamine) to his cannabis product. At no time does ARCHER have anything to do with the cultivation or preparation of the cannabis. The police raid the house and both men are arrested.

In relation to the offence of production of a controlled drug (contrary to s. 4(2) of the Misuse of Drugs Act 1971), which of the following statements is correct?

A ARCHER and ZIEGLER have committed the offence in these circumstances.

B ARCHER has not committed the offence. ZIEGLER has committed the offence but only when he cultivates the cannabis plants.

C ARCHER has not committed the offence. ZIEGLER has committed the offence when he cultivates and harvests the cannabis plants and also when he adds the bulking agents to his product.

D The offence under s. 4(2) has not been committed as all of the controlled drugs in question (cannabis and ketamine particularly) are Class B drugs—this offence is only committed in relation to the production of Class A drugs.

Question 6.9

MITCHUM has some cocaine (a controlled drug) in his pocket, which he intends to supply to someone else. Seeing a police officer in the distance, he hands the cocaine to his friend, WAGNER, and says 'Hold on to this cocaine for me and I will give you £20'. WAGNER agrees and takes possession of the cocaine intending always to hand it back to MITCHUM to enable MITCHUM to supply it to someone else. The officer stops both men and carries out a lawful search and discovers the cocaine that WAGNER has in his possession.

In relation to the cocaine, which offence(s) has WAGNER committed?

A Possession only as he at that point returned the drugs.

B Possession with intent to supply only, as the drugs were meant by MITCHUM for supply.

C Possession with intent to supply only as he was going to benefit from that supply.

D Possession of a controlled drug and also possession with intent to supply as he intended returning the drugs; the money is irrelevant.

Question 6.10

McNIFF owns a garden centre which sells plant foods. He is aware that one of the items he sells has been known to cause a psychoactive effect on humans and that young people have been buying it for that effect. He has labelled each bottle as 'plant food' and also added a notice saying 'not for human consumption' on the shelf on which the substance is kept. If someone apparently under the age of 21 buys the substance, he makes sure his staff always ask if it is for a proper purpose and not for their own use. However, customers buy it and consume it for its psychoactive effect.

At what point, if any, could McNIFF successfully claim a defence in relation to the supply of a psychoactive substance contrary to s. 5 of the Psychoactive Substances Act 2016?

A By insisting that staff challenge under-21s about using it for themselves.

B By labelling the product as 'plant food'.

C By putting 'not for human consumption' on the shelf the substance is on.

D McNIFF has no defence as he is still reckless as he knows what people are using the product for.

Question 6.11

SAUNDERS and TWEED are both drug addicts and bought a quantity of heroin together, which SAUNDERS carried back to a house. At the house, SAUNDERS divided the heroin equally and gave a share to TWEED. Unfortunately, TWEED had been drinking all day and fell asleep. SAUNDERS then injected TWEED with her own drugs while she was asleep.

At what point, if at all, does SAUNDERS commit the offence of supplying a controlled drug under s. 4(3)(a) of the Misuse of Drugs Act 1971?

A When SAUNDERS divided the heroin and gave it to TWEED.

B Only when SAUNDERS injected TWEED with the heroin.

C On both occasions, when SAUNDERS divided the heroin and gave it to TWEED and later when TWEED was injected with the heroin.

D The offence is not committed at all, because the heroin was jointly purchased by SAUNDERS and TWEED.

Question 6.12

Travel restriction orders made under the Criminal Justice and Police Act 2001 restrict the travel of convicted drug traffickers.

For how long a period does this travel restriction order last?

A Two years.

B Four years.

C Ten years.

D Unlimited period; no set maximum.

Question 6.13

MAY was the sole tenant and occupier of a flat which was raided by the police. They found MAY, along with seven others, and a number of items used for the smoking of drugs. They also found a quantity of cannabis resin. MAY admits he had given permission for drug smoking to take place. During the search of the premises, the police could detect no smell of cannabis. MAY was charged with allowing the offence of permitting the smoking of cannabis, cannabis resin or prepared opium on premises under s. 8 of the Misuse of Drugs Act 1971.

Is MAY guilty of this offence?

A No, as he was not the owner of the premises.

B No, as there was no evidence actual smoking took place.

C Yes, as there was cannabis and drugs paraphernalia in the premises.

D Yes, as he admits that he gave permission for drug smoking.

Question 6.14

VICKERS is sailing a yacht from Spain to the Netherlands and on board the yacht are speakers containing a large amount of cannabis. The speakers were delivered from his home address in London to Spain by PAYNE who knew they were going to be used to hide and transport the cannabis. The yacht is stopped in UK territorial waters en route to the Netherlands and VICKERS is arrested.

Considering the assisting a misuse of drugs offence outside the UK contrary to s. 20 of the Misuse of Drugs Act 1971, who, if either, has committed the offence?

A VICKERS only as he is delivering the drugs.

B PAYNE only as VICKERS was not in the UK when the speakers were delivered or the drugs loaded.

C Both, as PAYNE delivered the speakers and VICKERS is delivering the drugs.

D Neither, as PAYNE had no part in delivering the drugs and VICKERS was not in the UK when the drugs were loaded.

Question 6.15

Police officers have obtained a warrant to search a premises under s. 23 of the Misuse of Drugs Act 1971. When they enter the premises, there are a number of persons present, including one who is clearly repairing the washing machine.

Which of the following is true in relation to searching individuals on the premises?

A They can search all individuals in the premises under authority of the warrant.

B They can search all individuals in the premises under authority of the warrant, but only if it states individuals may be searched.

C They can search only individuals named on the warrant when using that warrant as authority to search.

D They could search everyone except those who are there for an ancillary purpose.

Question 6.16

RIDDICK was approached by CRAWLEY and asked to deliver a package to a nearby address. CRAWLEY gave RIDDICK £200 for taking the package. RIDDICK was very drunk at the time he was asked to take the package and did not realise that he had been given so much money. He takes the package but is stopped by police officers who have had CRAWLEY, a known drug dealer, under surveillance. The package is found to contain a very large quantity of a Class A drug and RIDDICK is charged with possession of, and possession with intent to supply, a Class A drug.

Consider RIDDICK's use of the defence under s. 28(2) of the Misuse of Drugs Act 1971 (lack of knowledge of some alleged fact) due to the fact that he was drunk and he had no 'reason to suspect' what he was doing.

Which of the following is correct?

A The defence could be used for possession of the drugs, but not for the intention to supply.

B The defence could not be used for either charge as 'reason to suspect' is a factual test and not subject to individual peculiarities.

C The defence could be used for either charge as 'reason to suspect' is subject to individual peculiarities and is not a factual test.

D The defence could be used for intention to supply but not for mere possession of the drugs.

Question 6.17

EWINGS is a drug dealer who supplies drugs from his girlfriend's flat. Police have been watching the premises and when his girlfriend arrives in a car, the police strike. In the car there is a large quantity of heroin. The car belongs to EWINGS and the girlfriend states that she was just delivering the drugs to EWINGS who sells the drugs for profit—she states that she is not involved in, and does not gain any benefit from, the supplying that EWINGS commits.

For what offence(s) under the Misuse of Drugs Act 1971 will the girlfriend be liable?

A Possession of a controlled drug only.

B Possession of a controlled drug and possession with intent to supply.

C Possession of a controlled drug and being concerned in the supply of a controlled drug.

D Possession of a controlled drug and being concerned in the supply of a controlled drug and possession with intent to supply.

Question 6.18

PERKIS suffers from multiple sclerosis (MS) and has heard that cannabis can assist to reduce the impact the condition has on her daily life. She is making inquiries regarding purchasing the drug but does not want to commit any offences contrary to the Misuse of Drugs Act 1971 so approaches PC FLANAGHAN for some advice regarding the drug and in particular the use of cannabis-based products for medicinal use. PC FLANAGHAN researches the law and discovers that the Misuse of Drugs (Amendments) (Cannabis and Licence Fees) (England, Wales and Scotland) Regulations 2018 (SI 2018/1055) amended the Misuse of Drugs Regulations 2001 to allow the wider use of cannabis-based products for medicinal use in humans, essentially for medical purposes.

In relation to those Regulations which of the following is correct?

A These unlicensed prescriptions can be issued for particular conditions like MS only.

B These unlicensed prescriptions can be issued by a specialist doctor.

C These unlicensed prescriptions can be issued by a GP but they must seek approval from an expert panel.

D These unlicensed prescriptions can be issued in any case where there is an unmet clinical need for patients with certain conditions.

Question 6.19

CAFFERATTA is convicted of an offence under s. 4(2) of the Misuse of Drugs Act 1971 (production of a controlled drug) and is sentenced to a period of three years in prison.

In these circumstances, can a court impose a travel restriction order on CAFFERATTA (under s. 33 of the Criminal Justice and Police Act 2001)?

A Yes, and if imposed the order must run for a minimum of three years.

B Yes, although the maximum period the order can run for is five years.

C No, as CAFFERATTA has not been sentenced to a period of imprisonment of four or more years.

D No, as production of a controlled drug under s. 4(2) of the Misuse of Drugs Act 1971 is not classed as a 'drug trafficking offence'.

ANSWERS

Answer 6.1

Answer **A** — This question does not ask if TURVEY has committed an offence, merely if he satisfies what the law requires for 'possession' of the drug. In order to be in possession of anything, the common law requires physical control of the object plus knowledge that it contains something, making answers B and C incorrect. The fact that TURVEY does not know of the existence of the cocaine within the cigarette packet may afford him a defence to a charge of possession but he still 'possesses' the drug, making answer D incorrect.

Crime, paras 1.6.3 to 1.6.3.7

Answer 6.2

Answer **A** — A person has possession of a drug if they have physical control of it plus knowledge of the presence of the drug. HINDS is therefore in possession of a controlled drug and commits the offence under s. 5(2) of the Misuse of Drugs Act 1971 (making answers C and D incorrect). Where a person in possession claims not to realise what they possessed, they may have a defence under s. 28 of the Misuse of Drugs Act 1971 (making answer B incorrect). If HINDS proves that she neither knew nor suspected nor had reason to suspect that the tablets in the container were controlled drugs, she would have a defence under s. 5 of the Act (correct answer A).

Crime, paras 1.6.3 to 1.6.3.8, 1.6.9

Answer 6.3

Answer **A** — The definition of this offence under s. 19 of the Misuse of Drugs Act 1971 is that it is an offence for a person to incite another to commit an offence under *any* other provisions of this Act. This covers all sections, including supplying.

A person inciting an undercover police officer may commit an offence under this section even though there was no possibility of the officer actually being induced to commit the offence, and therefore answer B is incorrect. As the offence is committed at the time the incitement is made, and is not conditional on either the supply or receipt of the controlled drugs, therefore answer C is incorrect.

Crime, para. 1.6.14

Answer 6.4

Answer **A** — The Misuse of Drugs Act 1971, s. 5 states:

(2) Subject to section 28 of this Act and to subsection (4) below, it is an offence for a person to have a controlled drug in his possession in contravention of subsection (1) above ...

The *actus reus* of this offence is simple possession; there are, however, defences supplied by the 1971 Act. These relate to knowledge of the drug and its use whilst in possession. The fact that MORRISON knows it is a drug and that she intends giving it to her partner negates these defences; answer B is therefore incorrect.

MORRISON's profession means she can lawfully possess Class A drugs (methadone is Class A) but not in these circumstances; answers C and D are therefore incorrect.

Crime, para. 1.6.3.7

Answer 6.5

Answer **A** — Section 4 of the Misuse of Drugs Act 1971 states:

(3) Subject to section 28 of this Act, it is an offence for a person—
  (a) to supply or offer to supply a controlled drug to another in contravention of subsection (1) above; or
  (b) to be concerned in the supplying of such a drug to another in contravention of that subsection; or
  (c) to be concerned in the making to another in contravention of that subsection of an offer to supply such a drug.

In *R v Maginnis* [1987] AC 303, the House of Lords held that 'supply' involves more than a mere transfer of physical control of the item from one person to another and includes a further concept, namely that of 'enabling the recipient to apply the thing handed over to purposes for which he desires or has a duty to apply it'. In other words, *the person to whom the drug is given must derive some benefit from being given the drug.* So the key to working out if there has been a 'supply' is to ask: 'Does being given the drug benefit the person to whom the drug has been given?' If the answer is 'Yes' then the person *giving the drug* is 'supplying' it. In this question, CORCORAN offers SHAW £20 to look after the cannabis—so SHAW benefits from being given the drug and therefore CORCORAN supplies it to him. When SHAW hands the cannabis back to CORCORAN, CORCORAN benefits from it as he can smoke the cannabis— therefore SHAW supplies CORCORAN.

So, at this stage, CORCORAN and SHAW have committed the offence under s. 4(3) meaning that answers C and D are incorrect.

Section 4A of the Misuse of Drugs Act 1971 requires courts to treat certain conditions as 'aggravating' factors when considering the seriousness of the offence under s. 4(3) if committed by a *person aged 18 or over*. This means that s. 4A will not apply to SHAW as he is 17 years old and means that answer B is incorrect.

Crime, paras 1.6.4.1 to 1.6.4.2

Answer 6.6

Answer **A** — Section 4 of the Misuse of Drugs Act 1971 states:

(3) Subject to section 28 of this Act, it is an offence for a person—
    (a) to supply or offer to supply a controlled drug to another in contravention of subsection (1) above; or
    (b) to be concerned in the supplying of such a drug to another in contravention of that subsection; or
    (c) to be concerned in the making to another in contravention of that subsection of an offer to supply such a drug.

The offence of offering to supply a controlled drug is complete when the offer is made. It is irrelevant whether or not the defendant actually has the means to meet the offer or even intends to carry it out (*R v Goodard* [1992] Crim LR 588); answers B and C are therefore incorrect. If the offer is made by conduct alone (i.e. without any words), it may be difficult to prove this offence. If words are used, the defence under s. 28 does not appear to apply (*R v Mitchell* [1992] Crim LR 723). If the offer is made to an undercover police officer, the offence is still committed and the defendant cannot claim that such an offer was not a 'real' offer (*R v Kray* [1998] EWCA Crim 3211); answer D is therefore incorrect.

Crime, para. 1.6.4.1

Answer 6.7

Answer **B** — Section 4 of the Misuse of Drugs Act 1971 states:

(2) Subject to section 28 of this Act, it is an offence for a person—
    (a) to produce a controlled drug in contravention of subsection (1) … ; or
    (b) to be concerned in the production of such a drug in contravention of that subsection by another.

'Produce' means producing by manufacture, cultivation or any other method and 'production' has a corresponding meaning (Misuse of Drugs Act 1971, s. 37). This is further than merely possessing the equipment to match such a production; answer A is therefore incorrect.

Converting one form of a Class A drug into another has been held to be 'producing' (*R v Russell* (1991) 94 Cr App R 351). So although crack and cocaine are essentially the same drug, it is production to change powdered cocaine into rock crack; answers C and D are therefore incorrect.

Crime, para. 1.6.7

Answer 6.8

Answer **C** — Section 4 of the Misuse of Drugs Act 1971 states that it is an offence to produce a controlled drug. The offence is relevant to all classes of drug (not just Class A), making answer D incorrect.

'Produce' means producing by manufacture, cultivation or any other method, and 'production' has a corresponding meaning (s. 37 of the Misuse of Drugs Act 1971). So ZIEGLER commits the offence when he cultivates the cannabis plants. Harvesting, cutting and stripping a cannabis plant is 'producing' (*R v Harris* [1996] 1 Cr App R 369), so ZIEGLER once again 'produces' when he harvests the cannabis plants. The addition of adulterants or bulking agents can amount to the production of a controlled drug (*R v Williams* [2011] EWCA Crim 232), so ZIEGLER commits the offence at this point as well. All of this means that answer B is incorrect. Being 'concerned in the production' requires evidence that the accused played an identifiable role in the production of the drug in question. This was not satisfied where the accused simply permitted two others who were producing drugs to use his kitchen (*R v Farr* [1982] Crim LR 745), which means ARCHER does not commit the offence (answer A is incorrect).

Crime, para. 1.6.7

Answer 6.9

Answer **D** — WAGNER has possession of the controlled drug (an offence under s. 5 of the Act) which makes options B and C incorrect.

So, if someone leaves drugs with a third person temporarily, what criminal liability is incurred by the third person? This situation was faced by the House of Lords in *R v Maginnis* [1987] AC 303. In that case, their Lordships decided that Maginnis would have been 'supplying' the controlled drug had he returned it to the drug trafficker who had left a package of cannabis resin in Maginnis's car (the drug trafficker would 'benefit' from this activity). Therefore he was in possession with intent to supply and so committed an offence under s. 5(3) of the Misuse of Drugs Act 1971. The same can be said of WAGNER as he intends to return the drugs so that MITCHUM can supply them to others (a benefit), meaning that answer A is incorrect and that answer D is correct.

Crime, paras 1.6.4 to 1.6.5

Answer 6.10

Answer **D** — Section 5 of the Psychoactive Substances Act 2016 states:

(1) A person commits an offence if—
  (a) the person intentionally supplies a substance to another person, (b) the substance is a psychoactive substance,
  (c) the person knows or suspects, or ought to know or suspect, that the substance is a psychoactive substance, and
  (d) the person knows, or is reckless as to whether, the psychoactive substance is likely to be consumed by the person to whom it is supplied, or by some other person, for its psychoactive effects.
(2) A person ('P') commits an offence if—
  (a) P offers to supply a psychoactive substance to another person ('R'), and
  (b) P knows or is reckless as to whether R, or some other person, would, if P supplied a substance to R in accordance with the offer, be likely to consume the substance for its psychoactive effects.
(3) For the purposes of subsection 2(b), the reference to a substance's psychoactive effects includes a reference to the psychoactive effects which the substance would have if it were the substance which P had offered to supply to R.
(4) ...

There are three mental elements of the supply offence.

- First, the prosecution must show that the supplying of the substance is intentional.
- Secondly, the defendant must have known or suspected, or ought to have known or suspected, that the substance is a psychoactive substance.
- Thirdly, the defendant must know, or be reckless as to whether, the psychoactive substance is likely to be consumed by the person to whom it is supplied or another person for its psychoactive effects.

The recklessness test would prevent a head shop proprietor escaping liability by arguing that because the psychoactive substances sold in his/her shop were labelled as 'plant food', 'research chemicals' or 'not for human consumption', he/she did not know that the substances were likely to be consumed; this offence covers the supply/offer to supply of a psychoactive substance to a person of *any age*; answers A, B and C are therefore incorrect.

Crime, para. 1.6.18

Answer 6.11

Answer **A** — It is an offence under s. 4(3)(a) of the Misuse of Drugs Act 1971 to supply a controlled drug to another. It has been held that dividing up controlled drugs which have been jointly purchased will amount to 'supplying' (*R* v *Buckley* (1979) 69 Cr App R 371).

Further, injecting another with his/her own controlled drug has been held *not* to amount to 'supplying' in a case where the defendant assisted in pushing down the plunger of a syringe that the other person was already using. Parker CJ's comments in that case suggest that simply injecting another person with their own drug would not amount to 'supplying' (*R* v *Harris* [1968] 1 WLR 769). It may, however, amount to an offence of 'poisoning' under s. 23 of the Offences Against the Person Act 1861.

Answers B, C and D are therefore incorrect.

Crime, para. 1.6.4

Answer 6.12

Answer **D** — The Criminal Justice and Police Act 2001 makes provision for courts (in practice the Crown Court) to impose travel restrictions on offenders convicted of drug trafficking offences. The offender has to have been sentenced by that court to a term of imprisonment of four years or more (s. 33(1)). The effect of the order is to restrict the offender's freedom to leave the UK for a period specified by the court, and it may require delivery up of his/her passport. The minimum duration of a travel restriction order is two years, starting from the date of the offender's release from custody. There is no maximum period prescribed in the legislation, therefore answers A, B and C are incorrect. The court must always consider whether such an order should be made and must give reasons where it does not consider such an order to be appropriate (s. 33(2)).

Crime, para. 1.6.16

Answer 6.13

Answer **B** — Section 8 of the Misuse of Drugs Act 1971 states:

A person commits an offence if, being the occupier or concerned in the management of any premises, he knowingly permits or suffers any of the following activities to take place on those premises, that is to say:

(a) producing or attempting to produce a controlled drug in contravention of section 4(1) of this Act;

(b) supplying or attempting to supply a controlled drug to another in contravention of section 4(1) of this Act, or offering to supply a controlled drug to another in contravention of section 4(1);

(c) preparing opium for smoking;

(d) smoking cannabis, cannabis resin or prepared opium.

As can be seen, it applies to occupiers and not just owners; answer A is therefore incorrect. It does, however, require that it was necessary to establish that the activity of smoking had taken place and not merely that the permission had been given (*R v Auguste* [2003] EWCA Crim 3929); answer D is therefore incorrect. It is also not sufficient that the drugs and paraphernalia were present—it seems the police may have timed their raid a bit too soon as no smoking had taken place; answer C is therefore incorrect.

Crime, para. 1.6.11

Answer 6.14

Answer **B** — Section 20 of the Misuse of Drugs Act 1971 states:

A person commits an offence if in the United Kingdom he assists in or induces the commission in any place outside the United Kingdom of an offence punishable under the provisions of a corresponding law in force in that place.

This offence relates to actions taking place in the UK that would assist the commission of an offence in another country. As VICKERS is at sea (albeit in UK waters) his actions cannot assist the commission of an offence in Spain as he has already left and having been stopped from delivering there will be no offence in the Netherlands, therefore he cannot commit this offence and answers A and C are incorrect.

PAYNE does commit the offence as 'assisting' has been held to include taking containers to another country in the knowledge that they would later be filled with a controlled drug and sent on to a third country (*R v Evans* (1977) 64 Cr App R 237) and once the drugs leave Spain the offence is committed; answer D is therefore incorrect.

Crime, para. 1.6.13

Answer 6.15

Answer **B** — Section 23 of the Misuse of Drugs Act 1971 is a very wide statutory provision granting authority for a broad range of enforcement measures in connection with controlled drugs.

Particular care will need to be taken when drafting the application for a warrant under s. 23. Where police officers are on premises under the authority of such a warrant it will be important to have established the precise extent of the warrant. If such a warrant authorises the search of premises only, that in itself will not give the officers authority to search people found on those premises unless the officer can point to some other power authorising the search (*Hepburn* v *Chief Constable of Thames Valley Police* [2002] EWCA Civ 1841); answers A and C are therefore incorrect.

However, where the warrant authorises the search of premises and people, the Divisional Court has held that it is reasonable to restrict the movement of people within the premises to allow the search to be conducted properly (*DPP* v *Meaden* [2003] EWHC 3005 (Admin)); answer D is therefore incorrect.

Crime, para. 1.6.17.1

Answer 6.16

Answer **B** — Section 28(2) allows a defence where the defendant did not know, suspect or have reason to suspect the existence of some fact which is essential to proving the case. In relation to this defence, RIDDICK could discharge the evidential burden by showing that he neither knew nor suspected that the package contained a controlled drug, and that he neither knew nor suspected that he was supplying it to another. Both of these elements would be facts which the prosecution would have to allege in order to prove the offence.

However, external factors can impact on this defence. For example, if RIDDICK knew the person to be a local drug dealer, or the reward for his errand was suspiciously large, then he may not be able to discharge this, albeit evidential, burden.

However, it has been held that the test for 'reason to suspect' is an objective (factual) one (*R* v *Young* [1984] 1 WLR 654). Consequently, where a 'reason to suspect' was not apparent to a defendant because he/she was too intoxicated to see it, the defence will not apply. So if you're offered a package to deliver whilst drunk ...

Consequently answers A, C and D are incorrect.

Crime, para. 1.6.9.1

Answer 6.17

Answer **B** — The offence of possession of a controlled drug is clear.

In *R v Maginnis* [1987] AC 303, the House of Lords held that 'supply' involves more than a mere transfer of physical control of the item from one person to another and includes a further concept, namely that of 'enabling the recipient to apply the thing handed over to purposes for which he desires or has a duty to apply it'—in other words, the person to whom the drug is given must derive some benefit from it. By supplying the drugs, EWINGS receives a benefit so therefore, although the girlfriend does not benefit, the person she supplies to does benefit and consequently it fits the offence.

There is no actual 'supplying' or being concerned in the supplying as the drugs were intercepted prior to supply; answers C and D are therefore incorrect. But there is possession with intent to supply; answer A is therefore incorrect.

Crime, paras 1.6.4, 1.6.4.1

Answer 6.18

Answer **B** — The Misuse of Drugs (Amendments) (Cannabis and Licence Fees) (England, Wales and Scotland) Regulations 2018 (SI 2018/1055), in force as of 1 November 2018, amend the Misuse of Drugs Regulations 2001 to allow the wider use of cannabis-based products for medicinal use in humans, essentially for medical purposes.

The law does not limit the types of conditions that can be considered for treatment and doctors will no longer need to seek approval from an expert panel in order for patients to access the medicines; answers A and C are therefore incorrect.

The decision to prescribe these unlicensed medicines must be made by a specialist doctor—not a GP (answer C is further incorrect).

The specialist doctor must make decisions on prescribing cannabis-based products for medicinal use on a case-by-case basis, and only when the patient has an unmet special clinical need that cannot be met by licensed products; answer D is incorrect as that relates to all patients not just individuals and there must be consideration that licensed products will not work.

Crime, para. 1.6.10

Answer 6.19

Answer **C** — The minimum period a travel restriction order can run for is two years, making answer A incorrect. There is no maximum period the order can run for making answer B incorrect. Answers A and B are further incorrect as they state that a travel restriction order could be made in these circumstances when that is not the case. Such an order can only be made when the court has convicted a person of a drug trafficking offence (and production of a controlled drug under s. 4(2) of the Misuse of Drugs Act 1971 is a 'drug trafficking offence', making answer D incorrect) and it has determined that a sentence of four years or more is appropriate. As CAFFERATTA has been sentenced to a period of imprisonment of three years, the order could not be made (correct answer C).

Crime, para. 1.6.16

7 | **Firearms and Gun Crime**

QUESTIONS

Question 7.1

GRIER is 17 years old and is fascinated by firearms. He is friendly with BREEM who has an imitation firearm in his possession. GRIER offers to buy the imitation firearm from BREEM for £100 and as BREEM is short of money he sells the imitation firearm to GRIER.

Under s. 40 of the Violent Crime Reduction Act 2006 (supplying imitation firearms to minors), which of the following is correct?

A Only BREEM commits an offence as he has sold the imitation firearm to a person under 18 years of age.

B Both BREEM and GRIER commit the offence in these circumstances.

C The offence has not been committed as GRIER is 17 years old (rather than being under 16 as the offence requires).

D Only BREEM commits this offence as he has sold an imitation firearm to a person under 21 years of age.

Question 7.2

SWEENEY was stopped by Constable RUBY while driving a motor vehicle on a road. Constable RUBY stood outside the vehicle and conducted a check which revealed that the vehicle had just been circulated for its involvement in an armed robbery at a petrol station less than an hour previously. SWEENEY overheard Constable RUBY calling for assistance and got out of the car. SWEENEY placed his hand in his pocket and, with his fingers extended, pretended that he had a pistol in his pocket and told the officer to back away. Constable RUBY was not fooled by SWEENEY's attempt and told him so. SWEENEY then gave up without resisting the officer.

Would SWEENEY be guilty of an offence under s. 17(1) of the Firearms Act 1968 (using a firearm/imitation firearm to resist arrest) in these circumstances?

A No, holding his fingers like this will not amount to an imitation firearm.

B No, because he did not have with him something which had been adapted or altered so as to resemble a firearm.

C No, because the officer was not fooled by his attempt.

D Yes, because his fingers had the appearance of a firearm.

Question 7.3

OWEN was asked to carry a rucksack by his friend SHORT; unknown to OWEN, inside the rucksack was a box and inside the box were several bullets for a semi-automatic rifle.

Which person, if either, would have possession of ammunition contrary to s. 5 of the Firearms Act 1968?

A Only OWEN, as he has taken physical possession of the ammunition which SHORT no longer has.

B Only SHORT, as OWEN has no knowledge of the ammunition or the box it is contained in.

C Both OWEN and SHORT have possession of the ammunition.

D Neither, as SHORT does not have physical control of the ammunition and OWEN has no knowledge of the ammunition or the box it is contained in.

Question 7.4

BROWN's marriage has broken down because his wife had an affair with MEADE. BROWN was very upset and drove his car to MEADE's home, where his wife was staying—in the boot of the car BROWN is driving is an imitation firearm and a shotgun and ammunition for the shotgun. BROWN intended to threaten them both in an effort to end the affair. BROWN left the shotgun and ammunition in the car but put the imitation pistol in the pocket of his coat and approached the house. BROWN was let into the house by MEADE; however, his wife was upstairs, refusing to see him. BROWN produced the imitation firearm and said to MEADE, 'Tell her to come down or I'll shoot you with this and I'll get my shotgun from the car and take it upstairs to shoot her.' BROWN's intent to shoot his wife was genuine if his wife did not speak to him.

In relation to an offence under s. 16 of the Firearms Act 1968 (possession with intent to endanger life), which of the following statements is correct?

A This offence has been committed in relation to the imitation firearm, the shotgun and the ammunition for the shotgun.

B This offence has been committed but only in relation to the shotgun and ammunition for it.

C This offence has been committed in relation to the shotgun alone.

D This offence has not been committed as it does not apply to imitation firearms and BROWN does not have the shotgun and ammunition 'with him'.

Question 7.5

NORMANTON buys a plastic toy gun which, from a distance, could pass as a real gun although closer inspection would reveal it to be a toy. As NORMANTON is walking along a street, he sees CHADWICK, who owes him money, and uses the toy gun to threaten him, intending that CHADWICK will fear he will be shot unless he repays the debt. However, as CHADWICK is quite close to the toy gun, he realises that the gun is not real and is not at all frightened by NORMANTON.

Has NORMANTON committed an offence under s. 16A of the Firearms Act 1968 (possession with intent to cause fear of violence)?

A No, this offence may not be committed with an imitation firearm.

B Yes, provided NORMANTON intended to use violence against CHADWICK at that time.

C No, because CHADWICK realises that the gun is an imitation firearm.

D Yes, the offence is complete in these circumstances.

Question 7.6

SHATTOCK owed KUSACK money. KUSACK drove to SHATTOCK's house with a shotgun in the boot of the car. On arriving, KUSACK left the shotgun in the car and approached SHATTOCK. KUSACK threatened SHATTOCK with violence if the money was not paid back. SHATTOCK was in fear that KUSACK would use violence and paid the money. Even though the shotgun was left in the car, KUSACK fully intended using it if SHATTOCK failed to pay the money.

Has KUSACK committed an offence of possession of a firearm with intent to cause fear of violence contrary to s. 16A of the Firearms Act 1968?

A Yes, provided SHATTOCK feared that KUSACK would use violence.

B No, SHATTOCK was not aware that KUSACK was in possession of the shotgun.

C Yes, even though SHATTOCK was not aware that KUSACK was in possession of the shotgun.

D No, the shotgun was not in KUSACK's physical possession at the time the threats were made.

Question 7.7

Constable CHAVEZ stopped PETERS in his car. When he conducted a Police National Computer check, Constable CHAVEZ found that PETERS was wanted for attempted robbery, having threatened a garage cashier with a knife. Constable CHAVEZ searched the car and discovered a firearm in the boot. There was no evidence to show that PETERS was in possession of a firearm at the time of the original offence.

Would PETERS be guilty of an offence contrary to s. 17(2) of the Firearms Act 1968 (possession of a firearm at the time of committing or being arrested for a sch. 1 offence)?

A No, he was not in possession of the firearm during the original offence.

B Yes, because he has attempted to commit an indictable offence.

C No, because he did not commit the full offence of robbery.

D Yes, because he has been arrested for attempting to commit a sch. 1 offence.

Question 7.8

MAYER was in a public house and went upstairs to look to steal something. He found a loaded air rifle in a bedroom and decided to take it with him; but he heard a noise downstairs and thought the licensee was coming so he put the gun back.

At the time he had the air rifle, has MAYER committed an offence under s. 20 of the Firearms Act 1968 (trespassing with a firearm)?

A Yes, provided he entered the private part of the pub as a trespasser and then took possession of the firearm.

B Yes, as he was in the private part of the premises as a trespasser, and then picked up the firearm.

C No, he was only in possession of an air weapon.

D No, as he did not leave the private part of the pub with the firearm.

Question 7.9

SAUNDERS, a drug dealer, keeps a handgun and an imitation firearm on his person for protection. One day he drove to a local shop, where he entered and stole goods worth £30 (an offence that would be classed as 'low-value shoplifting'). As he was leaving the shop, he was asked what he was doing by the store owner. SAUNDERS punched the store owner (committing an offence of s. 39 battery (contrary to the Criminal Justice Act 1988) in the process) and ran to his car and escaped. The handgun and the imitation firearm remained in his coat during the incident.

Has SAUNDERS committed an offence relating to the handgun and imitation firearm under s. 18(1) of the Firearms Act 1968 (having a firearm with intent to commit an indictable offence or resist arrest), in these circumstances?

A No, he did not use the handgun or imitation firearm during the commission of the offences.

B Yes, but only in relation to the handgun.

C Yes, in relation to the handgun and the imitation firearm.

D No, as it cannot be shown that he committed an indictable offence.

Question 7.10

WATKINS is a drug dealer and is seeking to take over the drugs market in a large town. He has acquired a Samurai sword and intends using it to threaten other dealers. WATKINS has been tipped off that the police are about to execute a warrant at his home in the next few days. WATKINS has persuaded his friend MAYO, who is aged 18, to hide the sword in his house until the police lose interest in him.

Could WATKINS be guilty of an offence under s. 28(1) of the Violent Crime Reduction Act 2006 (using another to look after etc. a dangerous weapon)?

A No, this offence can only be committed in relation to a firearm.

B Yes, this offence can be committed in relation to a firearm or an offensive weapon.

C No, this offence can only be committed when the person looking after the weapon is under 18.

D Yes, this offence can be committed in relation to a firearm, including an air weapon, or an offensive weapon.

Question 7.11

DENCH has had a restriction on him in respect of his possession of a shotgun by virtue of s. 21 of the Firearms Act 1968 due to his conviction and subsequent sentence for an offence. He wishes to have this prohibition removed as it is affecting his ability to carry out his farming job.

Where, if at all, could DENCH apply to have the prohibition removed?

A The prohibition cannot be removed.

B A magistrates' court.

C The Crown Court.

D The High Court.

Question 7.12

DE'SOUZA is 18 years of age and has recently been released from a young offenders' institution, having served two years of a three years and six months sentence of detention.

What restrictions, if any, are placed on DE'SOUZA being in possession of a firearm?

A He may only possess a firearm after five years from the date of his release.

B He may not possess a firearm at any time from the date of his release.

C He may only possess a firearm after three years from the date of his release.

D There are no restrictions as he was not sentenced to a term of imprisonment.

Question 7.13

Constable PEARCE attended a noisy house party. As Constable PEARCE arrived, one of the party-goers, BELSHAW, was leaving the party. BELSHAW told Constable PEARCE that he had seen ERNEST, the house owner, in a bedroom of the house with what appeared to be a real pistol. Also, BELSHAW had overheard ERNEST and another man discussing a robbery that was to take place at an all-night petrol station that night.

What powers, if any, would be available to Constable PEARCE under s. 47 of the Firearms Act 1968?

A No power under the Act, as ERNEST was not in a public place.

B Power to enter the house and arrest ERNEST for an offence under the Act.

C Power to enter and search the house without warrant, but only if Constable PEARCE suspects an offence has been committed.

D Power to enter the house without warrant and search ERNEST for the firearm.

Question 7.14

MARTIN owns a section 1 firearm and holds a certificate allowing its possession. MARTIN has decided to sell the firearm because it has not been used for a number of months.

What obligation does MARTIN now have, in respect of the sale of the firearm, under s. 32(2) of the Firearms (Amendment) Act 1997?

A MARTIN must notify the chief officer of police within 24 hours.

B MARTIN must notify the chief officer of police within 72 hours.

C MARTIN must notify the chief officer of police within 7 days.

D MARTIN must notify the chief officer of police within 21 days.

Question 7.15

CONRAD is sentenced to three years' imprisonment for an offence of burglary. He serves 18 months of the sentence and is then released. Several weeks after being released, CONRAD accompanies his friend, ZUCCARO, to a private estate where ZUCCARO is shooting (using a shotgun) in a competition. Whilst on the private estate, ZUCCARO asks CONRAD to hold on to his shotgun and a box of shotgun ammunition while he changes his clothes. CONRAD does so and several minutes later hands the shotgun and ammunition back to ZUCCARO.

Does CONRAD commit an offence under s. 21 of the Firearms Act 1968 (possession of a firearm by a convicted person)?

A Yes, CONRAD commits an offence in relation to the shotgun and the ammunition.

B No, CONRAD does not commit an offence as s. 21 only applies to offenders who have been sentenced to imprisonment for five years or more.

C Yes, CONRAD commits an offence but this would only be in respect of possession of the shotgun.

D No, CONRAD does not commit an offence as the possession activity takes place on private land.

ANSWERS

Answer 7.1

Answer **B** — Section 24A of the Firearms Act 1968 states that it is an offence to sell an imitation firearm to a person under 18 (making answers C and D incorrect). It also makes it an offence for a person under 18 to purchase an imitation firearm (answer A is therefore incorrect).

Crime, para. 1.7.6.1

Answer 7.2

Answer **A** — Section 17(1) of the Firearms Act 1968 states:

> It is an offence for a person to make or attempt to make any use whatsoever of a firearm or imitation firearm with intent to resist or prevent the lawful arrest or detention of himself or another person.

The issue of whether a person's fingers could be an imitation firearm was examined in the case of *R* v *Bentham* [2005] 1 WLR 1057. The Court of Appeal held that holding your fingers inside a jacket and threatening to shoot someone could amount to an offence involving an imitation firearm. However, the House of Lords overturned this decision, finding that the definition of an imitation firearm under s. 57 of the Firearms Act 1968 requires the defendant to carry a 'thing' which is separate and distinct from him/herself and therefore being capable of being possessed. Holding your fingers under your coat will not amount to an imitation firearm for the relevant offences, because an unsevered hand or finger is part of oneself and therefore could not be 'possessed'. Answer D is therefore incorrect.

The 'imitation' must have the appearance of a firearm but it is not necessary for any object to have been constructed, adapted or altered so as to resemble a firearm (*R* v *Williams* [2006] EWCA Crim 1650). Answer B is therefore incorrect. (Further, in *K* v *DPP* [2006] EWHC 2183 (Admin) it was held that in some circumstances a realistic toy gun, in this case a plastic ball-bearing gun, could become an imitation firearm.)

The offence allows for a person to make or attempt to make use of a firearm or imitation firearm; therefore answer C is incorrect.

Crime, paras 1.7.2.4, 1.7.9.3

Answer 7.3

Answer **C** — Section 5 of the Firearms Act 1968 states:

(1) A person commits an offence if, without the authority of the Secretary of State or the Scottish Ministers, he has in his possession, or purchases, or acquires [a prohibited weapon or ammunition] ...

As an offence contrary to s. 5 of the 1968 Act is a strict liability offence, it is irrelevant whether or not a person knew he/she was in possession of a firearm or ammunition (*R* v *Deyemi* [2007] EWCA Crim 2060); answers B and D are therefore incorrect.

In *Sullivan* v *Earl of Caithness* [1976] QB 966, it was held that a person can remain in possession of a firearm even if someone else has custody of it; answer A is therefore incorrect.

Crime, para. 1.7.7.2

Answer 7.4

Answer **C** — It is an offence under s. 16 of the Firearms Act 1968 for a person to have in his/her possession a firearm or ammunition with intent by means thereof to endanger the life of another. It does not apply to imitation firearms (making answer A incorrect). The ammunition is covered by the definition, making answer B incorrect. There is no requirement to show that a person had the firearm/ammunition 'with him', making answer D incorrect.

Crime, para. 1.7.9.1

Answer 7.5

Answer **D** — Under s. 16A of the 1968 Act, a person commits an offence if he/she has in his/her possession a firearm or imitation firearm, with intent by means thereof to cause any person to believe that unlawful violence will be used against him/her or another.

Because the offence can be committed with an imitation firearm, answer A is incorrect. There is no requirement to show that the person using the firearm actually intended to use violence against another, merely that he/she intended the other person to believe unlawful violence would be used. Answer B is therefore incorrect. Answer C is incorrect as the fact that CHADWICK realises the gun is not real would not prevent the offence being committed.

Crime, para. 1.7.9.2

Answer 7.6

Answer **B** — Under s. 16A of the Firearms Act 1968, a person commits an offence if he/she has in his/her possession a firearm or imitation firearm, with intent by means thereof to cause any person to believe that unlawful violence will be used against him/her or another. There is no need to prove the person had the firearm in his/her physical possession—therefore answer D is incorrect.

There is no requirement to prove that the victim actually feared that violence would be used against him/her; it is the intention of the suspect to cause that fear that is important and for that reason answer A is incorrect.

While there is no need for a firearm/imitation firearm to be produced or shown to anyone, possession of a firearm/imitation firearm while making a general threat to someone who does not know of its presence is unlikely to fall within this section. Therefore, even though KUSACK was in possession of a firearm and made a threat of violence towards SHATTOCK, the firearm did not provide the 'means' of the threat and consequently answer C is incorrect.

Crime, para. 1.7.9.2

Answer 7.7

Answer **D** — Under s. 17(2) of the Firearms Act 1968, a person is guilty if he/she is in possession of a firearm (or imitation) at the time of committing or being arrested for either committing or attempting an offence listed in sch. 1.

There is a list of offences in sch. 1 and some of these are indictable offences. However, as not all the offences mentioned in sch. 1 are indictable, answer B is incorrect.

Answer A is incorrect because the offence may be committed by possessing the firearm while being arrested for a sch. 1 offence regardless of any timescales between the arrest and the original offence (or whether the offender even had the firearm with him/her when that offence was committed).

The offence includes attempting to commit a sch. 1 offence and therefore answer C is incorrect.

Crime, para. 1.7.9.5

Answer 7.8

Answer **B** — Section 20 of the Firearms Act 1968 states:

(1) A person commits an offence if, while he has a firearm or imitation firearm with him, he enters or is in any building or part of a building as a trespasser and without reasonable excuse (the proof whereof lies on him).

So it is irrelevant whether he entered as a trespasser; if he enters and then becomes a trespasser this offence can still be committed; answer A is incorrect as it states that entry as a trespasser is required. It is possession in the building that makes the offence, not leaving the building with the firearm; answer D is therefore incorrect.

Air weapons are covered by this legislation; if the relevant firearm is an imitation or an air weapon, the offence is triable summarily; answer C is therefore incorrect.

Crime, para. 1.7.10.2

Answer 7.9

Answer **C** — An offence under s. 18(1) requires a person to have with him a firearm or imitation firearm with intent to commit an indictable offence or when resisting arrest or preventing the arrest of another, in either case while he has the firearm with him (correct answer C). As imitation firearms are included, that would make answer B incorrect. There is no need to use the firearm/imitation during the offence, making answer A incorrect.

Answer D is incorrect as 'indictable offence' will include offences which are triable either way and whilst that may not include a s. 39 assault (a summary only offence), the fact that a low-value shoplifting offence has been committed is enough as this is still an offence of theft (triable either way).

Crime, para. 1.7.9.4

Answer 7.10

Answer **B** — Under s. 28(1) of the Violent Crime Reduction Act 2006, a person is guilty of an offence if he/she uses another to look after, hide or transport a dangerous weapon for him/her, and he/she does so under arrangements or in circumstances that facilitate, or are intended to facilitate, the weapon being available to him/her for an unlawful purpose.

A 'dangerous weapon' includes a firearm *other than* an air weapon or a component part of, or accessory to, an air weapon. Answer D is therefore incorrect. Also included are weapons to which ss. 141 and 141A of the Criminal Justice Act 1988 apply. These include specified offensive weapons, such as knuckledusters, stealth knives and a host of other weapons (s. 141). Answer A is therefore incorrect.

One of the reasons this offence was introduced was to prevent adults from using children to hide weapons. Using a minor to mind a dangerous weapon is an aggravating factor, attracting a harsher sentence. However, this does not mean that the offence is incomplete when the weapon is being looked after by another adult and the offence is complete in these circumstances alone. Answer C is therefore incorrect.

Crime, para. 1.7.9.6

Answer 7.11

Answer **C** — Section 21 of the Firearms Act 1968 places restrictions on convicted persons in respect of their possession of firearms and/or ammunition.

Section 21(6) provides that a person prohibited under this section from having in his/her possession a firearm or ammunition may apply to the Crown Court for a removal of the prohibition and, if the application is granted, that prohibition shall not then apply to him/her; answers A, B and D are therefore incorrect.

Crime, para. 1.7.12

Answer 7.12

Answer **B** — Under s. 21 of the Firearms Act 1968, a person who has been sentenced to life imprisonment or three years' imprisonment (which includes detention in a youth offender institution) must not at any time have a firearm in his/her possession.

Note that the restriction applies to a person sentenced, and therefore it is immaterial that DE'SOUZA did not serve his whole sentence.

Answer A would be correct if DE'SOUZA had been sentenced to less than three years' detention (also covered by s. 21 of the Act). Answer C is merely a false statement and therefore incorrect.

As detention in a young offenders' institution is included therefore answer D is incorrect.

Crime, para. 1.7.12

Answer 7.13

Answer **D** — Under s. 47 of the Firearms Act 1968, a constable may require a person in a public place to hand over a firearm for examination (the purpose being to detect offences).

A further power is provided by s. 47 to examine a firearm from a person elsewhere than in a public place—provided the officer has reasonable cause to suspect the person is committing or is about to commit a relevant offence (offences in ss. 18 and 20 of the Act apply). Consequently, answers A and C are incorrect.

Answer B is incorrect because the power is provided to enter premises to search for or examine a firearm only—not to arrest (although an arrest may well be necessary if a firearm is found).

Crime, para. 1.7.11

Answer 7.14

Answer **C** — Section 32(2) of the Firearms (Amendment) Act 1997 requires that any person who is the holder of a certificate or permit who is involved in selling, letting on hire, lending or giving a section 1 firearm or ammunition (which includes lending a shotgun for a period of more than 72 hours) to another, must, within seven days of the transfer, give notice to the chief officer of police who granted the certificate or permit (s. 33(2)).

Answers A, B and D are therefore incorrect.

Crime, para. 1.7.5

Answer 7.15

Answer **A** — Section 21 of the Firearms Act 1968 places restrictions on convicted persons in respect of their possession of firearms and/or ammunition.

Any person who has been sentenced to:

- custody for *life*; or
- preventive detention, imprisonment, corrective training, youth custody or detention in a young offender institution for three years or more;

must not, *at any time*, have a firearm or ammunition in his/her possession, i.e. a life-time ban.

So s. 21 applies to CONRAD (making answer B incorrect). It does not matter where the possession activity takes place (making answer D incorrect). The ban on possession applies to firearms and ammunition (making answer C incorrect).

Crime, para. 1.7.12

8 | Weapons

QUESTIONS

Question 8.1

VAUGHAN owns a butterfly knife and a swordstick which he keeps in his house and never takes outside into a public place. He keeps them in a locked and secure drawer and only keeps them out of pure curiosity. From time to time, when friends visit him, he takes the items out of the drawer and shows them to his friends.

Does VAUGHAN commit the offence under s. 141(1A) of the Criminal Justice Act 1988 (possession of offensive weapons in private)?

A Yes, the offence is committed in relation to both items and the fact that they are kept in a locked and secure drawer does not change that.

B Yes, the offence is committed but only when VAUGHAN removes the items from the locked and secure drawer.

C Yes, the offence is committed by possessing the butterfly knife in private (it does not apply to the swordstick).

D Yes, the offence is committed by possessing the swordstick in private (it does not apply to the butterfly knife).

Question 8.2

BURTON is walking along a road when he becomes involved in an altercation with RICE. RICE has a flick-knife in his pocket, which he has as a general precaution in case he is attacked, which he pulls out on BURTON and threatens him with. BURTON is a carpet fitter and has a bag of tools with him, which he carries in the course of his trade, which includes a hammer. In reaction to the threat from RICE, he pulls out the hammer and hits RICE with it.

Who, if anyone, is guilty of an offence of having an offensive weapon in a public place (contrary to s. 1(1) of the Prevention of Crime Act 1953)?

A Only RICE commits the offence.

B Only BURTON commits the offence.

C Both RICE and BURTON will commit the offence.

D This offence is not committed by either RICE or BURTON.

Question 8.3

PENFOLD was stopped and searched on his way to a football match while he was walking in High Street. The searching officer, Constable MARRIOTT, discovered in PENFOLD's pocket a number of 50 pence pieces that had been sharpened around the edges. Believing that they were offensive weapons, the officer arrested PENFOLD.

In order to prove that PENFOLD was guilty of possessing an offensive weapon, would Constable MARRIOTT need to prove intent by PENFOLD to use the coins to cause injury?

A No, provided it can be shown that the coins have been made to cause injury.

B Yes, because there is no apparent victim in these circumstances.

C Yes, because the coins are not offensive weapons per se.

D No, provided it can be shown the coins have been adapted to cause injury.

Question 8.4

Constable BRADY stopped and searched CLOUGH in a park one evening, after receiving information that he was carrying a knife. Constable BRADY found a folding knife with a blade of approximately 3.5 inches in length in CLOUGH's pocket. CLOUGH claimed that he was a scout and bought the knife from a camping shop and it was intended for cutting string.

Which of the following statements is correct in relation to the knife that Constable BRADY found?

A The knife could be an offensive weapon or a bladed article depending on CLOUGH's intention.

B The knife could be an offensive weapon depending on CLOUGH's intentions, or a bladed article regardless of his intention.

C The knife would be an offensive weapon or a bladed article regardless of CLOUGH's intention.

D The knife could be an offensive weapon depending on CLOUGH's intention but it may not be a bladed article if the length of the blade is under 3.5 inches.

Question 8.5

McGREGOR had been to a traditional Scottish wedding and was wearing the traditional ceremonial outfit; this included carrying a 'Skean Dhu' knife (with a 3-inch blade) in a sheath in his right sock. Later in the evening, Constable KEEN was on foot patrol in the city centre and saw McGREGOR standing with a group of people in the street outside a pub. The officer saw that McGREGOR was holding the knife and approached to speak to him. McGREGOR stated that he was simply showing the knife to his friends and had no intention of using it to hurt anyone.

Under what circumstances could McGREGOR claim a defence in relation to the knife under s. 139 of the Criminal Justice Act 1988?

A If he could demonstrate to the court that he had no intention of using the knife to cause injury and it was part of a national costume.

B If he could demonstrate to the court that he had a good reason for having it with him and it was part of a national costume.

C If he could demonstrate to the court that he had it with him as part of a national costume.

D If he could demonstrate to the court that he had no intention of using the knife to cause injury.

Question 8.6

Constable O'NEIL attended a local school providing secondary education in relation to the behaviour of SPEARS, who had been involved in a violent incident. On arrival, the officer discovered that SPEARS, aged 17, had been excluded the year before and had gone to the premises whilst drunk in possession of a knife with a 6-inch blade and had threatened one of the teachers.

Which of the following statements is correct in relation to an offence under s. 139AA of the Criminal Justice Act 1988 (threatening with article with blade or point or offensive weapon)?

A This offence is incomplete in these circumstances because SPEARS was not a pupil at the school.

B This offence is complete if it can be shown that SPEARS threatened someone with the knife.

C This offence is complete if it can be shown that SPEARS threatened someone with the knife and there was an immediate risk of serious physical harm to that person.

D This offence is incomplete in these circumstances because school premises are not a public place.

Question 8.7

CRUZ was employed as a computer software programmer but was sacked for selling material to a rival company. CRUZ returned to the company offices one night, entering the gated compound using an electronic pass that had not been confiscated. CRUZ's intention was to sabotage the company software by loading a virus onto the server. CRUZ was in possession of a knife, intending to use it to threaten the night security guard if necessary. However, CRUZ was unable to get into the main company building as the electronic pass did not work. CRUZ does manage to get into a vehicle in the compound and cause some criminal damage to it but is then disturbed by the security guard and runs off.

Has CRUZ committed an offence contrary to s. 8(1) of the Criminal Law Act 1977 (trespassing with a weapon of offence)?

A No, CRUZ has not entered a dwelling with a weapon of offence.

B Yes, the offence is committed when he enters the gated compound with a weapon of offence.

C No, CRUZ has not entered a building with a weapon of offence.

D Yes, the offence is committed but only when he enters the vehicle in the compound with a weapon of offence.

Question 8.8

STONE owns a shop which sells second-hand goods and has a reputation for being able to supply unusual weapons. COLLINS entered the shop looking for some weapons for himself and his friends for a football match the following week. STONE indicated that he could get his hands on some knuckledusters, which he could sell at a good price. COLLINS agreed to return three days later to buy them.

At what point would STONE commit an offence under s. 141 of the Criminal Justice Act 1988 (manufacture, sale and hire of offensive weapons)?

A Not until he actually sells the weapons to COLLINS.
B Not until he is in possession of the weapons with intent to sell them.
C When he offered to sell the weapons to COLLINS.
D Not until he has the weapons with him with intent to sell them.

Question 8.9

FAHEY is aged 19 and works in a hardware shop. McKAY, aged 17, came into the shop one day and selected a pocket-knife from the display, intending to buy it. The pocket-knife had a blade with a cutting edge of 3.5 inches.

Considering offences under s. 141A of the Criminal Justice Act 1988 (selling knives to minors), could FAHEY lawfully sell this pocket-knife to McKAY?
A Yes, because FAHEY is over 18.
B Yes, because McKAY is over 16.
C No, because McKAY is under 18.
D Yes, this offence does not apply to folding pocket-knives with a cutting edge not exceeding 3.5 inches.

Question 8.10

ENLOE (aged 15) is a pupil at St Craymore's School (which is a school offering secondary education to children between the ages of 11 and 16). ENLOE is in the playground of the school when he becomes involved in an argument with INGFIELD who is another pupil at the school. ENLOE produces a knife with a 6-inch blade and threatens INGFIELD with it. FROBISHER, a teacher monitoring the playground, sees what has happened and confiscates the knife from ENLOE. INGFIELD is very upset at what has happened and contacts the police via his mobile phone. PC TRINDER is sent to the school and arrives 15 minutes after the call by INGFIELD has been made.

In relation to s. 139B of the Criminal Justice Act 1988 and the power of entry and search associated with it, which of the following comments is right?
A PC TRINDER may enter the school premises and search the premises and any person on the premises if she has reasonable suspicion that an offence under s. 139A of the Criminal Justice Act 1988 (having a bladed or sharply pointed article or offensive weapon on school premises) is being, or has been, committed.
B The power can be used although Code A of the PACE Codes of Practice does not apply to any search carried out under s. 139B.

C There is a power of entry and search available to the officer but it will not extend to the search of members of staff or employees of the school (such as a search of FROBISHER).

D The threshold for the use of the power under s. 139B is that the officer reasonably believes that an offence under s. 139A (having a bladed or sharply pointed article or offensive weapon on school premises) is being, has been or will be committed. If PC TRINDER has that belief then she may enter the school premises and search the premises and anyone in it for the item concerned.

ANSWERS

Answer 8.1

Answer **A** — Section 141 of the Criminal Justice Act 1988 was amended by the Offensive Weapons Act 2019 to create an offence of possession of an offensive weapon in private.

Under s. 141(1A), any person who possesses a weapon in private to which this section applies is guilty of an offence. The weapons to which the 1988 Act applies are set out in the schedule to the Criminal Justice Act 1988 (Offensive Weapons) Order 1988 (SI 1988/2019). The weapons listed include swordsticks and butterfly knives (making answers C and D incorrect). The fact that these items are, from time to time, kept in a locked and secure drawer has no bearing on the matter (answer B is incorrect).

Crime, paras 1.8.7.1, 1.8.8

Answer 8.2

Answer **A** — The offence is committed by RICE as a person commits this offence if, without lawful authority or reasonable excuse, the proof of which shall lie on him, he has in any public place any offensive weapon. A flick-knife is an offensive weapon *per se* and there is not a reasonable excuse to have such a weapon with you as a general precaution in case you are attacked; this makes answers B and D incorrect. BURTON does not commit the offence as per the decision in *Ohlson* v *Hylton* [1975] 1 WLR 724. Here the defendant had a bag of tools with him in the course of his trade and produced a hammer and hit someone with it. The court held that, as he had formed the intention to use the hammer after it came into his possession, the offence was not made out (answer C is incorrect).

Crime, paras 1.8.2 to 1.8.2.5

Answer 8.3

Answer **D** — The prosecution would have to show that the coins have been adapted to cause injury in order to show that they are offensive weapons. However, once the prosecution has proved this, there is no need to show an intention to use them to cause injury (*Davis* v *Alexander* (1970) 54 Cr App R 398).

Answer A is incorrect because the coins have not been 'made' to cause injury; they are not offensive weapons *per se*. However, the fact that they are not offensive weapons *per se* still does not place a burden upon the prosecution to prove intent to use them (*Davis* v *Alexander*), which is why answer C is incorrect.

Answer B is incorrect because it is the adaptation of the article that is relevant, not the intention of the person carrying it (*Bryan* v *Mott* (1976) 62 Cr App R 71).

If PENFOLD were charged in relation to the third element of the definition, where the weapon is intended to cause injury, the prosecution would have to prove an intention to cause injury by PENFOLD. This would obviously be a harder case to prove than adaptation in these circumstances.

Crime, para. 1.8.2.5

Answer 8.4

Answer **B** — Under s. 1(1) of the Prevention of Crime Act 1953, any person who without lawful authority or reasonable excuse, the proof whereof shall lie on him, has with him in any public place any offensive weapon shall be guilty of an offence.

Under s. 139 of the Criminal Justice Act 1988, a person commits an offence if he/she has a bladed or sharply pointed article in a public place.

Offensive weapons (under s. 1(1)) fall into three categories for the purposes of this offence; namely, articles:

- made for causing injury (offensive weapons *per se*);
- adapted for causing injury; and
- intended by the person who has them for causing injury.

The knife carried in this scenario would not count as an offensive weapon *per se* (such as a flick knife or gravity knife) as it was not made for causing injury. Neither has it been adapted for causing injury. It is simply a knife that may be used as a tool; therefore, to prosecute the person under this section, you would have to prove that the person who had the knife intended using it for causing injury. Answer C is incorrect because the person's intention *is* relevant.

Turning to offences under the Criminal Justice Act 1988, a person commits the offence either by carrying a sharply pointed instrument or a bladed instrument. There is no mention of the intent to use the article for any purpose—having it with you is enough. Answer A is therefore incorrect.

There are defences of lawful authority and reasonable excuse (or good reason) for both offences, and folding pocket-knives are excluded *unless* the cutting edge of the blade exceeds 3 inches (7.62 cm) and not 3.5. Answer D is therefore incorrect.

Crime, paras 1.8.2.4 to 1.8.2.5

Answer 8.5

Answer **C** — Under s. 139 of the Criminal Justice Act 1988, a person commits an offence if he/she has a bladed or sharply pointed article in a public place.

Section 139 contains two specific defences:

(4) It shall be a defence for a person charged with an offence under this section to prove that he had good reason or lawful authority for having the article with him in a public place.

(5) Without prejudice to the generality of subsection (4) above, it shall be a defence for a person charged with an offence under this section to prove that he had the article with him—
 (a) for use at work;
 (b) for religious reasons; or
 (c) as part of any national costume.

Therefore, under s. 139 the intention of the person is irrelevant when it comes to these specific defences and answers A and D are incorrect.

The general defence under s. 139(4) is available for people who are carrying weapons that are not covered by the defence contained in subs. (5). McGREGOR would only have to demonstrate to the court that he had it with him as part of a national costume and answer B is incorrect.

Crime, para. 1.8.4.1

Answer 8.6

Answer **C** — Under s. 139AA(1) of the Criminal Justice Act 1988, a person is guilty of an offence if that person:

(a) has an article to which this section applies with him or her in a public place or on school premises,

(b) unlawfully and intentionally threatens another person with the article, and

(c) does so in such a way that there is an immediate risk of serious physical harm to that other person.

This offence is similar to that created in s. 1A of the Prevention of Crime Act 1953 and includes threats to those made on school premises or in a public place. Answer D is incorrect.

The fact that the person is not a pupil of the school is irrelevant and answer A is incorrect.

It must be shown that the person threatened someone with an offensive weapon or a sharply pointed article or article having a blade *and* that there was an immediate risk of serious physical harm to that person. Answer B is therefore incorrect.

Crime, para. 1.8.5.1

Answer 8.7

Answer **B** — Under s. 8(1) of the Criminal Law Act 1977, a person who is on any premises as a trespasser, after having entered as such, is guilty of an offence if, without lawful authority or reasonable excuse, he/she has with him/her on the premises any weapon of offence.

Under s. 12 of the 1977 Act, 'premises' for this purpose means:

(1) any building; or
(2) any part of a building under separate occupation;
(3) *any land adjacent to and used/intended for use in connection with a building;*
(4) the site comprising any building(s) together with ancillary land;
(5) any fixed structure;
(6) any movable structure, *vehicle* or vessel designed or adapted for residential purposes.

So CRUZ would commit the offence when he enters the gated compound (correct answer B) therefore answers A, C and D are incorrect.

Crime, para. 1.8.6

Answer 8.8

Answer **C** — Section 141 of the Criminal Justice Act 1988 makes it an offence to manufacture, sell, hire, offer for sale or hire, expose, have in possession for the purpose of sale or hire, or lend or give to another person, any weapon listed in the schedule to the Act (knuckle dusters are included).

The offence may be committed by making an offer—the Act makes no mention of being in possession of the article when the offer is made, which is why answer C is correct (this is similar to a case of offering to supply drugs under the Misuse of Drugs Act 1971).

Although offences would be made out in answers A and B, the offence has already been committed.

Answer D would be an incorrect answer in any circumstances, as unlike the original 1953 Act which requires a person to have the weapon with him, this offence deals with possession for the purpose of sale or hire.

Crime, para. 1.8.7

Answer 8.9

Answer **C** — Under s. 141A of the Criminal Justice Act 1988, it is an offence for any person to sell to a person under 18 a knife, blade, razor blade, axe or any article which has a blade or sharp point and is made or adapted for causing injury, therefore answer B is incorrect.

The offence does not apply to a razor blade in a cartridge, where not more than 2 mm of the blade is exposed or to a folding pocket-knife with a blade of less than 3 inches. Since the blade in this question was 3.5 inches, it is covered by s. 141A and therefore answer D is incorrect.

The age of the person making the sale is not relevant (which is why answer A is incorrect).

Crime, para. 1.8.9.1

Answer 8.10

Answer **A** — Section 139B of the Criminal Justice Act 1988 states:

(1) A constable may enter school premises and search those premises and any person on those premises for—
   (a) any article to which section 139 of this Act applies, or
   (b) any offensive weapon within the meaning of section 1 of the Prevention of Crime Act 1953,
   if he has reasonable grounds for suspecting that an offence under section 139A of this Act is being, or has been, committed.

The threshold for the constable to use his/her power is 'reasonable grounds for *suspecting*', making answer D incorrect.

'School', under s. 4 of the Education Act 1996, means:

(1) … an educational institution which is outside the further education sector and the higher education sector and is an institution for providing—
   (a) primary education,
   (b) secondary education, or
   (c) both primary and secondary education,
   whether or not the institution also provides further education.

PACE Code A applies to searches under s. 139B, making answer B incorrect.

The power of entry and search is to search any person—this would include members of staff and other employees of the school, making answer C incorrect.

Crime, para. 1.8.5.5

9 | Racially and Religiously Aggravated Offences

QUESTIONS

Question 9.1

OLLERTON and PATEL are neighbours and are in dispute over the boundary between their respective back gardens. One evening, OLLERTON comes home to find that PATEL has erected a fence between the two gardens. OLLERTON loses her temper and begins to break the fence. As OLLERTON is breaking the fence, PATEL comes out into the back garden. Motivated by frustration over the fence and also her intense hostility to Hindus, OLLERTON says to PATEL, 'How dare you put up a fence, you Hindu dickhead.' PATEL is not personally upset by OLLERTON's comments—in fact, PATEL is not Hindu.

Would this offence of criminal damage be 'racially aggravated' under s. 28 of the Crime and Disorder Act 1998?

A Yes, as it is immaterial whether OLLERTON's hostility is also based, to any extent, on any other factor.

B No, because PATEL is not personally upset by the situation.

C Yes, but only because the words uttered were said during the commission of the offence rather than after the offence.

D No, as 'simple' criminal damage (under s. 1(1) of the Criminal Damage Act 1971) is not capable of being 'aggravated' under the Crime and Disorder Act 1998.

Question 9.2

PC BRAHM is on uniform patrol when he is sent to a report of two men arguing outside a pub. PC BRAHM attends the scene and sees O'GRADY and ARCHER arguing in the pub car park. PC BRAHM approaches the pair and asks what is happening.

Without warning, O'GRADY punches PC BRAHM in the face causing slight injury to the officer (amounting to a s. 39 battery contrary to the Criminal Justice Act 1988). As he struck the blow, O'GRADY said 'Nothing to do with a black copper!' (PC BRAHM is black). PC BRAHM falls to the floor and, as he does so, ARCHER kicks PC BRAHM's back causing significant bruising (amounting to a s. 47 assault contrary to the Offences Against the Person Act 1861) saying, 'There is absolutely nothing worse than a black copper!'

Would these activities amount to racially aggravated assaults against PC BRAHM?

A No, as police officers are not protected by racially/religiously aggravated offences under the Crime and Disorder Act 1998.

B Yes, by O'GRADY and ARCHER.

C No, as only a s. 20 GBH/wounding offence (contrary to the Offences Against the Person Act 1861) can be racially or religiously aggravated.

D Yes, but only by O'GRADY.

Question 9.3

SPEIGHT has a hatred of Muslims. He sees PATHAN in the street one day and assaults him occasioning actual bodily harm. When questioned, he states that he assaulted him because he thought he was a Muslim based on the colour of his skin. In fact, PATHAN is an agnostic of Indian origin.

Would this be a religiously aggravated assault?

A Yes, as the hostility was based on the victim's presumed membership of a religious group.

B Yes, as the hostility was based on the colour of the victim's skin.

C No, as PATHAN is not a member of the religious group against whom the hostility was meant.

D No, as PATHAN is not a member of any religious group.

Question 9.4

PC GODDARD is part of a team of officers investigating a serious disorder incident that took place in a street after rival gangs clashed after a funeral. Witnesses state that during the disorder they heard language that suggests that some of the offences committed may have been motivated by racial hostility. PC GODDARD is considering whether some of the offences that have been disclosed could therefore be racially aggravated (under the Crime and Disorder Act 1998).

Which of the following offences that PC GODDARD is investigating could be racially aggravated under the Act?

A An offence of s. 20 wounding (contrary to s. 20 of the Offences Against the Person Act 1861).

B An offence of threats to kill (contrary to s. 16 of the Offences Against the Person Act 1861).

C An offence of affray (contrary to s. 3 of the Public Order Act 1986).

D An offence of threats to destroy or damage property (contrary to s. 2 of the Criminal Damage Act 1971).

Question 9.5

PLATT is in a bad mood as the football team he supports have just lost in a Cup Final. He was watching the match in a pub and decides to leave and walk home. On his way home, he sees a car parked at the side of the road which has a football scarf on the rear parcel shelf demonstrating support for Tottenham Hotspur (the team that PLATT's side has just lost the Cup Final to). Sitting in the front passenger seat of the car is HATCHIN. PLATT automatically presumes HATCHIN is a supporter of Tottenham Hotspur and also that HATCHIN is a Jew. PLATT opens the door of the car and drags HATCHIN out of the car, punching him in the face several times. The injuries caused to HATCHIN amount to a s. 39 battery (contrary to the Criminal Justice Act 1988). Immediately after the battery is committed, PLATT shouts, 'You filthy Jew bastard. I hate all Spurs fans.'

Considering the law under the Crime and Disorder Act 1998 and a 'demonstration' of hostility in particular, which of the following comments is correct?

A The circumstances could not amount to a 'demonstration' of hostility as the words were used immediately after the offence was committed, not before or during the commission of the offence.

B This could not be a racially aggravated offence as Jewish people are not protected by the legislation.

C The circumstances of this offence mean that it could be classed as a racially aggravated offence.

D This could not be an 'aggravated' offence as a s. 39 battery under the Criminal Justice Act 1988 cannot be racially or religiously aggravated.

Question 9.6

WOODS appeared in court charged with a racially aggravated assault (a s. 47 assault contrary to the Offences Against the Person Act 1861) against ADAMS, a door supervisor, who had refused him entry into a nightclub. It is alleged that at the time of assaulting ADAMS, WOODS shouted, 'Let me in, you black bastard'. WOODS did not deny assaulting ADAMS, or uttering the words, but contested the racially aggravated element of the offence, stating that he was motivated by frustration rather than racism when he uttered the words. When giving evidence in court, ADAMS said that he was not personally upset by what WOODS had said, stating that he suffered such abuse frequently in his job.

What facts should the court take account of when considering the racially aggravated element of the offence, as set out in s. 28(1)(a) of the Crime and Disorder Act 1998?

A WOODS's motivation when he uttered the words.
B ADAMS's own perception of the words and whether he was personally upset by the situation.
C Neither WOODS's motivation nor ADAMS's own perception of the words.
D Whether ADAMS or an innocent bystander would have been personally upset by the words.

ANSWERS

Answer 9.1

Answer **A** — Section 28(3) of the Crime and Disorder Act 1998 states that it is immaterial whether or not the offender's hostility is also based, to any extent, on any other factor (correct answer A). Answer B is incorrect as the Administrative Court has held that the victim's own perception of the words used was irrelevant, as was the fact that the victim was not personally upset by the situation (*DPP* v *Woods* [2002] EWHC Admin 85). Answer C is incorrect as a racially aggravated offence can take place *immediately before, at the time of committing an offence or after committing the offence*. Answer D is incorrect as s. 1(1) 'simple' damage is capable of being an 'aggravated' offence under the Crime and Disorder Act 1998.

Crime, paras 1.9.1 to 1.9.3.1

Answer 9.2

Answer **B** — Police officers can be victims of these offences and are entitled to the same protection as anyone else (*R* v *Jacobs* [2001] 2 Cr App R (S) 38) so answer A is incorrect). The offences that can become racially or religiously aggravated can be grouped in four categories—one of those is assaults. The assault offences that can be racially or religiously aggravated are:

- common assault—Criminal Justice Act 1988, s. 39;
- causing actual bodily harm—Offences Against the Person Act 1861, s. 47;
- wounding or grievous bodily harm—Offences Against the Person Act 1861, s. 20.

This makes answer C incorrect. As both assaults by O'GRADY and ARCHER are covered, answer D is incorrect.

Crime, paras 1.9.2 to 1.9.3.4

Answer 9.3

Answer **A** — The test for racial or religious aggravation is set out at s. 28 of the Crime and Disorder Act 1998:

(1) An offence is racially or religiously aggravated for the purposes of sections 29 to 32 ... if—

(a) at the time of committing the offence, or immediately before or after doing so, the offender demonstrates towards the victim of the offence hostility based on the victim's membership (or presumed membership) of a racial or religious group ...

'Presumed' means presumed by the offender and as that is what the offender presumes here the offence is complete. Answer B would be correct if the offence was racially motivated but you were asked about religious motivation which makes that answer incorrect.

Irrespective of actual membership of a group, the offence is complete where the accused presumes that membership; answers C and D are therefore incorrect.

Crime, para. 1.9.3

Answer 9.4

Answer **A** — Some offences under the Public Order Act 1986 are covered (ss. 4, 4A and 5) but not s. 3, making answer C incorrect. Criminal damage under s. 1(1) is covered but not threats to commit damage under s. 2 of the Criminal Damage Act 1971, therefore answer D is incorrect. Threats to kill (under s. 16 of the Offences Against the Person Act 1861) are not covered, making answer B incorrect; s. 20 wounding is covered, making answer A correct.

Crime, para. 1.9.2

Answer 9.5

Answer **C** — The timing of a 'demonstration' of hostility is immediately before, during or immediately after the trigger offence is committed, making answer A incorrect. Answer B is incorrect as Jews are a racial group. Answer D is incorrect as a s. 39 battery is covered by the Crime and Disorder Act 1998.

Crime, paras 1.9.2 to 1.9.3.9

Answer 9.6

Answer **C** — The test for racial or religious aggravation is set out at s. 28(1) of the Crime and Disorder Act 1998, which states that an offence is racially or religiously aggravated for the purposes of ss. 29 to 32 if—

(a) at the time of committing the offence, or immediately before or after doing so, the offender demonstrates towards the victim of the offence hostility based on the victim's membership (or presumed membership) of a racial or religious group; or

(b) the offence is motivated (wholly or partly) by hostility towards members of a racial or religious group based on their membership of that group.

In a case involving the abuse and assault of a doorman, the Administrative Court held that a racial insult uttered a few moments before an assault was enough to make the offence racially aggravated for the purposes of the Crime and Disorder Act 1998. The court also held that the victim's own perception of the words used was irrelevant, as was the fact that he was not personally upset by the situation. Similarly, the fact that the defendant might have been motivated to utter the words merely by frustration rather than racism was also irrelevant (*DPP* v *Woods* [2002] EWHC Admin 85).

Simply, under s. 28(1)(a), when the person has *demonstrated* hostility based on the victim's membership (or presumed membership) of a racial or religious group at the time of committing the offence, or immediately before or after doing so, the offence is complete regardless of his/her motivation or the perception of the victim (or some other bystander).

Answers A, B and D are therefore incorrect.

Crime, paras 1.9.2 to 1.9.3.5

10 Non-Fatal Offences Against the Person

QUESTIONS

Question 10.1

Sergeant HEALY is custody officer when Constable MOORE brings in a prisoner whom he has arrested for criminal damage. The prisoner claims that he has been unlawfully arrested as the property he damaged was his own, and this in fact is correct. During the booking-in process, the prisoner assaults Sergeant HEALY and during the investigation it becomes clear that the prisoner was unlawfully arrested by Constable MOORE.

Has an offence of 'assault police' contrary to s. 89 of the Police Act 1996 been committed in these circumstances?

A Yes, provided the custody officer at the time of the assault believed the arrest to be lawful.

B Yes, the custody officer is entitled to assume that the arrest has been lawful even if the original arrest turns out to have been unlawful.

C No, the custody officer should have made inquiries to establish the lawfulness of the arrest as the prisoner has alleged it was unlawful therefore she was not acting in the execution of her duty.

D No, as the original arrest was unlawful any detention would be unlawful and therefore the custody officer was not acting in the execution of her duty.

Question 10.2

STANFORD and HARTELL are neighbours who have had a long-standing dispute over car parking outside their respective houses. One afternoon, STANFORD parks his car directly outside HARTELL's house. HARTELL sees this and, grabbing hold of an imitation pistol, he runs outside and confronts STANFORD. Intending to make STANFORD believe he will be subject to immediate unlawful violence, HARTELL points the imitation pistol at STANFORD and says, 'If you don't move your car, I'll shoot you!' HARTELL believes the threat and moves his car.

Considering the offences of assault and battery only (under s. 39 of the Criminal Justice Act 1988), which of the following comments is true?

A STANFORD's actions would constitute a 'battery'.
B STANFORD does not commit an assault as this is a conditional threat.
C STANFORD has committed an offence of 'assault'.
D STANFORD does not commit an assault as he cannot physically harm STANFORD with an imitation pistol.

Question 10.3

GUNNING is walking his dog in a park. Although he knows his dog is bad-tempered, there is nobody else in the park and so he lets his dog off its lead and allows it to run free. Just after GUNNING lets his dog free, O'HARE walks into the park. Because GUNNING has omitted to keep his dog on the lead, the dog runs towards O'HARE. O'HARE is frightened of the dog and believes it will bite him. GUNNING runs up to his dog and puts it back on the lead. O'HARE says, 'You bloody idiot, if your dog wasn't with you I'd kick your head in!' GUNNING is annoyed by the comment and lets his dog off the lead again saying, 'Bite him boy!' The dog bites O'HARE.

At what point, if at all, is an assault committed?

A When, because of GUNNING's omission, his dog causes O'HARE to believe he will be bitten.
B When O'HARE threatens GUNNING.
C When GUNNING sets his dog on O'HARE.
D An assault has not taken place in these circumstances.

Question 10.4

ILLINGWORTH makes a series of telephone calls to FENNEL over a period of several days. One day, he makes 14 phone calls and each time FENNEL answers the phone, ILLINGWORTH remains silent, sometimes for several minutes. FENNEL suffers psychiatric harm as a result.

Which of the following comments is true?

A ILLINGWORTH could only be charged with a s. 39 assault (Criminal Justice Act 1988) or s. 47 assault (Offences Against the Person Act 1861), as psychiatric injuries can never amount to grievous bodily harm.

B No assault is committed because 'silence' would not constitute the *actus reus* of an assault.

C ILLINGWORTH could be charged with a s. 20 assault (contrary to the Offences Against the Person Act 1861) if the psychiatric injury amounted to really serious harm.

D In these circumstances, no assault is committed as the victim and the defendant are not face to face.

Question 10.5

ELVIN is a store detective who witnesses YEUNG stealing a bottle of whisky from a supermarket. ELVIN arrests YEUNG outside the supermarket, at which point YEUNG punches ELVIN in the face and runs off. ELVIN chases after YEUNG and catches her 200 metres away where the two begin fighting. GILLIGAN sees the struggle and believes that ELVIN is trying to rob YEUNG. GILLIGAN punches ELVIN in the face and as a result YEUNG manages to escape.

Who, if anyone, has committed the offence of assault with intent to resist arrest (contrary to s. 38 of the Offences Against the Person Act 1861)?

A Only YEUNG commits the offence.

B Only GILLIGAN commits the offence as he is preventing the lawful apprehension of another.

C Both YEUNG and GILLIGAN commit the offence.

D Neither YEUNG nor GILLIGAN commits the offence because ELVIN is not a police officer.

Question 10.6

CATON steals a car and is pursued by PC STONE, who is driving a police livery vehicle. CATON drives into a cul-de-sac and is followed by the officer. CATON realises that there is no way out of the cul-de-sac and that he will be arrested if he does not ram PC STONE's vehicle. Intending to escape and avoid arrest, CATON drives into the officer's car. CATON realises that this may cause some harm to PC STONE. The resulting crash causes multiple cuts to PC STONE's face, requiring 200 stitches and causing really serious harm to the officer. CATON is caught several minutes later.

With regard to assaults under the Offences Against the Person Act 1861, which of the following statements is correct?

A In these circumstances, CATON has 'inflicted' the injury and so the appropriate offence would be one of a s. 20 wounding.

B CATON commits s. 20 wounding as there was no intent to wound the officer.

C CATON's actions were malicious and carried out in order to resist arrest. This means that he commits s. 18 wounding.

D CATON's actions would not provide the evidence required for a successful prosecution under s. 18 or 20 of the Offences Against the Person Act.

Question 10.7

PC AVERY is assisting officers of the National Crime Agency (NCA) during the course of an operation the NCA is carrying out on business premises belonging to MILLS. As MILLS is being escorted from the premises, he kicks out at LOGUE (the NCA officer escorting him from the premises) and, as the officer releases him from his grip, MILLS pushes PC AVERY against a wall. LOGUE receives a slight injury to his leg and PC AVERY receives slight injuries to his shoulder (the injuries in each case amount to a s. 39 battery (Criminal Justice Act 1988). PC AVERY and officer LOGUE are both acting in the exercise of functions as emergency workers.

Would these injuries amount to an assault on an emergency worker (as per the Assaults on Emergency Workers (Offences) Act 2018)?

A No, as the legislation only applies to situations where the injuries would amount to serious or really serious harm under s. 20 or 18 of the Offences Against the Person Act 1861.

B Yes, but only against PC AVERY.

C No, as the Act does not apply to officers carrying out the functions of a police officer or to an officer of the National Crime Agency.

D Yes, against PC AVERY and officer LOGUE.

Question 10.8

PLEGGE and his girlfriend (HARBER) were having a stormy time in their relationship. PLEGGE was very upset when he discovered that HARBER had been having an affair with her beauty therapist, who had helped manicure and maintain HARBER's long nails and hair. It had taken over two years for HARBER to grow her nails and get them to the point where she thought they were perfect and HARBER's hair had not been cut for over ten years. Whilst HARBER was sleeping, PLEGGE took some nail clippers and cut off one nail from each of HARBER's hands and cut off a substantial length of her hair; HARBER is distraught and complains to the police regarding the incident.

In relation to a s. 47 offence (contrary to the Offences Against the Person Act 1861), which of the following is correct?

A Cutting the hair can amount to a s. 47 assault; cutting the nails could not.

B Cutting the nails could amount to a s. 47 assault; cutting the hair could not.

C Cutting the nails and the hair could amount to a s. 47 assault.

D Cutting the nails and the hair cannot amount to a s. 47 assault.

Question 10.9

PC COPPLE is dealing with an incident where several assaults and public order offences were committed. The officer is considering the possibility of charging several of the participants in the disorder with the offence of obstruct police (contrary to s. 89 of the Police Act 1996) and approaches you for some advice on the matter. The officer tells you that during the incident HARTELL was spoken to by the police but refused to answer any questions, NORRIS stood in the doorway of a house and blocked police access to the premises for several minutes, STANSFIELD made a telephone call on his mobile phone providing a false location of the disorder to the police resulting in other officers attending the incorrect address several streets away from the incident and CARTER stood in his doorway several feet from the incident and did nothing to assist the police when the disorder began. All four were later arrested for assaults.

Which of the following comments is correct?

A Obstruct police requires some sort of physical opposition so the only person who commits the offence is NORRIS.

B NORRIS and STANSFIELD commit the offence, HARTELL does not. CARTER would only commit the offence if he were under some duty towards the police to assist them.

C All four commit the offence of obstruct police in these circumstances.

D HARTELL, NORRIS and STANSFIELD commit the offence.

Question 10.10

BALDWIN hates HIGGS as the two have had numerous fights with each other. BALDWIN is drinking in his local pub when he sees ROBERTS, a friend of HIGGS's, walk into the pub. BALDWIN approaches ROBERTS and says, 'Next week I'm getting a gun and I'm gonna use it to kill HIGGS.' BALDWIN does not intend ROBERTS to believe the threat will be carried out; he just enjoys intimidating HIGGS's friends. ROBERTS believes BALDWIN and passes the threat on to HIGGS, who does not fear the threat at all.

Which of the following statements is correct in relation to the offence of making a threat to kill (s. 16 of the Offences Against the Person Act 1861)?

A The offence has not been committed because BALDWIN has made a threat to kill another person at some time in the future.

B No offence has been committed because the person to whom the threat is directed (HIGGS) does not fear that the threat will be carried out.

C The offence has not been committed because the threat has been made to a third party (ROBERTS), rather than the person to whom the threat is directed.

D No offence has been committed because the person making the threat does not do so with the intention that the person receiving it (ROBERTS) will fear that it will be carried out.

Question 10.11

TAPSTER is using an internet chat room with DODD and ANGUS. TAPSTER has an argument with DODD and becomes so angry that he writes a message saying 'I'm gonna kill DODD next week' and sends it to ANGUS. TAPSTER does not intend to make ANGUS think he is going to kill DODD, he is just incredibly angry and is venting his frustration. Unfortunately, ANGUS sees the message and believes it and contacts the police; DODD never sees the message and is oblivious of its existence.

In relation to the offence of threats to kill (contrary to s. 16 of the Offences Against the Person Act 1861), which of the following comments is correct?

A The offence has not been committed because TAPSTER did not intend ANGUS to fear that DODD would be killed.

B The offence has not been committed as the threat was to kill a person in the future, not there and then.

C The offence has not been committed because the person who was to be killed was unaware of the threat.

D The offence has not been committed because the offence cannot be committed via a third party.

Question 10.12

PC WHITLEY is making inquiries regarding an offence of robbery that has just taken place at a bookmakers. The officer is visiting shops that are in the same street as the bookmakers and is looking for witnesses to the offence. He enters a florists shop which is situated opposite the bookmakers and speaks to STREDWICK who is working behind the serving counter. When PC WHITLEY asks STREDWICK if she has seen anything, she replies, 'I don't have to tell you anything, you pig!' PC WHITLEY asks STREDWICK to be reasonable and help if she can, to which STREDWICK responds, 'OK, the bloke responsible was wearing a green jacket and ran off towards the town hall.' This is deliberately misleading information provided by STREDWICK as the offender was wearing a different colour jacket and ran off in the opposite direction to that which she said he did.

Does STREDWICK commit the offence of obstructing a police officer (contrary to s. 89(2) of the Police Act 1996)?

A No, as STREDWICK does not offer any form of physical resistance to PC WHITLEY.

B Yes, when she tells PC WHITLEY that she does not have to tell him anything and also when she provides the deliberately misleading information.

C No, as this offence can only be committed by a person who is under a positive obligation to assist the police and STREDWICK is not in that position.

D Yes, but only when she provides the deliberately misleading information to PC WHITLEY.

Question 10.13

INGRAM (a British citizen) is on holiday in Germany. Whilst in a bar in Berlin, INGRAM strikes up a conversation with BALSIGER (a German citizen) and the two agree to have sexual intercourse at INGRAM's hotel in Berlin. The two leave the bar and go straight to INGRAM's hotel room where they have sexual intercourse. During sexual intercourse INGRAM asks BALSIGER if she will allow him to strangle her — BALSIGER agrees. During the act of strangulation INGRAM gets carried away and injures BALSIGER causing slight bruising to BALSIGER's throat (an injury that would amount to a s. 39 battery (contrary to the Criminal Justice Act 1988)).

In relation to the offence of strangulation (under s. 75A of the Serious Crime Act 2015), which of the below comments is correct?

A The offence has been committed by INGRAM but he would have a defence in this situation as BALSIGER consented to the act of strangulation.

B The offence has not been committed by INGRAM as the act of strangulation occurred outside the United Kingdom.

C The offence has been committed by INGRAM and the fact that BALSIGER consented to the act would not afford INGRAM a defence in this situation.

D The offence has not been committed as the victim was not a United Kingdom national.

ANSWERS

Answer 10.1

Answer **B** — Section 89 of the Police Act 1996 states:

(1) Any person who assaults a constable in the execution of his duty, or a person assisting a constable in the execution of his duty, shall be guilty of an offence ...

This offence requires that the officer was acting in the execution of his/her duty when assaulted.

Where a prisoner is arrested and brought before a custody officer, that officer is entitled to assume that the arrest has been lawful. Therefore, if the prisoner goes on to assault the custody officer, that assault will nevertheless be an offence under s. 89(1) even if the original arrest turns out to have been unlawful (*DPP* v *L* [1999] Crim LR 752).

There is no need to believe or establish whether the original arrest was lawful as there is an automatic entitlement to assume it was lawful for the custody officer to still be acting in the execution of his/her duty; answers A, C and D are therefore incorrect.

Crime, para. 1.10.7.2

Answer 10.2

Answer **C** — A 'battery' is the actual application of force requiring some degree of contact; there has been no such contact so answer A is incorrect. Answer D is incorrect as even though the pistol is an imitation and incapable of firing, it is the intention of the defendant coupled with the belief of the victim that is important. These circumstances would constitute an assault (answer C). Answer B is incorrect as this *is not* a conditional threat. A conditional threat would be something like STANFORD approaching HARTELL and pointing the pistol at him and saying, 'If you ever park your car outside my house I'll shoot you!' The threat in the question is different as it is an immediate threat conditional upon some real circumstance—move your car or else!

Crime, paras 1.10.2 to 1.10.3

Answer 10.3

Answer **C** — Answer A is incorrect as an assault cannot be committed by an omission. When O'HARE threatens to assault GUNNING it is a conditional threat; the assault will not be committed because of the presence of the dog and, therefore, GUNNING cannot fear immediate application of force (therefore answer B is incorrect). An assault is committed at point C because the 'indirect' application of force (via the dog) qualifies as an assault.

Crime, paras 1.10.2 to 1.10.2.4

Answer 10.4

Answer **C** — In *R* v *Ireland* [1998] AC 147, it was held that telephone calls to a victim, followed by silence, could amount to an assault. This makes answers B and D incorrect. The harm caused in *R* v *Ireland* was psychiatric harm and the offender was charged and convicted of a s. 47 assault. This does not mean that psychiatric harm caused to the victim will limit the charge to a s. 47 assault only; there is nothing to stop an offence of s. 20 (or even s. 18) being committed when the harm is of a psychiatric nature, making answer A incorrect.

Crime, paras 1.10.2 to 1.10.2.4

Answer 10.5

Answer **A** — This offence applies to arrests made by several groups of people including store detectives, making answer D incorrect. To commit the offence, the offender must assault any person knowing that the person assaulted was trying to make or help in an arrest. This knowledge is not present in GILLIGAN's mind, making answers B and C incorrect.

Crime, para. 1.10.7.1

Answer 10.6

Answer **C** — Whilst there is no intention to wound, CATON's actions are 'malicious'. Maliciousness means that the defendant must realise that there is a risk of some harm being caused to the victim. The defendant does not need to foresee the degree of harm that is eventually caused, only that his/her behaviour may bring about some harm to the victim. When the harm is caused with *intent* to *resist or prevent lawful apprehension* (arrest), the s. 18 grievous bodily harm/wounding offence is made out. This makes answers A, B and D incorrect.

Crime, paras 1.10.6.4, 1.10.6.5

Answer 10.7

Answer **D** — The Assaults on Emergency Workers (Offences) Act 2018 applies to police officers and officers of the National Crime Agency, making answers B and C incorrect. It applies to offences of common assault and battery (s. 39 of the Criminal Justice Act 1988) which rules out answer A and makes answer D correct.

Crime, para. 1.10.6.2

Answer 10.8

Answer **C** — It was held in *DPP* v *Smith (Ross Michael)* [2006] EWHC 94 (Admin), that the substantial cutting of a person's hair against his/her will could amount to actual bodily harm even though no pain or other injury may be involved (making answers B and D incorrect). In *Smith*, the defendant cut off his ex-partner's ponytail, deliberately and without her permission. Even though, medically and scientifically speaking, the hair above the surface of the scalp is no more than dead tissue, it remains part of the body and is attached to it. While it is so attached, it falls within the meaning of 'bodily' in the phrase 'actual bodily harm' as it is concerned with the body of the individual victim. Therefore the same would be true of fingernails (making answer A incorrect).

Crime, para. 1.10.6.3

Answer 10.9

Answer **B** — HARTELL's refusal to answer police questions is not obstruction, making answers C and D incorrect. Although obstruct police may involve some sort of physical opposition (NORRIS), it can also be committed by making it more difficult for a constable to carry out his/her duty (STANSFIELD), making answer A incorrect. Obstruction can be caused by omission (CARTER) but only where the defendant was already under some duty towards the police or the officer.

Crime, para. 1.10.7.3

Answer 10.10

Answer **D** — The offence of making a threat to kill can only be committed if it can be shown that the threat was made with the *intention* that *the person receiving it* would fear it would be carried out. It is the *intention* of the person who makes the threat that is important in this offence. It is immaterial that the threat to kill is a threat to kill another in the future, making answer A incorrect. It is also immaterial that the person to whom the threat is directed does not believe the threat and that that threat has been made via a third party, making answers B and C incorrect.

Crime, para. 1.10.8

Answer 10.11

Answer **A** — An offence under s. 16 of the Offences Against the Person Act 1861 is committed by a person who, without lawful excuse, makes to another a threat, *intending* that that other will fear that it will be carried out, to kill that other or a third person. TAPSTER did not have the relevant intention so answer A is correct. The threat can be to kill in the future (making answer B incorrect). It does not matter if the person who would be killed does not know of the threat (making answer C incorrect). The threat can be delivered by a third party (making answer D incorrect).

Crime, para. 1.10.8

Answer 10.12

Answer **D** — Section 89 of the Police Act 1996 states:

(2) Any person who resists or wilfully obstructs a constable in the execution of his duty, or a person assisting a constable in the execution of his duty, shall be guilty of an offence.

There is no need for a physical 'obstruction' to be offered to the officer for the offence to be committed, making answer A incorrect. Answer C is incorrect as whilst obstruction can be caused by omission, this will only be where the defendant was already under some duty towards the police or the officer and that is not the case with an ordinary member of the public being asked questions by a police officer. Answer B is incorrect as refusing to answer an officer's questions is not obstruction (*Rice* v *Connolly* [1966] 2 QB 414). Obstruction may take many forms, e.g. deliberately providing misleading information (*Ledger* v *DPP* [1991] Crim LR 439), meaning that the correct answer is D.

Crime, para. 1.10.7.3

Answer 10.13

Answer **A** — Section 75A of the Serious Crime Act 2015 states:
A person ('A') commits an offence if—

(a) A intentionally strangles another person ('B'), or (b) A does any other act to B that—
(i) affects B's ability to breathe, and (ii) constitutes battery of B.

On the face of it this means that INGRAM has committed the offence but then the fact that the activity occurred in Germany and involved a German citizen needs to be considered. That is dealt with by s. 75B which states:

(1) If—
(a) a person does an act in a country outside the United Kingdom, (b) the act, if done in England and Wales, would constitute an offence under HYPERLINK "https://www.pnld.co.uk/members/legal-narrative-detail/?id=3fa2b8a3-47ed-44d1-9f91-173081009b06" section 75A, and (c) the person is a United Kingdom national or is habitually resident in England and Wales, the person is guilty in England and Wales of that offence.

Section 75B(2) In this section, a United Kingdom national means (amongst other things) a British citizen (INGRAM). The fact that the offence occurred in Germany (outside the United Kingdom) and the victim was a German citizen (BALSIGER) would not prevent the offence being committed. This means that answers B and D are incorrect. Answer C is incorrect as s. 75A(2) states that it is a defence to an offence under this section for A to show that B consented to the strangulation or other act. That defence does not apply if B suffers serious harm and A either intended to cause B serious harm, or was reckless as to whether B would suffer serious harm. As BALSIGER did not suffer 'serious harm' the defence would be available, making answer C incorrect (and answer A correct).

Crime 1.10.9

11 | Offences Involving the Deprivation of Liberty

QUESTIONS

Question 11.1

MOORE stopped his car at a bus stop and told a lone woman waiting for the bus that the bus had broken down about half a mile down the road (this was not in fact true). He offered the woman a lift. She accepted, but then asked to be let out of the car after a short distance. MOORE refused and kept the woman in his car. He reached his house and forced her down into the basement.

At what point, if any, does MOORE 'kidnap' the woman?

- **A** He does not kidnap her, she consents to get in the car.
- **B** He kidnaps her when she first gets into the car.
- **C** He kidnaps her when he refuses to let her out.
- **D** He kidnaps her when he takes her into his house.

Question 11.2

WILSON sees a young couple out walking on the common. He approaches the girl and tells her that he is a police officer and is taking her to be searched for drugs. He tells the boyfriend to go home. He then walks her to his car about 25 metres away. Her boyfriend, suspecting something is not right, returns with two other friends and rescues the girl prior to WILSON putting her in his car. WILSON is not a police officer and had an unlawful purpose in mind.

Has WILSON committed the offence of kidnapping?

- **A** Yes, as he has taken the girl away without her consent.
- **B** Yes, as he has taken the girl away without her consent and had an unlawful purpose.

C No, as the girl went willingly with him.

D No, as he never really took her anywhere as they were still on the common.

Question 11.3

MALPASS and FROBISHER are friends and have a bet with each other. MALPASS bets £500 that FROBISHER would not have the nerve to pick up a prostitute and have sex with her. FROBISHER takes the bet and the two men drive to an area that is well known to be frequented by prostitutes. FROBISHER drops MALPASS off on a street corner so he can witness what happens. FROBISHER then drives to the other side of the road and winds his car window down to speak to WARNER who is standing on the street corner dressed provocatively. FROBISHER asks WARNER to get into his car to 'discuss terms' and WARNER complies. Once inside the car, WARNER tells FROBISHER that sexual intercourse is £100. FROBISHER tells her that is too much and at this point locks the doors of the car and tells WARNER to drop her price or he will not let her go. WARNER panics and tells FROBISHER to let her out. FROBISHER repeats his demand that she drop her price so WARNER says she will drop it to £50; FROBISHER tells her it is still too much. At this point, WARNER starts to scream so FROBISHER unlocks the doors and tells WARNER to get out. She does so and FROBISHER drives away.

Considering the offence of false imprisonment (contrary to common law), which of the following comments is true?

A FROBISHER commits the offence when he locks the doors of his car and restrains WARNER's freedom of movement.

B FROBISHER does not commit the offence as he has not touched WARNER and has therefore not physically restrained her freedom of movement.

C FROBISHER commits the offence but the prosecution would have to prove that he intended to restrain WARNER's freedom of movement, as recklessness in respect of this element of the offence is not enough.

D FROBISHER does not commit the offence as WARNER's freedom of movement was only restrained for a very short period of time.

Question 11.4

DOYLE answered his door to a cold-caller and invited him in to discuss life insurance. As the conversation continued, DOYLE began to suspect that the salesperson was in fact trying to obtain money by fraud and, as the conversation between the two continues, that suspicion becomes a genuine belief. DOYLE decides to call the police and leaves the room with the salesperson still in there and locks the door to prevent him from escaping until the police arrive.

Has DOYLE committed an offence of false imprisonment contrary to common law?

A Yes, as he has falsely imprisoned another person as he restrained the person's freedom of movement.

B Yes, as he has falsely imprisoned another person and had no evidence that person was trying to commit a fraud offence.

C No, as the salesperson voluntarily entered the house.

D No, provided he genuinely believed he was acting in defence of his property.

Question 11.5

DUNBAR (a UK national) visits Cairo (in Egypt) with a view to recruiting a number of adults to come to England and beg on the streets of London. DUNBAR intends to exploit any adults he recruits and to use or threaten force against them to make them carry out begging activities once they are in London. He intends to keep any money they make. In Egypt, DUNBAR speaks to AHMED (an adult) and tells him that he can provide him with transport to England and get him a job in London. AHMED is delighted and voluntarily agrees to travel with DUNBAR from Cairo to Alexandria (also in Egypt) where he will be transported by boat to mainland Europe and onwards to the UK. DUNBAR and AHMED travel to Alexandria together but, in Alexandria, AHMED changes his mind about going to England and returns to Cairo.

Considering only the offence of human trafficking (contrary to s. 2 of the Modern Slavery Act 2015), which of the following comments is correct?

A DUNBAR does not commit the offence as he did not intend to sexually exploit AHMED.

B The offence has not been committed because the travel that took place only took place within Egypt.

C As no actual exploitation of AHMED occurred, the offence has not been committed.

D DUNBAR has committed the offence in these circumstances.

Question 11.6

TRAVIS has been arrested for an offence of human trafficking contrary to s. 2 of the Modern Slavery Act 2015 and the officer in the case, PC BAPTISTA, is preparing to interview TRAVIS and in doing so is considering the meaning of the term 'exploitation' which is a key part of this offence.

Which of the following best describes 'exploitation' within the meaning given by the 2015 Act?

A Exploitation includes slavery, servitude and forced or compulsory labour.

B Exploitation includes slavery, servitude, forced or compulsory labour and sexual exploitation.

C Exploitation includes slavery, servitude, forced or compulsory labour, sexual exploitation and organ removal.

D Exploitation includes slavery, servitude, forced or compulsory labour, sexual exploitation, organ removal and prostitution.

ANSWERS

Answer 11.1

Answer **B** — Kidnapping is an offence at common law. It involves the taking or carrying away of one person by another without the consent of the person so taken or carried away, and without lawful excuse.

The issue here is consent, and certainly the woman consents to get into the car. However, the Court of Appeal held in *R v Cort* [2003] 3 WLR 1300 that if the consent is obtained by fraud, as it was here through the lies told, then this would not be true consent. Without such consent, the offence is made out when the woman gets in the car and, as MOORE has kidnapped her, therefore answer A is incorrect. Although he further detains her, this is more the offence of false imprisonment and happens after she is kidnapped; answers C and D are therefore incorrect.

Crime, para. 1.11.3

Answer 11.2

Answer **A** — Kidnapping is defined at common law as follows:

It is an offence at common law to take or carry away another person without the consent of that person and without lawful excuse.

The required elements of this offence are the unlawful taking or carrying away of one person by another by force or fraud (*R v D* [1984] AC 778). These requirements go beyond those of mere restraint needed for false imprisonment. Parents may be acting without lawful excuse, for instance if they are acting in breach of a court order in respect of their children.

The taking or carrying away of the victim must be without the consent of the victim. If the victim consents to an initial taking but later withdraws that consent, the offence would be complete. If the consent is obtained by fraud, the defendant cannot rely on that consent and the offence—or attempted offence—will be made out (see *R v Cort* [2003] 3 WLR 1300); answer C is therefore incorrect. There is no limit as to how far the taking should be; answer D is therefore incorrect.

There need only be a 'taking'; the purpose is irrelevant which makes answer B incorrect.

Crime, para. 1.11.3

Answer 11.3

Answer **A** — It is an offence at common law to falsely imprison another person. The elements required for this offence are the unlawful and intentional/reckless restraint of a person's freedom of movement, making answer C incorrect. Locking someone in a vehicle or keeping him/her in a particular place for however short a time may amount to false imprisonment if done unlawfully, so answer D is incorrect. Physical contact is not required between offender and victim, meaning that answer B is incorrect.

Crime, para. 1.11.2

Answer 11.4

Answer **D** — It is an offence at common law falsely to imprison another person.

The elements required for this offence are the unlawful and intentional/reckless restraint of a person's freedom of movement (*R* v *Rahman* (1985) 81 Cr App R 349); this is the case whether or not the person voluntarily entered the place they were being held; answer C is therefore incorrect.

In *R* v *Shwan Faraj* [2007] EWCA Crim 1033, the court stated that there was no reason why a householder should not be entitled to detain someone in his house whom he genuinely believed to be a burglar; he would be acting in defence of his property in doing so (a lawful detention of the person). This action would be correct for other offences and not restricted only to burglary; answers A and B are therefore incorrect.

Crime, para. 1.11.2

Answer 11.5

Answer **D** — Exploitation takes many forms and covers sexual and non-sexual exploitation, making answer A incorrect. Section 2(5) states that 'travel' means: (a) arriving in, or entering, any country, (b) departing from any country, (c) travelling within any country. Section 2(6) states that a person who is a UK national commits an offence under this section regardless of where the arranging or facilitating takes place or where the travel takes place, so the journey from Cairo to Alexandria would be covered, making answer B incorrect. The fact that AHMED changed his mind and that no actual exploitation took place is immaterial, making answer C incorrect.

Crime, para. 1.11.4.2

Answer 11.6

Answer **C** — Exploitation is defined in s. 3 of the Modern Slavery Act 2015 and includes slavery, servitude and forced or compulsory labour, sexual exploitation and removal of organs, etc. but not specifically prostitution; answers A, B and D are therefore incorrect.

Crime, para. 1.11.4.2

12 Sexual Offences

Question 12.1

WRIGHT works with LAKER and during an office party he suggests to LAKER that they have sex together; LAKER refuses. This annoys WRIGHT and later on he follows LAKER into the female toilets. WRIGHT demands that LAKER talk with him in one of the toilet cubicles and, once inside, WRIGHT locks the door. WRIGHT demands to know why LAKER refused to have sex with him and when LAKER begins to cry, WRIGHT tells her he would be happy if she took part in oral sex with him. LAKER asks to be let out of the cubicle but WRIGHT refuses. LAKER realises that WRIGHT will not let her out, so agrees to have oral sex with him and allows WRIGHT to put his penis in her mouth.

Considering the offence of rape only (contrary to s. 1 of the Sexual Offences Act 2003), which of the following statements is correct?

A No offence of rape has been committed because LAKER consented to the act of oral sex.

B Rape can only be committed if WRIGHT penetrates the vagina or anus of LAKER.

C WRIGHT commits rape (the presumptions under s. 75 of the Sexual Offences Act 2003 would be relevant here as LAKER was unlawfully detained at the time of the relevant act).

D WRIGHT has not committed rape because he has not used violence or caused LAKER to believe immediate violence will be used against her.

Question 12.2

DUPONT approaches THOMPSON in the street. He shows her a photograph of her 3-year-old son and says, 'Me and my mate have been watching you and your boy, my mate's watching him now. Unless you do as I say, my mate will hurt your kid.' THOMPSON believes that her son is in immediate danger and that DUPONT's associate will harm him. DUPONT demands that THOMPSON follow him into a nearby alleyway where he puts his fingers into DUPONT's vagina. DUPONT does not have a friend watching THOMPSON's child, who is in no actual danger at the time of the act.

Has DUPONT committed an offence of rape (contrary to s. 1 of the Sexual Offences Act 2003)?

A Yes, because at the time of the relevant act he has caused THOMPSON to believe that immediate violence will be used against another person.

B No, because he did not use violence against THOMPSON or cause her to believe that immediate violence would be used against her.

C Yes, because he has intentionally deceived THOMPSON into taking part in the relevant act.

D No, because intentionally penetrating THOMPSON's vagina with his fingers is not the *actus reus* of rape.

Question 12.3

STONE is walking through the park in the summer when he comes across a girl sunbathing wearing only her bikini bottoms, exposing her breasts. Seeing STONE staring at her, she invites him over and says 'I can show you more'. He nods and she pulls her pants aside and exposes her vagina. STONE thanks her and walks off. A female was also walking past and was distressed at this behaviour and informs the police. The girl exposed herself to STONE for her own sexual gratification.

In relation to exposure (contrary to s. 66 of the Sexual Offences Act 2003), which of the following is correct?

A The girl has committed the offence of exposure by deliberately exposing her breasts.

B The girl has committed the offence of exposure by deliberately exposing her vagina.

C The girl has not committed the offence of exposure as STONE was clearly not alarmed or distressed.

D The girl has not committed the offence of exposure as when she did so she did not intend to cause anyone alarm or distress.

Question 12.4

WALSH is 15 years of age and has been infatuated with his neighbour's 18-year-old daughter for some time, and wishes to have sex with her. One night they are alone in WALSH's house and he asks to have oral sex, the girl agrees and he has oral sex with the girl (who is aware that WALSH is 15 years of age).

Has the girl committed an offence contrary to s. 9 of the Sexual Offences Act 2003 (sexual activity with a child)?

A Yes, she commits this offence when she agrees to have oral sex with him.

B Yes, she commits this offence when she actually has oral sex with him.

C No, as she did not penetrate him, he penetrated her.

D No, as this offence is committed by a person over 18 years of age.

Question 12.5

McNALLY and his girlfriend, who are both 17 years of age, are in their bedroom and are joined by McNALLY's younger brother, who is 13 years of age. Whilst the younger brother watches, McNALLY and his girlfriend participate in mutual masturbation and oral sex. They both know the child is present, and both are getting sexual gratification from the fact they are being watched by the brother. The brother is not offended and enjoys watching.

Is this engaging in sexual activity in the presence of a child (contrary to s. 11 of the Sexual Offences Act 2003)?

A Yes, as they are over 17 years of age.

B Yes, because the brother is under 14 years of age.

C No, because they are not 18 years of age or over.

D No, because the child is not offended or forced to watch.

Question 12.6

ULLESTHORPE sneaks into a care home which specifically caters for people with mental illnesses who are unable to look after themselves. ORTON is a patient at the home and is in a constant vegetative state, unable to speak or move. ULLESTHORPE is fully aware of the nature of the home and the condition of the people who are in it and creeps into ORTON's room where he fondles ORTON's breasts to obtain sexual gratification. ULLESTHORPE becomes sexually aroused and places his erect penis in ORTON's hand. He then uses ORTON's hand to masturbate himself.

At what point, if at all, does ULLESTHORPE first commit an offence of sexual activity with a person with a mental disorder (contrary to s. 30 of the Sexual Offences Act 2003)?

A When he fondles ORTON's breasts.

B When he places his erect penis in ORTON's hand.

C When he uses ORTON's hand to masturbate himself.

D The offence has not been committed by ORTON.

Question 12.7

CASE and her boyfriend PRIZEMAN (both aged 25 years) are babysitting SHIPMAN (aged 12 years). CASE and PRIZEMAN are watching television in the downstairs lounge when PRIZEMAN sees SHIPMAN looking through an open doorway into the lounge and watching the television. CASE is unaware of the presence of SHIPMAN. PRIZEMAN undresses CASE and begins to have sexual intercourse with her. He intends that SHIPMAN should see the act and wishes to obtain sexual gratification from that fact. Unknown to PRIZEMAN, who believes SHIPMAN is watching, SHIPMAN has in fact returned to her bedroom on the first floor and does not see PRIZEMAN undress CASE and have sexual intercourse with her.

Is PRIZEMAN guilty of an offence of engaging in sexual activity in the presence of a child (contrary to s. 11 of the Sexual Offences Act 2003)?

A Yes, even though SHIPMAN is not present PRIZEMAN intended the act to be viewed by her.

B No, because SHIPMAN is not present or in a place where she can observe the act.

C Yes, because PRIZEMAN believes that SHIPMAN is watching the sexual activity.

D No, because CASE was never aware of SHIPMAN's presence.

Question 12.8

CORNELIUS lives with his girlfriend and has recently encouraged her to go to work as a prostitute for DIBLEY, a local drug dealer. CORNELIUS hopes that in providing his girlfriend, DIBLEY will supply him with cheap drugs in the future, which is likely. CORNELIUS receives no money from DIBLEY for the deal. His girlfriend is happy with this arrangement as she will make more money working for DIBLEY.

Has CORNELIUS committed an offence of controlling prostitution for gain (contrary to s. 53 of the Sexual Offences Act 2003)?

A No, there has been no gain as yet, only future hopes of gain.

B No, as CORNELIUS's girlfriend is not forced into prostitution.

C Yes, as there will be future financial advantage.

D Yes, as the prostitute will make money and she lives with CORNELIUS.

Question 12.9

ALLDAY and MASSEY (both males) have consensual anal intercourse. Immediately after the act, ALLDAY feels extremely guilty and begs MASSEY not to tell either of their wives what they have done. MASSEY punches ALLDAY in the face and tells him he will do what he likes. MASSEY then demands that ALLDAY place his penis in MASSEY's mouth or he will beat ALLDAY up. Compelled under the threat of violence, ALLDAY does so. Several minutes later, MASSEY demands anal intercourse. ALLDAY refuses but MASSEY tells him that he will tell their wives of their activities and, as a result (in fear of MASSEY exposing what has taken place between the two men), ALLDAY allows MASSEY to have anal sexual intercourse with him.

At what stage, if at all, is the offence of rape (contrary to s. 1 of the Sexual Offences Act 2003) committed?

A When MASSEY punches ALLDAY in the face immediately after the act of anal sexual intercourse.

B When ALLDAY is compelled to put his penis into MASSEY's mouth.

C When ALLDAY, out of fear, allows MASSEY to have anal sexual intercourse for a second time.

D The offence of rape is not committed.

Question 12.10

COLLINS is very upset that his daughter's ex-boyfriend was unfaithful to her and plans revenge. COLLINS finds out the email address of the ex and uses a messaging service to induce him to masturbate in front of his webcam. The ex-boyfriend believes, however, that he is masturbating for the gratification of a 20-year-old girl.

Has COLLINS committed an offence of causing a person to engage in sexual activity without consent (contrary to s. 4 of the Sexual Offences Act 2003)?

A Yes, as he deceived the ex-boyfriend as to the purpose of the masturbation.

B Yes, as he deceived the ex-boyfriend as to the purpose of the masturbation and by impersonating someone else.

C No, as the ex-boyfriend was not deceived as to the actual sexual activity; he knew he was being asked to masturbate.

D No, as COLLINS did not impersonate someone known personally to the ex-boyfriend.

Question 12.11

BUTCHER wants to have sexual intercourse with a prostitute. He has never had any dealings with prostitutes in any way and is unsure of how to go about getting a prostitute to have sexual intercourse with him. He gets into his car and drives to a residential area he believes, mistakenly, to be a well-known red-light area. He notices a lone woman standing near a bus stop. He stops beside her and says, 'Are you doing business?' (meaning will she have sexual intercourse with him). Not knowing what he means, she says, 'No I'm waiting for a bus, what sort of business are you looking for?' Confused, BUTCHER drives straight home.

Which of the following is correct in relation to the offence of 'kerb-crawling' (contrary to s. 51A of the Sexual Offences Act 2003)?

A He has committed an offence of 'kerb-crawling' as his behaviour is likely to cause annoyance to the woman.

B He has committed an offence of 'kerb-crawling' as he has solicited the woman from his car.

C He has not committed an offence of 'kerb-crawling' as the woman was not offended or annoyed.

D He has not committed an offence of 'kerb-crawling' as he did not solicit the woman on more than one occasion.

Question 12.12

LINTERN has a 15-year-old daughter, FAY, who looks older than her age. LINTERN introduced FAY to his friend, GREGORY, who is a pimp. Between them, LINTERN and GREGORY persuaded FAY to become a prostitute. She agreed and went out with GREGORY on weekends only, and solicited in the street for prostitution. FAY's mother was aware of what was happening to her daughter and encouraged her, but refused to accept any money from what the child earned.

In relation to offences under s. 48 of the Sexual Offences Act 2003 (sexual exploitation of children), which of the following is true?

A GREGORY has committed the offence, but LINTERN has not.

B LINTERN has committed the offence, but GREGORY has not.

C LINTERN and GREGORY have committed the offence in these circumstances.

D LINTERN, GREGORY and the child's mother have committed the offence.

Question 12.13

GATRELL (aged 21 years) is living with his partner HADLOW (aged 17 years) in an enduring family relationship. GATRELL takes a dozen photographs of HADLOW taking part in simulated sex acts with INGLEY (aged 25 years). HADLOW and INGLEY are both naked in the photographs and both consent to the photographs being taken by GATRELL. GATRELL wishes to keep the photographs for his own pleasure and does not intend to distribute them in any way.

With regard to the taking of indecent photographs (contrary to s. 1 of the Protection of Children Act 1978 (as amended by s. 45 of the Sexual Offences Act 2003)), has GATRELL committed an offence?

A Yes, as the photographs show a person other than GATRELL and HADLOW.

B No, because GATRELL and HADLOW were living together in an enduring family relationship.

C Yes, because indecent photographs of a child under 18 years of age cannot be taken in any circumstances.

D No, because HADLOW consented to the photographs being taken and she is over 16 years of age.

Question 12.14

ABLITT is in a nightclub where he begins talking to RICHARDS, who is an actress. ABLITT tells RICHARDS that he is only in the country for a week, after which he will fly out to America where he will be directing a film starring a major Hollywood actor; this is a lie as ABLITT is in fact a plumber. ABLITT tells RICHARDS that he can get her a part in the film but he will only do so if she has sexual intercourse with him. To further her acting career, RICHARDS goes to ABLITT's house where she has sexual intercourse with him.

What effect will s. 76 of the Sexual Offences Act 2003 (conclusive presumptions about consent) have on ABLITT's actions?

A As ABLITT has deceived RICHARDS regarding the nature of the act, RICHARDS will be presumed not to consent to it.

B RICHARDS will be presumed not to have consented to the act as ABLITT has intentionally deceived her by impersonating a film director.

C It will have no effect as ABLITT has not impersonated a person known personally to RICHARDS.

D It will have no effect as this section relates to the use of violence to obtain consent from the victim.

Question 12.15

REYNOLDS, aged 48 years, owns a sweet shop which he uses as a means to meet children under the age of 16 and carry out sexual activities with them. He sees BEN, who is 12 years old, in the shop and has desires to touch him sexually. He arranges to meet BEN later in the local park. He has never met BEN prior to seeing him in the sweet shop. REYNOLDS walks to the park at about 7 pm, and meets BEN by the swings. BEN realises something is wrong and runs off before REYNOLDS can touch him.

At what point, if any, does REYNOLDS first commit an offence under s. 15 of the Sexual Offences Act 2003 (meeting a child following sexual grooming)?

A When he arranges to meet the child.

B When he starts walking to meet the child.

C When he first meets the child in the park.

D He does not commit the offence as he has not previously communicated with the child.

Question 12.16

FEARING applies for a job as a lifeguard at his local swimming pool. Part of his prospective duties will include giving swimming lessons to children between the ages of 5 and 12 years old. FEARING's ulterior motive is to gain employment at the swimming pool and then take indecent photographs of the children (contrary to s. 1 of the Protection of Children Act 1978). To help him get the job, he forges several certificates that state he has passed examinations as a lifeguard. As a result, FEARING is given the job as a lifeguard.

Considering the offence of committing a criminal offence with intent to commit a sexual offence (s. 62 of the Sexual Offences Act 2003), which of the following statements is right?

A FEARING does not commit the offence as taking indecent photographs of children under s. 1 of the Protection of Children Act 1978 is not a 'relevant sexual offence'.

B This offence can only be committed if the criminal offence is one of kidnapping or false imprisonment, therefore FEARING has not committed the offence.

C Until FEARING commits a sexual assault on one of the children, he cannot be arrested for committing this offence.

D FEARING has initially committed an offence of obtaining a pecuniary advantage by deception (s. 16 of the Theft Act 1968) and therefore commits this offence.

Question 12.17

Police are investigating a hotel they believe is being used by a criminal gang for child sexual exploitation. The gang are allowing men to watch children on the toilet; this action would amount to an offence of voyeurism contrary to s. 67 of the Sexual Offences Act 2003. Police are keen to get information about the guests from the hotel using s. 116 of the Anti-social Behaviour, Crime and Policing Act 2014.

In relation to this, which of the following is correct?

A They may get this information provided an officer of at least the rank of inspector serves notice that the officer reasonably believes the premises have been or will be used for the purposes of child sexual exploitation.

B They may get this information provided an officer of at least the rank of superintendent serves notice that the officer reasonably believes the premises have been or will be used for the purposes of child sexual exploitation.

C They may get this information provided a magistrate serves notice that the evidence has been laid giving reasonable grounds to believe the premises are currently being used for the purposes of child sexual exploitation.

D They will not get the information using this Act as an offence of voyeurism is not classed as sexual exploitation by this Act.

Question 12.18

SANDBROOK (aged 25 years) has several indecent photographs of TAFANO (aged 14 years) posted through his front door. SANDBROOK had not made any prior request for these photographs to be delivered. SANDBROOK opens the envelope containing the photographs and, having examined them, he leaves them on a shelf in his flat. Six months later, SANDBROOK's flat is raided by the police and the photographs of TAFANO are discovered. SANDBROOK states that he has not shown or distributed the photographs of TAFANO to anyone else nor did he intend to do so.

With regard to s. 160 of the Criminal Justice Act 1988 (possession of indecent photographs of children), which of the following statements is correct?

A SANDBROOK does not commit the offence as the photographs are of a child aged over 13 years of age.

B SANDBROOK has committed the offence but would have a defence because the photographs were sent to him without any prior request.

C As SANDBROOK has not shown or distributed the photographs to anyone else, he has not committed an offence under this Act.

D SANDBROOK has committed the offence, which is punishable with up to five years' imprisonment.

Question 12.19

BEDDOW is at a nightclub and approaches GRAINGER and tries to talk to her as he finds her sexually attractive. GRAINGER is not interested in BEDDOW and tells him to go away. Later in the evening, GRAINGER is standing at the bar waiting to be served when BEDDOW approaches her from behind. To obtain sexual gratification, he takes out his penis and lightly touches GRAINGER's buttocks (through her clothing) with the tip of his penis. BEDDOW is aroused by this contact and ejaculates onto GRAINGER's skirt while he is touching her. GRAINGER is completely unaware that BEDDOW has behaved in this way.

Considering the offence of sexual assault (contrary to s. 3 of the Sexual Offences Act 2003), which of the following comments is correct?

A The offence has not been committed as no violence was used by BEDDOW.

B The offence has not been committed as BEDDOW has not touched GRAINGER's sexual organs.

C The offence has not been committed as GRAINGER is unaware that she has been touched.

D BEDDOW commits the offence in these circumstances.

Question 12.20

PARISH has recently had gender reassignment surgery where the penis was removed and replaced with a surgically constructed vagina. Whilst out in a pub, PARISH meets a man she finds very attractive and she invites him back to her flat.

They begin kissing and PARISH allows the male to digitally penetrate her vagina. The male then removes a small dildo from his back pocket and starts to use it to penetrate PARISH's vagina. She asks him to stop as she does not want to risk damaging her reconstructive surgery. She firmly tells him 'no', but he does so anyway, laughing.

Which of the following statements is correct in relation to a sexual assault (contrary to s. 2 of the Sexual Offences Act 2003)?

A A surgically constructed vagina is not included in this offence.

B This offence is only committed by using a body part for penetration not an inanimate object.

C The offence here is not committed as PARISH agreed to digital penetration.

D The offence is committed as PARISH did not consent to penetration by the dildo.

Question 12.21

HALLAM's car breaks down in a country lane late one night. Rather than risk getting lost, she decides to sleep in her car and seek assistance in the morning. Several hours later, MILLENSTED walks past HALLAM's car and sees her sleeping inside. He decides to sexually touch HALLAM (an activity that would constitute an offence under s. 3 of the Sexual Offences Act 2003). MILLENSTED smashes the front window of the car and crawls inside. HALLAM, who is woken by the noise, manages to open one of the car doors and gets away from MILLENSTED.

With regard to the offence of trespass with intent to commit a sexual offence (contrary to s. 63 of the Sexual Offences Act 2003), which of the following statements is correct?

A The only intention that would make MILLENSTED guilty of this offence would be an intention to rape HALLAM.

B MILLENSTED has not committed the offence as a car would not be classed as a structure or part of a structure for the purposes of this offence.

C MILLENSTED has committed the offence as the term 'premises' for the purpose of s. 62 will include a vehicle.

D As HALLAM escaped before MILLENSTED committed the relevant sexual offence, he does not commit the offence.

Question 12.22

BURRELL was found with an image on his computer of a woman and a dead horse. The woman had the horse's penis in her mouth.

Considering s. 63 of the Criminal Justice and Immigration Act (possession of extreme pornographic images), which of the following is correct?

A This would be an offence if the 'reasonable person' looking at the image would think it was grossly offensive.

B This would be an offence provided it was produced solely or principally for the purpose of sexual arousal.

C This would not be an offence as the animal was dead at the time the photograph was taken.

D This would not be an offence as the animal was dead at the time the photograph was taken, and the 'reasonable person' looking at the image would think that the animal was dead.

Question 12.23

MARKU is involved in exploiting girls for prostitution. He accepts payment from CROSS for the services of a prostitute. MARKU then persuades a young illegal immigrant to have sex with CROSS and tells her that if she does he will ensure that she will get political asylum in the UK. MARKU has absolutely no way of being able to influence the immigration status of the girl; however, he intends giving the girl half of the money paid by CROSS. CROSS has no idea that MARKU has used a deception on the girl.

Considering the offence of paying for sexual services of a prostitute subjected to force (contrary to s. 53A of the Sexual Offences Act 2003), which of the following is correct?

A Both MARKU and CROSS have committed this offence as CROSS has made payment and MARKU has benefited.

B Only CROSS has committed this offence as he has made payment; MARKU has not committed this offence at all.

C Only CROSS has committed this offence as he has made payment; MARKU has not committed this offence as he has offered to share the benefits with the prostitute.

D Only MARKU commits this offence as CROSS knows nothing about the exploitative conduct committed by MARKU.

Question 12.24

Henry SINCLAIR is an 18-year-old male and lives with his step-sister, Jayne RAYNOR, who is 16 years old and both their respective parents, his father and her mother; both the parents are widowed. Henry and Jayne have been step-brother and step-sister for the last five years. During this time, they have become very close and have

fallen in love; however, because of their very religious upbringing they have remained totally celibate. Henry asks Jayne to marry him and her mother gives the
appropriate legal consent. They marry two weeks before Jayne's 17th birthday.

Considering offences contrary to s. 25 of the Sexual Offences Act 2003 (sexual
activity with child family members), which of the following statements is correct?

A Henry and Jayne cannot have sex until she is 17.

B Henry and Jayne can have sex because they are married.

C Henry and Jayne cannot have sex until she is 18.

D Henry and Jayne can have sex as they are not blood relatives and she is 16 years
or over.

Question 12.25

BRANNIGAN and HURLEY are in a relationship and regularly have sexual intercourse
together. One evening, after sexual intercourse, BRANNIGAN takes a picture of
HURLEY as she lies naked on a bed with her vagina exposed and 30 minutes later
a further 'selfie' picture of BRANNIGAN and HURLEY kissing each other when they
are fully clothed — this is done with HURLEY's consent but only on the strict condition BRANNIGAN will keep the pictures private. Two weeks later the relationship
breaks up and to get revenge against HURLEY and cause her distress, BRANNIGAN
telephones her and threatens to place the picture he took of her lying naked on
the bed with her vagina exposed and also the picture of the pair kissing on a social
media site so that 100s of their contacts on the social media site will see the pictures.
HURLEY is extremely upset and begs BRANNIGAN not to do as he has threatened
- BRANNIGAN feels extremely guilty about the threat he has made and does not disclose the pictures, instead, he deletes them.

Des BRANNIGAN commit an offence of disclosing or threatening to disclose a private
sexual photograph (contrary to s. 33 of the Criminal Justice and Courts Act 2015)?

A No, as the pictures did not show HURLEY engaging in sexual activity.

B No, as BRANNIGAN did not make the threat for the purposes of obtaining sexual
gratification.

C Yes, but only in relation to the picture that shows HURLEY's genitals.

D Yes, in relation to both pictures.

ANSWERS

Answer 12.1

Answer **C** — Rape can be committed if a male penetrates the vagina, anus or mouth of his victim, making answer B incorrect. Although the use of or threat to use violence would negate consent (s. 72(2)(a) and (b)), this is not the only way that a complainant can be deemed to have refused consent to the relevant act, making answer D incorrect. Consent will only be true consent if the person agrees by choice and has the freedom and capacity to make that choice. Under s. 75(2)(c) of the Act, the complainant is taken not to have consented to the relevant act if the complainant was, and the defendant was not, unlawfully detained at the time of the relevant act, making answer A incorrect.

Crime, paras 1.12.3 to 1.12.3.4

Answer 12.2

Answer **D** — Although answer A is correct insofar as the consent obtained from THOMPSON is not true consent as it is obtained by threatening immediate violence against another person, the *actus reus* of rape is the penetration of the vagina, anus or mouth of another person with the penis, making this answer incorrect. Answer B is incorrect as had DUPONT used violence, this would still not be rape. The deception in rape must be as to the nature or purpose of the relevant act not the circumstances leading up to the act, making answer C incorrect.

Crime, paras 1.12.3 to 1.12.3.4

Answer 12.3

Answer **D** — Section 66 of the Sexual Offences Act 2003 states:

A person commits an offence if—
(a) he intentionally exposes his genitals, and
(b) he intends that someone will see them and be caused alarm or distress.

This offence requires only the intentional exposure of the genitals with the dual intention of them being seen by someone else and that this other person will be caused alarm or distress.

Without that intent, this offence is not made out even if someone is actually offended; answer B is therefore incorrect. However, it does not matter that someone is not distressed, provided the exposure was done with the relevant intent; answer C is therefore incorrect. A woman who exposes her breasts will not be guilty of an offence under s. 66; answer A is therefore incorrect.

Crime, para. 1.12.18.1

Answer 12.4

Answer **B** — Section 9 of the Sexual Offences Act 2003 makes it an offence for a person aged 18 or over (answer D is therefore incorrect) intentionally to engage in sexual touching of a child under 16.

It involves penetration of the victim's anus or vagina by a part of the defendant's body or anything else, of the victim's mouth with the defendant's penis, of the defendant's anus or vagina by a part of the victim's body or of the defendant's mouth by the victim's penis; answer C is therefore incorrect. It is not committed until the act actually takes place; answer A is therefore incorrect.

Crime, para. 1.12.7.1

Answer 12.5

Answer **C** — Section 11 makes it an offence for a person aged 18 or over intentionally to engage in sexual activity when a child under 16 is present, or in a place from which he can be observed by the child, the purpose of which is for obtaining sexual gratification from the presence of the child. 'Sexual' is defined by s. 78. The offence is met where the child is under 16 years of age, therefore answer B is incorrect; and is committed by those who are aged 18 or over, therefore answer A is incorrect. The offence is committed even where the child apparently consents to watching the sexual act, and does not need to cause offence; answer D is therefore incorrect.

This offence is intended to cover the situation where someone seeks sexual gratification not from the sexual act itself, but rather from the fact that he is performing that act in the presence or intended presence of a child. The motive of sexual gratification is a necessary safeguard intended to avoid capturing those who engage in sexual activity in front of a child for a legitimate reason. For example, a teacher who sexually kisses his partner just outside the school gates could be deemed to be engaging in sexual activity intentionally in front of a child, and might otherwise be caught by the offence. Note that in the circumstances of the question, an offence contrary to s. 13 of the 2003 Act would have been committed as the assailant was under 18, but you were asked specifically about s. 11.

Crime, para. 1.12.7.3

Answer 12.6

Answer **A** — A person commits an offence under s. 30(1) if:

(a) he intentionally touches another person (B),
(b) the touching is sexual,
(c) B is unable to refuse because of or for a reason related to a mental disorder, and
(d) A knows or could reasonably be expected to know that B has a mental disorder and that because of it or for a reason related to it B is unlikely to refuse.

ULLESTHORPE clearly commits the offence when he fondles ORTON's breasts, making answers B, C and D incorrect.

Crime, para. 1.12.14.2

Answer 12.7

Answer **B** — This offence is committed if a person aged 18 or over (A) engages in sexual activity, for the purpose of obtaining sexual gratification and the activity is engaged in *when another person is present or is in a place from which (A) can be observed.* The fact that PRIZEMAN intended SHIPMAN to view the act (answer A) or the fact that he believed her to be watching the activity (answer C) are both immaterial if SHIPMAN is not present or in a place from which PRIZEMAN can be observed. Answer D is incorrect as the fact that CASE was unaware of SHIPMAN's presence would not preclude PRIZEMAN committing the offence if SHIPMAN was present when the activity took place.

Crime, para. 1.12.7.3

Answer 12.8

Answer **C** — Section 53 makes it an offence for a person intentionally to control another person's activities relating to prostitution, in any part of the world, where it is done for, or in the expectation of, gain for him/herself or a third party. Clearly, CORNELIUS is controlling his girlfriend's activity even although she is happy to go along with it, and it was done with a view to gain, therefore answer B is incorrect.

'Gain' is defined by s. 54 of the Act as any financial advantage, including the discharge of a debt or obligation to pay, or the provision of goods or services (including sexual services) for free or at a discount. It also covers the goodwill of any person likely to bring such a financial advantage. So this would cover CORNELIUS inciting his girlfriend to work as a prostitute for DIBLEY, where CORNELIUS expects this will lead to DIBLEY providing him with cheap drugs at a later date. This future gain therefore makes answer A incorrect. It is immaterial that CORNELIUS will be in a household with extra income due to his girlfriend's 'activities'; the offence is complete with the goodwill, and answer D is therefore incorrect.

Crime, para. 1.12.15.2

Answer 12.9

Answer **C** — Rape is committed when a person (A) intentionally penetrates the vagina, anus or mouth of another person (B) with his penis and that other person (B) does not consent to the penetration and A does not reasonably believe that B consents. The first act of anal sexual intercourse was consensual and, although violence was used by MASSEY after this act, that will not alter the true consent given to anal intercourse on the first occasion, making answer A incorrect. Answer B is incorrect as rape is committed when the defendant intentionally penetrates the vagina, anus or mouth of the complainant with his penis—it is not committed when the defendant (A) forces the complainant (B) to penetrate A's mouth with B's penis. The offence is committed at point C as at this point, although ALLDAY allows the penetration to take place, it is only allowed because of ALLDAY's fear that his activities will be exposed to his wife. As a result, this is not 'true' consent. 'True' consent is given by a person who agrees by choice and has the freedom and capacity to make that choice. Therefore, if a person does not have any choice in the matter, or their choice is not a genuine exercise of their free will (and ALLDAY's choice is not), they will not have consented, making answer D incorrect in the process.

Crime, paras 1.12.3 to 1.12.3.4

Answer 12.10

Answer **A** — An offence of causing a person to engage in sexual activity without consent contrary to s. 4 of the Sexual Offences Act 2003, is committed where a person intentionally causes another person to engage in an activity, the activity is sexual and the other person does not consent to engaging in the activity. This question only relates to 'consent' and to answer this we have to turn to s. 76 of the Sexual Offences Act 2003 which states that, if it is proved in some sexual offences (including s. 4) that the defendant did the relevant act and that he/she:

(a) intentionally deceived the complainant as to the nature or purpose of the relevant act; or
(b) intentionally induced the complainant to consent to the relevant act by impersonating a person known personally to the complainant.

There will be a conclusive presumption both that the victim did not consent and also that the defendant did not believe he/she consented.

The 'or' between points (a) and (b) means that only one of the points applies, not both; answer B is therefore incorrect.

In *R v Devonald* [2008] EWCA Crim 527 (a case under s. 4 where the court held that s. 76 applied), the court held that it was open to the jury to conclude that the complainant was deceived into believing he was masturbating for the gratification of a 20-year-old girl via a webcam when in fact he was doing it for the father of a former girlfriend who was teaching him a lesson. Here 'purpose' has been given a wide meaning in that the deception was not as to sexual purpose, rather it was as to the purpose of the act of masturbation and, in particular, as to the identity of the observer. This ruling means answers C and D are incorrect, even though *Devonald* may seem out of step with *R v Jheeta* [2007] EWCA Crim 1699, where the defendant deceived the complainant into having sex more frequently than she would have done otherwise. In these circumstances, the conclusive presumptions under the Sexual Offences Act 2003 had no relevance as the complainant had not been deceived as to the nature or purpose of the sexual intercourse.

Crime, para. 1.12.5

Answer 12.11

Answer **B** — Section 51A of the Sexual Offences Act 2003 (as amended) states:

(1) It is an offence for a person in a street or public place to solicit another (B) for the purpose of obtaining B's sexual services as a prostitute.
(2) The reference to a person in a street or public place includes a person in a vehicle in a street or public place.

This offence is applicable to both sexes.

Kerb-crawling or soliciting is punishable on the first occasion the activity takes place; answer D is therefore incorrect.

In the case of kerb-crawling, there is no requirement for the soliciting to be shown to be likely to cause nuisance or annoyance to others or to actually go on to cause nuisance or offence; answers A and C are therefore incorrect.

Crime, para. 1.12.15.5

Answer 12.12

Answer **D** — Section 48 makes it an offence for a person intentionally to sexually exploit a child under 18 in any part of the world.

For the purposes of ss. 48 to 50, a person (B) is sexually exploited if:

* on at least one occasion and whether or not compelled to do so, B offers or provides sexual services to another person in return for payment or a promise of payment to B or a third person; or
* an indecent image of B is recorded;

and sexual exploitation is to be interpreted accordingly (s. 51(2)).

The sexual exploitation itself does not need to take place for the offence to be committed. The offence would be committed where a 'pimp' makes a living from the prostitution of others and encourages new recruits to work for him. It could also cover the situation where the defendant forces the victim to take part in child pornography for any reason.

Unlike the equivalent adult offence at s. 52, there is no requirement that the sexual exploitation must be done for the gain of any of the persons involved, therefore FAY's mother is as culpable as the others. All three persons have incited the child, therefore answers A, B and C are incorrect.

Crime, para. 1.12.11.1

Answer 12.13

Answer **A** — Section 1(1)(a) of the Protection of Children Act 1978 makes it an offence for a person to take, or permit to be taken or to make, any indecent photograph or pseudo-photograph of a child. Section 45 of the Sexual Offences Act 2003 amends the Protection of Children Act so that, where photographs are concerned, a person will be considered a 'child' if they are 16 or 17 years of age. However, photographs taken and used within an established relationship will not be criminalised if: (a) the defendant proves that the photograph in question was of a child aged 16 or over and at the time of the taking or making, he and the child were married or living together as partners in an enduring family relationship; (b) the child consented to the photograph being taken or the defendant reasonably believed that the child consented; and (c) the photograph must not be one that shows a person other than the child and the defendant. If *any* of these conditions is not satisfied then the prosecution need only prove the offence as set out in s. 1(1)(a) of the 1978 Act. Answers B and D are incorrect as they only form part of the potential defence available to GATRELL. In addition, answer D is incorrect as it asserts that taking photographs of a child over the age of 16 is permissible with the consent of the child. Answer C is incorrect as this defence exists if all three elements are present.

Crime, para. 1.12.10.3

Answer 12.14

Answer **C** — This section of the Act relates to the use of some form of deception in order to obtain consent from the victim and not the use of violence to obtain consent (covered by s. 75 of the Act), making answer D incorrect. Answer A is incorrect as RICHARDS has not been deceived into the act by a misrepresentation as to the nature of the act; RICHARDS knew that what she was doing was sexual intercourse. Answer B is incorrect as the person impersonated must be known *personally* to the victim.

Crime, para. 1.12.3.5

Answer 12.15

Answer **A** — The Sexual Offences Act 2003, s. 15 states:

(1) A person aged 18 or over (A) commits an offence if—
   (a) A has met or communicated with another person (B) on one or more occasions and subsequently—
      (i)   A intentionally meets B,
      (ii) A travels with the intention of meeting B in any part of the world or arranges to meet B in any part of the world, or
      (iii) B travels with the intention of meeting A in any part of the world,
   (b) A intends to do anything to or in respect of B, during or after the meeting mentioned in paragraph (a)(i) to (iii) and in any part of the world, which if done will involve the commission by A of a relevant offence,
   (c) B is under 16, and
   (d) A does not reasonably believe that B is 16 or over.

The initial action of the defendant involves either a meeting or a communication with the victim (who must be under 16) on one or more occasions. The communications can include text messaging or interactions in Internet chat rooms. Such contact can have taken place in any part of the world.

Once the earlier meetings or communications have taken place, the offence is triggered by:

- an intentional meeting with the victim;
- a defendant travelling with the intention of meeting the victim;
- a defendant arranging to meet the victim;
- the victim travelling to meet the defendant in any part of the world.

In this scenario, REYNOLDS has met the child (one or more occasions) and the offence is triggered when he arranges a further meeting with the relevant intention. One previous meeting will suffice (answer D is therefore incorrect) and the offence is first committed on the arrangement to further meet; answers B and C are therefore incorrect.

Crime, para. 1.12.7.7

Answer 12.16

Answer **A** — Section 62 of the Sexual Offences Act 2003 states that a person commits an offence under this section if he commits any offence with the intention of committing a relevant sexual offence. There are no restrictions on the nature or type of offence committed as long as it can be shown that there was an intention, when committing the original offence, to commit a relevant sexual offence. This makes answer B incorrect. Answer C is incorrect as the offence under s. 62 is committed when the first offence is committed with the required intention. Answer D is incorrect as although FEARING has committed an offence, taking photographs of children (contrary to s. 1 of the Protection of Children Act 1978) is not a 'relevant offence' for the purposes of s. 62. A 'relevant offence' means a sexual offence under Pt 1 of the Sexual Offences Act 2003.

Crime, para. 1.12.16.2

Answer 12.17

Answer **A** — Section 116 of the Anti-social Behaviour, Crime and Policing Act 2014 confers a power on a police officer, of at least the rank of inspector (not superintendent, answer B is therefore incorrect), to serve a notice on the owner, operator or manager of a hotel that the officer reasonably believes has been or will be used for the purposes of child sexual exploitation or conduct preparatory to or connected with it. This takes it beyond just being used now and therefore answer C is incorrect.

Section 116(8) of the 2014 Act outlines which offences would amount to 'child sexual exploitation' and includes s. 67 of the Sexual Offences Act 2003 (voyeurism); answer D is therefore incorrect.

Crime, para. 1.12.11.3

Answer 12.18

Answer **D** — Answer A is incorrect as a 'child' is a person under the age of 18 years of age at the material time. Answer B is incorrect as although the photographs were sent to SANDBROOK without any prior request being made by him for such material (the first part of the defence under s. 160(2)(c)), he has kept them for an unreasonable time, thereby defeating the defence. Answer C is incorrect as showing or distributing the indecent photographs relates to an offence under s. 1 of the Protection of Children Act 1978 and not to the offence of possessing indecent photographs under this Act.

Crime, para. 1.12.10.4

Answer 12.19

Answer **D** — There is no requirement for force or violence for the offence to be committed, making answer A incorrect. Answer B is incorrect as the part of the body touched does not have to be a sexual organ. Answer C is incorrect as the victim need not be aware of being touched, so the offence was committed when the accused secretly took his penis out of his trousers and ejaculated onto a woman's clothing when pressed up against her dancing at a nightclub (*R* v *Bounekhla* [2006] EWCA Crim 1217).

Crime, paras 1.12.4.3, 1.12.4.4

Answer 12.20

Answer **D** — As with rape, s. 79(3) of the Sexual Offences Act references to a vagina include a surgically constructed vagina; answer A is therefore incorrect. The penetration may be penetration with a part of the offender's body, for example a finger or a fist, or with anything else, for example a dildo or a sharp object (the term 'anything else' will include an animal or other living organism); answer B is therefore incorrect.

Consent is an ongoing criterion; whilst she may have freely consented to one activity, ongoing consent to that activity, or any other activity, can be withdrawn at any time. Failure to conform to withdrawal of consent would be an assault; answer C is therefore incorrect.

Crime, para. 1.12.3.1

Answer 12.21

Answer **C** — Answer A is incorrect as MILLENSTED intends to commit a 'relevant sexual offence' (i.e. an offence under Pt 1 of the Sexual Offences Act 2003). Answer D is incorrect as this is an offence of intention rather than consequence, therefore there is no need to prove that the substantive sexual offence took place. The term 'premises' for the purposes of this offence is far wider than that which relates to burglary under the Theft Act 1968. Section 63(2) of the Sexual Offences Act 2003 defines 'premises' as including a structure or part of a structure and this will include a tent, a vehicle or vessel or other temporary or movable structure. This makes answer B incorrect.

Crime, para. 1.12.16.3

Answer 12.22

Answer **B** — Section 63 of the Criminal Justice and Immigration Act 2008 states:

(1) It is an offence for a person to be in possession of an extreme pornographic image.

There are three elements to the offence. An image must come within the terms of all three elements before it will fall foul of the offence. Those elements are:

- that the image is pornographic;
- that the image is grossly offensive, disgusting or otherwise of an obscene character; and
- that the image portrays in an explicit and realistic way, one of the following extreme acts:
  - an act which threatens a person's life (this could include depictions of hanging, suffocation or sexual assault involving a threat with a weapon);
  - an act which results in or is likely to result in serious injury to a person's anus, breasts or genitals (this could include the insertion of sharp objects or the mutilation of the breasts or genitals);

- an act involving sexual interference with a human corpse (necrophilia);
- a person performing an act of intercourse or oral sex with an animal (whether dead or alive) (bestiality);
- an act which involves the non-consensual penetration of a person's vagina, anus or mouth by another with the other person's penis;
- an act which involves the non-consensual sexual penetration of a person's vagina or anus by another with a part of the other person's body or anything else;
• and a reasonable person looking at the image would think that the people and animals portrayed were real.

All three elements must be covered. It makes no difference whether the animal is alive or dead; answers C and D are therefore incorrect. The 'reasonable person' test does not apply to the image, it will be grossly offensive by design; answer A is therefore incorrect.

An 'extreme pornographic image' is an image which is both pornographic and an extreme image. An image is 'pornographic' if it is of such a nature that it must reasonably be assumed to have produced solely or principally for the purpose of sexual arousal.

Crime, para. 1.12.19

Answer 12.23

Answer **B** — Section 53A of the Sexual Offences Act 2003 states:

(1) A person (A) commits an offence if—
   (a) A makes or promises payment for the sexual services of a prostitute (B),
   (b) a third person (C) has engaged in exploitative conduct of a kind likely to induce or encourage B to provide the sexual services for which A has made or promised payment, and
   (c) C engaged in that conduct for or in the expectation of gain for C or another person (apart from A or B).
(2) The following are irrelevant—
   (a) where in the world the sexual services are to be provided and whether those services are provided,
   (b) whether A is, or ought to be, aware that C has engaged in exploitative conduct.
(3) C engages in exploitative conduct if—
   (a) C uses force, threats (whether or not relating to violence) or any other form of coercion, or
   (b) C practises any form of deception.

This section creates an offence which is committed if someone pays or promises payment for the sexual services of a prostitute who has been subject to exploitative conduct of a kind likely to induce or encourage the provision of sexual services for which the payer has made or promised payment. The person responsible for the exploitative conduct must have been acting for or in the expectation of gain for him/herself or another person, other than the payer or the prostitute.

So only CROSS can commit this offence; answers A, C and D are therefore incorrect.

It does not matter where in the world the sexual services are to be provided. An offence is committed regardless of whether the person paying or promising payment for sexual services knows or ought to know or be aware that the prostitute has been subject to exploitative conduct. In other words, the offence is one of strict liability and no mental element is required in respect of the offender's knowledge that the prostitute was forced, threatened, coerced or deceived.

Crime, para. 1.12.15.3

Answer 12.24

Answer **B** — The Sexual Offences Act 2003, s. 25 states:

(1) A person (A) commits an offence if—
    (a) he intentionally touches a person (B),
    (b) the touching is sexual,
    (c) the relation of A to B is within section 27,
    (d) A knows or could reasonably be expected to know that his relation to B is of a description falling within that section, and
    (e) either—
        (i) B is under 18 and A does not reasonably believe that B is 18 or over, or
        (ii) B is under 13.

Under s. 25 of the Sexual Offences Act 2003, there are offences that apply to blood relatives, and certain persons who have lived in the same household but who are not blood relatives, until the victim is 18 years old. With these latter categories, there are exceptions under s. 27 where (a) either they were having sex before they became so related; for instance, a step-brother and step-sister who were in a sexual relationship before they became step-brother and step-sister when both 16 or over, or (b) they are legally married as in the case of Henry and Jayne, which makes B the correct answer.

Crime, para. 1.12.9.1

Answer 12.25

Answer **D** — Under s. 33(1) of the Criminal Justice and Courts Act 2015, a person commits an offence if -

the person discloses, or threatens to disclose, a private sexual photograph or film in which another individual ('the relevant individual') appears, by so doing, the person intends to cause distress to that individual, and the disclosure is, or would be, made without the consent of that individual.

There is no requirement that the 'private sexual photograph' involves a person engaging in sexual activity (incorrect answer A) or that the defendant discloses/ threatens to disclose for the purpose of sexual gratification (incorrect answer B).

Section 35 of the Criminal Justice and Courts Act 2015 defines the terms 'private' and 'sexual' used in section 33 of the Act in relation to the disclosure of, or threat to disclose, private sexual photographs and films with intent to cause distress and states that a photograph or film is private if it shows something that is not of a kind ordinarily seen in public and that a photograph or film is sexual if—

it shows all or part of an individual's exposed genitals or pubic area, it shows something that a reasonable person would consider to be sexual because of its nature, or it's content, taken as a whole, is such that a reasonable person would consider it to be sexual.

This would exclude from the ambit of the offence a photograph or film that shows something that is of a kind ordinarily seen in public. This means that a photograph or film of something sexual (such as people kissing) would not fall within the ambit of the offence if what was shown was the kind of thing that might ordinarily take place in public meaning that answer C is incorrect and that answer D is the correct answer.

Crime 1.12.20.1

13 | Child Protection

QUESTIONS

Question 13.1

HAYMAN (aged 16 years) and NICHOLL (aged 13 years) are in a park when they are approached by EAMES (aged 30 years). EAMES tells them that he has just had his bike stolen and asks them if they will help him to look for it. This is not true as EAMES's real motive is to attack the boys and sexually assault them at the first opportunity. Both boys willingly agree to EAMES's request and walk towards some nearby bushes where EAMES claims that he left the bike. After walking some 30 metres with EAMES, the boys have second thoughts and run off.

Has EAMES committed an offence of child abduction (contrary to s. 2 of the Child Abduction Act 1984)?

A Yes, but only in relation to NICHOLL.

B No, because both HAYMAN and NICHOLL consented to go with EAMES.

C Yes, both HAYMAN and NICHOLL are covered by the legislation.

D No, neither of the boys has been removed from the lawful control of any person.

Question 13.2

THOMAS is a registered childminder and is looking after a 6-month-old baby when she is called away to collect another minded child from the school. She leaves the baby in the care of her husband who is not a registered childminder whilst she goes to collect the other child. THOMAS's husband does not want to look after the child as it is crying loudly so he puts a duvet over the child's face to lessen the noise. By the time his wife returns, the child is quiet but quite blue from lack of oxygen, although otherwise uninjured.

Has an offence of child cruelty (contrary to s. 1 of the Children and Young Persons Act 1933) been committed and, if so, by whom?

A Both THOMAS and her husband may have committed this offence.

B THOMAS's husband only has committed this offence.

C THOMAS only has committed this offence.

D Neither has committed this offence, although the husband could have committed an assault offence.

Question 13.3

POTTS and OLDFIELD lived together as common law husband and wife but the relationship has ended. There were two children by this relationship, ANN (aged 12 years) and MARTIN (aged 16 years). Both children now live with their mother (OLDFIELD), who has lawful custody of the children. One evening, POTTS visits his children. While OLDFIELD goes out shopping, POTTS persuades the two children to go on holiday with him to Spain for two weeks. The children agree and all three leave for Spain without the consent of OLDFIELD.

Would this constitute an offence of child abduction (contrary to s. 1 of the Child Abduction Act 1984)?

A No, as POTTS has taken the children outside the UK for less than one month.

B Yes, but only in relation to ANN.

C No, because POTTS is the father of both children.

D Yes, in relation to ANN and MARTIN.

Question 13.4

In relation to the offence of child cruelty contrary to the Children and Young Persons Act 1933, a person will be presumed to have neglected a child where it is proved that the child was an infant under a certain age and that he/she died as a result of suffocation while in bed with someone of over a certain age who was under the influence of drink or a prohibited drug when he/she went to bed.

What are those relevant ages?

A An infant under 2 years of age and a person 16 years or older.

B An infant under 3 years of age and a person 16 years or older.

C An infant under 2 years of age and a person 18 years or older.

D An infant under 3 years of age and a person 18 years or older.

Question 13.5

ANITA, aged 15, agreed to babysit her neighbours' 2-year-old child while her neighbours went out for the evening. During the evening, ANITA's boyfriend rang her and asked if he could see her. ANITA checked that the child was asleep then slipped out of the house to meet her boyfriend. She had been gone from the house for about half an hour when neighbours found the child wandering down the street in his pyjamas. The child was not injured during the incident.

In relation to the offence of child cruelty (contrary to s. 1 of the Children and Young Persons Act 1933), which of the following is correct?

A ANITA has committed an offence of child cruelty through her neglect.

B ANITA has committed an offence of child cruelty as her actions are wilful.

C ANITA does not commit an offence of child cruelty in these circumstances.

D ANITA does not commit an offence of child cruelty as the child was not injured.

Question 13.6

JUDSON leaves FOXLEY, her common law husband, after their relationship breaks down and takes their 3-year-old child with her. FOXLEY contacts DC BANHAM and reports the child's absence. DC BANHAM later locates JUDSON, who is staying in a women's refuge with her 3-year-old child. At the request of JUDSON, DC BANHAM tells FOXLEY that the child is safe but refuses to tell him where the child is. FOXLEY hires a solicitor and *ex parte* (i.e. without telling the police) applies for an order from the County Court under s. 33 of the Family Law Act 1986, requiring the police to disclose the information.

Considering the law with regard to the disclosure of a child's whereabouts, which of the following statements is correct?

A If FOXLEY obtains such an order then DC BANHAM will have to provide him with details of the child's whereabouts.

B An order under s. 33 in respect of the police will be made without their presence (*ex parte*) in all cases.

C If FOXLEY's application is successful then DC BANHAM will have to tell FOXLEY's solicitor of the child's whereabouts.

D It has been held that only in exceptional circumstances will the police be asked to divulge the whereabouts of a child under a s. 33 order.

Question 13.7

DC GALVIN is investigating an allegation of child cruelty (contrary to s. 1 of the Children and Young Persons Act 1933). DC GALVIN has never dealt with this offence before and approaches her supervisor, DS WRATTEN, for some advice on the elements of the offence as she has been given contrary advice regarding the constituent elements of it.

Which of the following is correct in relation to that offence?

A The offence can only be committed by a positive act and not by omission.

B The acts must have occurred in a manner that caused unnecessary suffering or injury to health.

C The acts must have occurred in a manner that caused unnecessary suffering or injury to health with intention to do so.

D The acts must have occurred in a manner likely to cause unnecessary suffering or injury to health; there is no need to show that any such suffering or injury actually came about.

Question 13.8

LILLEY has three children who are profoundly deaf; he himself suffers from Usher's Syndrome, which means that he has tunnel vision and night blindness. He is registered blind and has been without a valid driving licence since it was withdrawn on medical grounds by the DVLA. Despite this, LILLEY regularly drove his children to school, but has been warned by social services that this must stop and he had agreed it would. Two days later, social services had information that LILLEY had driven the children several hundred miles to be assessed by another school for deaf children. On learning what had happened, the family's social worker instructed the council's legal department to apply for an emergency protection order (EPO) pursuant to s. 44 of the Children Act 1989, which was granted. The police were informed and they intercepted the vehicle on the motorway being driven home with the children as passengers. The officers invoked their powers under s. 46 of the Children Act 1989 and took the children into police protection.

In relation to police action, which of the following is correct?

A The s. 46 power to remove a child cannot be exercised where an EPO is in force in respect of the child.

B The police should invoke the powers under s. 46 as the statutory scheme accords primacy to that procedure.

C Where a police officer knows that an EPO is in force, he/she should not exercise the power of removing a child under s. 46 unless there are immediate and compelling reasons to do so.

D Where a police officer knows that an EPO is in force, he/she should not exercise the power of removing a child under s. 46 unless there are compelling reasons to do so.

Question 13.9

PC RAFIQ is on uniform patrol when he is sent to a report that two children (aged 12 and 14 years) living in a house with their mother could be harmed as the mother is addicted to drugs. Several neighbours have heard the children crying and there is genuine concern for the welfare of the children. Having spoken to the neighbours, PC RAFIQ is considering using the powers under s. 46 of the Children Act 1989 to take them into 'police protection'.

In relation to the use of the power under s. 46, which of the following statements is correct?

A A constable or social worker may remove a child to suitable accommodation.

B A constable in uniform may remove a child to suitable accommodation.

C A constable may only remove a child to a police station or hospital.

D A constable may remove a child to suitable accommodation.

Question 13.10

MICHAEL is 11 years old and is living with his 24-year-old cousin, although she has no parental responsibility for him. MICHAEL becomes subject to police protection in line with s. 46 of the Children Act 1989.

Which of the following is correct in relation to whether the designated officer can allow the cousin to have contact with MICHAEL whilst in police protection?

A The cousin can have no contact with MICHAEL as she has no parental responsibility for him.

B The cousin would be entitled to contact with MICHAEL as he is currently living with her even though she has no parental responsibility.

C The cousin should be allowed contact provided the designated officer believes it to be reasonable and in the child's best interest.

D The cousin must be allowed contact unless the designated officer believes it would not be reasonable and in the child's best interest.

Question 13.11

An 11-year-old child has been made the subject of an emergency protection order under s. 44 of the Children Act 1989 taken out by social services. The child has been placed into temporary foster care. The child's father contacts the child via her mobile phone and tells her that if she comes back to the family home she will be safe and taken away on a special holiday to see her grandmother who lives in France.

Has the father committed an offence of acting in contravention of a protection order (contrary to s. 49 of the Children Act 1989)?

A Yes, as the father has induced, assisted or incited the child to run away from foster care.

B Yes, as the father has induced, assisted or incited the child to run away from foster care and intends taking the child abroad.

C No, as the child was not directly in 'care' within the local authority area as foster care is not 'care' for the purposes of the legislation.

D No, as the offence would only be complete if the child actually leaves or is taken away from foster care by the father.

Question 13.12

PRINCE is the divorced father of three children aged 16, 14 and 12. He takes them on a skiing holiday to France for a week with the consent of his wife, and at the end of that time he calls her to say he will not be returning the children to her as he is going to settle in France with them.

Considering the offence under s. 1 of the Child Abduction Act 1984 (abduction by person connected with a child) only, which of the following statements is correct?

A PRINCE commits the offence in relation to all three children and has no defence.

B PRINCE commits the offence in relation to the two younger children and has no defence.

C PRINCE commits the offence but would have a defence as he is out of the UK for a period of less than one month.

D PRINCE does not commit this offence at all in these circumstances.

Question 13.13

LATIMER has been in an abusive relationship and has left home taking her child with her and has gone into a refuge. Her partner has reported the child missing and the police have traced LATIMER to the refuge. She states that for fear of her safety she does not want to tell her partner where she and the child are.

What should the police tell her?

A That due to concerns about her safety it is unlikely they would have to divulge her location.

B That due to concerns about her safety they guarantee they would not have to divulge her location.

C Even with concerns as to her safety, her partner could apply for a court order that would mean they would have to divulge her location to him.

D Even with concerns as to her safety, her partner could apply for a court order that would mean they would have to divulge her location to him or his solicitor.

ANSWERS

Answer 13.1

Answer **A** — The legislation covers children under the age of 16 years, making answer C incorrect. The fact that the boys consented to go with EAMES is irrelevant, making answer B incorrect. The Act talks about the taking or detaining of a child and this includes keeping a child where they are found or inducing the child to remain with the defendant or another person. Effectively, this taking or keeping is complete when the defendant substitutes his/her authority or will for that of the person in lawful control of the child and in this example the substitution takes place when EAMES walks with the boys towards the bushes (*R* v *Leather* (1993) 98 Cr App R 179). Therefore, answer D is incorrect.

Crime, para. 1.13.2.3

Answer 13.2

Answer **A** — Section 1 of the Children and Young Persons Act 1933 states:

> (1) If any person who has attained the age of 16 years and has responsibility for any child or young person under that age, wilfully assaults, ill-treats (whether physically or otherwise), neglects, abandons, or exposes him, or causes or procures him to be assaulted, ill-treated (whether physically or otherwise), neglected, abandoned, or exposed, in a manner likely to cause him unnecessary suffering or injury to health (whether the suffering or injury is of a physical or a psychological nature), that person shall be guilty of an offence.

This offence is committed by a person aged 16 years or over who has responsibility for a child. Even though he is not a registered childminder, whilst he is looking after the child the husband has responsibility for that child. However, anyone having parental responsibility or any other legal liability to maintain a child or young person will be presumed to have responsibility for that child and that responsibility does not cease simply because the person ceases to have care of the child. In these circumstances, THOMAS has legal responsibility and therefore even when not present he may still commit this offence; answers B, C and D are therefore incorrect.

Crime, para. 1.13.3

Answer 13.3

Answer **B** — This offence can be committed by any person listed under s. 1(2) of the Act who is connected to the child/children. The Act states that a person is connected with a child (at s. 1(2)(b)) in the case of a child whose parents were not married to each other at the time of his/her birth, if there are reasonable grounds for believing that he is the father of the child, i.e. POTTS. However, just because POTTS is the father of the children does not afford him immunity from this offence, making answer C incorrect. The offence can only be committed in relation to a child under the age of 16 so it cannot be committed in relation to MARTIN, making answer D incorrect. The fact that POTTS has taken the children outside the UK for less than one month is immaterial. The time factor is only relevant if there is a residence order in existence in favour of POTTS (and there is not); what is relevant is that POTTS has taken ANN outside the UK without the consent of OLDFIELD, making answer A incorrect.

Crime, paras 1.13.2 to 1.13.2.4

Answer 13.4

Answer **B** — Section 1(2) of the Children and Young Persons Act 1933 states:

(b) where it is proved that the death of an infant under three years of age was caused by suffocation (not being suffocation caused by disease or the presence of any foreign body in the throat or air passages of the infant) while the infant was in bed with some other person who has attained the age of sixteen years, that other person shall, if he was, when he went to bed, under the influence of drink, be deemed to have neglected the infant in a manner likely to cause injury to its health.

This is answer B; answers A, C and D are therefore incorrect.

Crime, para. 1.13.3

Answer 13.5

Answer **C** — To be guilty of an offence under s. 1 of the Children and Young Persons Act 1933, an accused must have been over the age of 16 at the time of the offence, and must have 'had responsibility' for the child or young person in question. Although s. 1 creates just one offence, it may take a number of different forms. It may take the form of positive abuse (assault, ill-treatment (whether physically or otherwise), abandonment or exposure) or of mere neglect, or it may take the form of causing or procuring abuse or neglect. The abuse or neglect in question must be committed 'in a manner likely to cause unnecessary suffering or injury to health', but the offence is essentially a conduct crime rather than a result crime. It need not therefore be shown that any such injury was caused (answer D is therefore incorrect). ANITA's actions may well have amounted to an offence under the Act but she is outside the scope of the legislation by virtue of her age; answers A and B are therefore incorrect.

Crime, para. 1.13.3

Answer 13.6

Answer **D** — This question relates to the circumstances in *S* v *S (Chief Constable of West Yorkshire Intervening)* [1998] 1 WLR 1716. In this case, Butler-Sloss LJ stated that an order under s. 33 provides for the information to be disclosed to the court and not to any other party or his/her solicitor, making answers A and C incorrect. She also stated that an order made under s. 33 should not normally be made in respect of the police without their being present, making answer B incorrect.

Crime, para. 1.13.4.3

Answer 13.7

Answer **D** — It is an offence of child cruelty when a person, in relation to a child:

wilfully assaults, ill-treats (whether physically or otherwise), neglects, abandons, or exposes him, or causes or procures him to be assaulted, ill-treated (whether physically or otherwise), neglected, abandoned, or exposed, in a manner likely to cause him unnecessary suffering or injury to health …

(Section 1 of the Children and Young Persons Act 1933.)

This section creates only one single offence, albeit one that can be committed in many different ways, by both positive acts and omission (see *R* v *Hayles* [1969] 1 QB 364); answer A is therefore incorrect. Although any aspect of neglect must be shown to have occurred in a manner likely to cause unnecessary suffering or injury to health, there is no need to show that any such suffering or injury actually came about; answers B and C are therefore incorrect.

Crime, para. 1.13.3

Answer 13.8

Answer **D** — This scenario mirrors the case of *Langley* v *Liverpool City Council and Chief Constable of Merseyside* [2005] EWCA Civ 1173. In that case, the police invoked their powers under s. 46 of the Children Act 1989 despite an EPO being in existence that the social services were going to raise when the children returned home.

The Court of Appeal considered the proper approach in these circumstances to be as follows:

- There is no express provision in the Act prohibiting the police from invoking s. 46 where an EPO is in place and it is not desirable to imply a restriction which prohibits a constable from removing a child under s. 46 where he/she has reasonable cause to believe that the child would otherwise be likely to suffer significant harm; answer A is therefore incorrect.
- The s. 46 power to remove a child can therefore be exercised even where an EPO is in force in respect of the child.
- Where a police officer knows that an EPO is in force, he/she should not exercise the power of removing a child under s. 46 unless there are compelling reasons to do so; answer C is therefore incorrect as there is no mention of 'immediately'.
- The statutory scheme accords primacy to the EPO procedure under s. 44 because removal under that section is sanctioned by the court and involves a more elaborate, sophisticated and complete process of removal than under s. 46; answer B is therefore incorrect.
- Consequently, the removal of children should usually be effected pursuant to an EPO, and s. 46 should only be invoked where it is not reasonably practicable to execute an EPO.
- In deciding whether it is practicable to execute an EPO, the police should always have regard to the paramount need to protect children from significant harm.
- Failure to follow the statutory procedure may amount to the police officer's removal of the child under s. 46 being declared unlawful; answer C is therefore incorrect.

Crime, para. 1.13.4

Answer 13.9

Answer **D** — Section 46 states that where a constable has reasonable cause to believe that a child would otherwise be likely to suffer significant harm, he/she may remove that child to suitable accommodation and keep him/her there. Answer A is incorrect as the section allows only a constable to remove the child (known as police protection). There is no requirement for the officer to be in uniform (answer B is therefore incorrect). The section does not specify that the child should only be taken to a police station or hospital (although these may be suitable places); the child may be taken to any suitable accommodation (which is why answer C is incorrect).

Crime, para. 1.13.4

Answer 13.10

Answer **C** — Section 46(10) of the Children Act 1989 states:

Where a child has been taken into police protection, the designated officer shall allow—

(a) the child's parents;
(b) any person who is not a parent of the child but who has parental responsibility for him;
(c) any person with whom the child was living immediately before he was taken into police protection;
(d) any person named in a child arrangements order as a person with whom the child is to spend time or otherwise have contact;
(e) any person who is allowed to have contact with the child by virtue of an order under section 34; and
(f) any person acting on behalf of any of those persons,

to have such contact (if any) with the child as, in the opinion of the designated officer, is both reasonable and in the child's best interests.

So, clearly, it is the decision of the designated officer what, if any, contact should be had with the child whilst in police protection (answer B is therefore incorrect) considering:

• what is reasonable;
• what is in the child's best interest.

There is no 'must' about the cousin's contact and therefore answer D is incorrect. Even though the cousin has no parental responsibility, contact could be allowed if the designated officer thinks it is appropriate; answer A is therefore incorrect.

Crime, para. 1.13.4.1

Answer 13.11

Answer **A** — Acting in contravention of a protection order or power exercised under s. 46 of the Children Act 1989 (police protection power) is an offence contrary to s. 49 of the 1989 Act.

Section 49 of the Children Act 1989 states:

(1) A person shall be guilty of an offence if, knowingly and without lawful authority or reasonable excuse, he—
   (a) takes a child to whom this section applies away from the responsible person;
   (b) keeps such a child away from the responsible person; or
   (c) induces, assists or incites such a child to run away or stay away from the responsible person.

So the offence is complete when a person induces, assists or incites a child to run away, and does not necessarily involve actually taking the child away although that action is also an offence under this section; answer D is therefore incorrect. In this section, 'the responsible person' means any person who for the time being has care of him/her by virtue of the care order, the emergency protection order or s. 46, as the case may be. This would include the foster carer; answer C is therefore incorrect.

The legislation does not mention an intention to take the child abroad, referring only to taking the child, or inducing the child to leave the place they were put if they were in care, subject to an EPO or police protection powers (s. 49(2)); answer B is therefore incorrect.

Crime, para. 1.13.4.2

Answer 13.12

Answer **D** — Section 1 of the Child Abduction Act 1984 states:

(1) Subject to subsections (5) and (8) below, a person connected with a child under the age of 16 commits an offence if he takes or sends the child out of the United Kingdom without the appropriate consent.

So the offence itself only relates to children under 16; for that reason alone answer A is incorrect.

The offence can only be committed by a person 'connected with' the child and this is defined in s. 1(2) of the Child Abduction Act 1984, which would include the children's father.

Such a person must either take, or be responsible for sending, the child out of the UK him/herself. This offence is not committed by holding the child within the jurisdiction or where the child is lawfully taken out the country and return is then refused; answers A, B and C are therefore incorrect.

Had the father taken the children to France without the consent of the mother, then the offence may have been committed. This would have led to the various defences kicking in, one of which is that the child is out of the UK for a period of less than one month. However, as the offence was not committed, no defence is necessary.

Crime, para. 1.13.2.1

Answer 13.13

Answer **A** — Where a child is reported missing, problems can arise once the child is discovered to be safe and well but one of the parents wants the police to disclose the whereabouts of the child. This situation arose in *S v S (Chief Constable of West Yorkshire Police Intervening)* [1998] 1 WLR 1716 and the Court of Appeal provided some clarification of the issues. The court stated that the police are not in a position to give 'categoric assurances' of confidentiality to those who provide information as to the whereabouts of a child. The most they could say is that, other than by removing the child, it would be most unlikely that they would have to disclose the information concerning the child's whereabouts; answer B is therefore incorrect.

Any court order provides for the information to be disclosed to the court not to the other party or his/her solicitor; answers C and D are therefore incorrect.

Crime, para. 1.13.4.3

14 Theft and Related Offences

QUESTIONS

Question 14.1

VENTHAM goes into a shop intending to steal a dress and she has brought a label with a barcode on it with her, much cheaper than the actual price of the dress she wants. She picks up the dress and replaces the label and starts to walk towards the till; however, she believes she is being followed by a store detective so she puts the dress down and walks off. Ten minutes later, she returns and picks the dress up again this time going through the till and buying the dress at a much cheaper price.

In relation to theft (contrary to s. 1 of the Theft Act 1968), which of the following is correct?

A VENTHAM commits theft when she picks up the dress initially.

B VENTHAM commits theft when she changes the price tag.

C VENTHAM commits theft when she picks up the dress for the second time.

D VENTHAM does not commit theft, she commits a Fraud Act offence when she pays for the dress at a cheaper price.

Question 14.2

BRUCE is in a stately home as part of an organised tour. Whilst on the tour, he sees a room that he really wants to enter as it is a part of the house he really wants to see but that room is closed due to refurbishment. He hangs back a little and when no one is looking he goes into the room. He sees a silver pocket watch that he has long looked at pictures of and can't stop himself picking it up to look at it. He decides to keep it for a while and return it the following week when he takes the tour again.

At what point, if any, does BRUCE commit burglary (contrary to s. 9 of the Theft Act 1968)?

A When he enters the room that is temporarily closed.

B When he picks up the pocket watch and leaves the room that is temporarily closed.

C He does not commit burglary as he does not commit theft.

D He does not commit burglary at any point—as the room is only temporarily closed he is not trespassing.

Question 14.3

MILSOM is shopping in his local supermarket when he notices that a member of staff has left a price-labelling machine on a display stand. He thinks it will be funny to create new price labels for goods in the store and cause chaos as a result. MILSOM walks around the store placing new and cheaper price labels on a wide variety of goods. MILSOM's only intention is to create confusion, not to benefit himself or any other customers in the supermarket.

Considering s. 3 of the Theft Act 1968 (appropriation) only, which of the following statements is correct?

A Although MILSOM swaps price labels, he is not appropriating the property. To do this effectively, he must pay for the goods.

B MILSOM's actions fall short of a full appropriation. This can only be accomplished by a combination of label swapping and the removal of an item from the shelf.

C It does not matter that MILSOM's further intention is to cause chaos and confusion; his conduct would constitute an appropriation.

D In order for MILSOM to appropriate property, he must have a dishonest intention. As this is not present, he does not appropriate.

Question 14.4

BEYNON believes that his neighbour's dog keeps excreting in his garden so he breaks into his house one night with the intention of committing GBH on his neighbour; however, no one is in so BEYNON breaks several items in the house.

In relation to the offence of burglary (under s. 9 of the Theft Act 1968), which of the following is correct?

A BEYNON commits both s. 9(1)(a) and s. 9(1)(b) offences when he enters the house.

B BEYNON only commits an offence contrary to s. 9(1)(a) when he enters the house.

C BEYNON commits an offence contrary to s. 9(1)(b) when he damages the property.

D BEYNON does not commit a burglary offence as he had no intention to commit damage when he entered and did not actually commit GBH.

Question 14.5

OLSEN is a homeless person and is walking along a canal bank late at night. He breaks into a canal barge to see if there is any food in there he can steal; however, he is tired and sleeps the night. The following day, he spends all day on the barge and sleeps there that night. He decides then to move on and steals some tins of food on his way out. The canal barge itself was in fact uninhabited at this time as it had been repossessed by the bank and was awaiting sale.

In considering only if the canal barge would be a 'building' for the purposes of burglary (under s. 9 of the Theft Act 1968), which of the following is correct?

A Yes, a canal barge is always a 'building' as it is a structure of a permanent nature.

B Yes, the canal barge is always a 'building' as it is capable of being inhabited.

C No, the canal barge will not be a 'building' as it was uninhabited at the time it was entered.

D No, the canal barge will not be a 'building' as it was unoccupied at the time it was entered.

Question 14.6

CUTHBERT organises a gang to carry out a burglary at a large country house. He plans it meticulously and has various roles for all his accomplices. One of those, BRITZ, is asked to carry a large knife in case they are disturbed; all the gang know that BRITZ will be carrying a knife and all agree that they will use it if they have to. The gang enter the house and steal several items. BRITZ stayed outside the house on guard with his knife.

Who, if anyone, has committed aggravated burglary (contrary to s. 10 of the Theft Act 1968)?

A All the gang commit aggravated burglary as they are all aware of the knife.

B All the gang commit aggravated burglary as they are all aware of the knife and all agree to its use if necessary.

C Only BRITZ as he was the one actually carrying the knife.

D No one at all commits aggravated burglary.

Question 14.7

GRIFFITHS asked his colleague MORGAN if he could borrow her motor vehicle (a van) to take his family on holiday for the weekend to Wales. MORGAN agreed; however,

GRIFFITHS had misled MORGAN and actually takes the motor van to a pop festival with some friends. He returns it in good condition at the end of the weekend.

Has GRIFFITHS committed an offence (under s. 12 of the Theft Act 1968) of taking a vehicle without the owner's consent?

A Yes, he obtained MORGAN's permission by deception.
B Yes, but only if the journey was further than the agreed destination.
C No, his deception did not negate the consent he obtained.
D Yes, unless he could show he believed MORGAN would have consented.

Question 14.8

ELLIS and McWHIRTER were in a supermarket car park when they saw a car with the keys in the ignition. They decided to take the vehicle and ELLIS got in the driver's seat; McWHIRTER sat in the front passenger seat. While he was reversing out of the parking place, ELLIS struck KANG, a shopper who was walking past. Both ELLIS and McWHIRTER got out of the car and ran off, leaving KANG behind with a bruised hip.

Has an offence been committed (under s. 12A of the Theft Act 1968) of aggravated vehicle-taking?

A No, the vehicle was not driven on a road.
B Yes, but only by ELLIS, the driver.
C Only if it can be shown that the vehicle was driven dangerously.
D Yes, by both ELLIS and McWHIRTER.

Question 14.9

RENNIE and ELLIOT met one evening to discuss breaking into an electrical warehouse. It was agreed that RENNIE would break in and hand the goods to ELLIOT outside in his van. They were joined in the meeting by SEDGMORE, who agreed to keep the goods in his house for a few weeks, and MALROW, who owned a second-hand store and would sell the goods. They agreed that the burglary would take place the following night.

Who, if anyone, has committed the offence of handling stolen goods (contrary to s. 22 of the Theft Act 1968) in these circumstances?

A ELLIOT, SEDGMORE and MALROW only.
B All four have committed the offence.
C Only SEDGMORE and MALROW have committed the offence.
D None of these people have committed the offence.

Question 14.10

STUARTSON has been arrested for handling stolen goods and the officers dealing with the case are deciding what they would need to prove in order to secure a conviction in relation to the 'stolen goods' aspect of the offence of handling stolen goods (contrary to s. 22 of the Theft Act 1968).

In relation to 'stolen goods', which of the following is correct?

A They only have to show that the goods were actually stolen.

B They would have to show that the goods were stolen by way of conviction of the 'thief'.

C They would have to show that the goods were actually stolen and by whom they were stolen.

D They would have to show that the goods were actually stolen and name the actual loser.

Question 14.11

LATIMER and BOWEN went for a meal at their favourite restaurant, one where they ate regularly. During the meal, they consumed two bottles of wine each. For a laugh, at the end of the meal they both went to the toilet and climbed out of the window. They intended returning the next day to pay for the meal; however, the restaurant owner did not know this and called the police.

Have LATIMER and BOWEN committed an offence (under s. 3 of the Theft Act 1978) of making off without payment?

A Yes, but they would have a defence if they could show that they thought the owner would have consented in the circumstances.

B No, because they have not deceived the owner into thinking they would pay for the meals.

C No, they have not committed the offence in these circumstances as they intended returning to pay.

D Yes, they have committed the offence, regardless of their intention to pay, and would have no defence in the circumstances.

Question 14.12

GWYNN was at his friend PETERS's flat and he had with him a stolen credit card, which he had recently used to obtain goods by fraud. GWYNN gave the card to

EDDINGTON so that EDDINGTON could use it the next day to commit offences of fraud. GWYNN had no intention of using the card again.

Which of the following statements is true, in relation to s. 25 of the Theft Act 1968, regarding 'going equipped'?

A An offence has been committed by EDDINGTON only as GWYNN did not intend using the card again.

B An offence has been committed by GWYNN and EDDINGTON in these circumstances.

C No offence has been committed by either EDDINGTON or GWYNN in these circumstances.

D An offence has been committed by GWYNN; EDDINGTON commits no offence in these circumstances.

Question 14.13

GARWOOD has placed a large bet on the outcome of a local Sunday league football match. Two days before the match is due to take place, he finds out that the team he has backed have lost four of their star players after they were involved in a car accident. Worried that he will lose his money, GARWOOD approaches the referee of the match. GARWOOD tells the referee, 'If you don't call off the game, my friends will rape your wife.' The referee takes no notice of GARWOOD and two days later the game goes ahead. GARWOOD loses his bet.

Considering the offence of blackmail (contrary to s. 21 of the Theft Act 1968) only, which of the following statements is true?

A GARWOOD does not commit the offence because he did not 'gain' any money.

B GARWOOD does not commit the offence because the threat is that his friends rather than GARWOOD would rape the referee's wife.

C As the game went ahead, GARWOOD commits an offence of attempted blackmail.

D In these circumstances, GARWOOD commits the offence as he intended to keep what he already had (his original bet).

Question 14.14

DRAPER is walking along the street when his friend pulls up next to him in a car. DRAPER gets in the car and notices that the ignition barrel is missing and asks if the vehicle has been stolen. His friend tells him it hasn't and that the ignition barrel is only broken. DRAPER does not believe him and suspects that the vehicle has been stolen. Despite this belief, DRAPER allows himself to be carried in the vehicle. However, a few miles into their journey they are stopped by police as the car was in fact taken without the owner's consent.

Has DRAPER committed the offence, under s. 12(1) of the Theft Act 1968, of allowing himself to be carried?

A Yes, the fact he suspects the car to be stolen and his presence in it is enough; movement of the car is irrelevant.

B Yes, as he suspects the car to be stolen and allows himself to be carried in it.

C No, mere suspicion is not enough, he must know the car is stolen and allow himself to be carried in it.

D No, mere suspicion is not enough, he must know the car is stolen; movement of the car is irrelevant.

Question 14.15

BECKET has been charged with an attempt to commit an offence of concealing criminal property contrary to s. 327 of the Proceeds of Crime Act 2002. During his interview, he said that he did not believe the money he was asked to put through his bank account amounted to criminal property but he said he suspected it may have been.

Is BECKET guilty of committing this offence in these circumstances?

A No, as he did not believe that the money amounted to criminal property.

B No, as he only suspected that the money amounted to criminal property.

C Yes, as suspecting the money amounted to criminal property is enough.

D Yes, if it can be proved that the money is criminal property then his suspicion that it was is enough.

Question 14.16

McIVOR visits his NHS doctor in absolute agony due to a back injury. He demands an injection of a new pain-killing drug but, as it is very expensive, his doctor refuses and prescribes a strong painkiller instead. Infuriated, McIVOR pulls a knife from his pocket and threatens to kill the doctor unless he gets the new drug. In fear for his life, the doctor gives him the injection. McIVOR apologises for his behaviour and leaves.

With respect to blackmail (contrary to s. 21 of the Theft Act 1968), which of the following is true?

A The offence is complete when McIVOR threatens the doctor and makes his demand for the pain-killing drug.
B The offence is complete when the doctor gives McIVOR the injection.
C This is not blackmail as McIVOR has had no 'gain'.
D This is not blackmail as the doctor has had no personal financial loss, the drug belonged to the NHS.

Question 14.17

GOODCHILD steals a car from TURVEY and sells it to CLIFF for £2,000. This is a cheap price for the car and, although CLIFF is suspicious of GOODCHILD, she buys the car nevertheless. CLIFF drives the car for several days and eventually finds papers in the car belonging to TURVEY. CLIFF telephones TURVEY, who tells her that the car is stolen. CLIFF quickly hangs up and retains the car for two days while she decides what she will do. Realising that she may lose the car if she returns it to TURVEY, CLIFF sells the car to MARTINEZ for £500.

At what stage, if at all, does CLIFF commit the offence of handling stolen goods (contrary to s. 22 of the Theft Act 1968)?
A When CLIFF buys the car for £2,000 from GOODCHILD.
B When CLIFF retains the car knowing it is stolen.
C When CLIFF sells the car to MARTINEZ.
D CLIFF does not commit the offence in these circumstances.

Question 14.18

DOUGLAS worked in a petrol station owned by RANKIN. At the end of her shift one day, she was told that her son had been in a car accident and was in hospital. DOUGLAS did not have a car and when she finished work she took £10 from the till to pay for a taxi to take her to the hospital as she had no cash on her. In fact, she had plenty of money in her bank account but she didn't want to waste time by going to a cashpoint. DOUGLAS intended paying the money back the next day, thinking that RANKIN would not mind and would consent to the appropriation of the money if he knew of it and the circumstances. RANKIN found that the till was short of money the next day and confronted DOUGLAS. RANKIN did mind that the money had been taken and contacted the police to report a theft.

Considering s. 2 of the Theft Act 1968 and the definition of 'dishonesty', would DOUGLAS be 'dishonest' in these circumstances?

A Yes, because RANKIN did not consent to the money being taken and therefore it was theft.

B Yes, as she could have got her own money had she taken reasonable steps to get it.

C No, if she believed that RANKIN would have consented if he had known she was taking the money and the circumstances in which it was taken.

D No, if she believed that RANKIN would have consented if he had known she was taking the money.

Question 14.19

CRAWFORD obtains several thousand pounds in cash by stealing it from his elderly neighbour. CRAWFORD deposits the cash in his own account but transfers it electronically to the bank account held by his friend, ELMS, who is initially unaware of the transfer. A few days later, ELMS discovers the money in his account and when he asks where it came from, CRAWFORD tells him the truth. ELMS agrees to keep it to assist CRAWFORD.

At what point, if any, does ELMS commit an offence of dishonestly retaining a wrongful credit (contrary to s. 24A of the Theft Act 1968)?

A He commits an offence under s. 24A as soon as the money is transferred into his account.

B He commits an offence under s. 24A as soon as he becomes aware that the money was stolen.

C He commits an offence under s. 24A as soon as he becomes aware that the money was stolen and fails to have it cancelled.

D He does not commit an offence contrary to s. 24A but will commit an offence of handling stolen goods as he assists in the retention of the funds.

Question 14.20

CARMEN approaches GREEN who is sitting in the cab of his HGV. The HGV load is several hundred thousand pounds' worth of cigarettes. CARMEN opens the passenger door and gets into the vehicle. He tells GREEN to hand over the keys to the vehicle or 'the next time I see you, I will shoot you'. GREEN refuses to do so. CARMEN then produces a photograph of GREEN's wife and tells GREEN that unless he hands the keys to the HGV over to him, GREEN's wife will be beaten up. GREEN does not believe CARMEN and refuses. CARMEN produces a mobile phone which shows live pictures of GREEN's living room (100 miles away from GREEN's present location).

GREEN can see that his wife is in the process of being assaulted by CARMEN's associate. CARMEN once again demands the keys and tells GREEN the assault will continue if he does not give in. At this point, GREEN hands over the keys and gets out of the cab of the HGV. CARMEN drives off with the load of cigarettes.

At what point, if at all, is an offence in respect of robbery (contrary to s. 8 of the Theft Act 1968) actually committed?

A When CARMEN threatens to shoot GREEN the next time he sees him.

B When CARMEN threatens GREEN's wife.

C When CARMEN shows GREEN pictures of his wife being assaulted.

D When CARMEN drives off with the load of cigarettes.

Question 14.21

ASTON is a career criminal involved in serious and high-value robbery offences. He carries out a robbery on a van carrying gold bullion and manages to get away with the contents of the van. To ship the gold abroad, he takes the gold to PULCHER and instructs PULCHER to melt the gold, turn it into Eiffel Tower-shaped paperweights and ship it abroad to France—PULCHER is well aware of where the gold has come from. ASTON promises to pay PULCHER a hefty fee from the sale of the gold as and when he finally disposes of it abroad. PULCHER does as ASTON asks and six months later he receives a bank transfer from ASTON for £50,000.

Considering only the offence of acquisition, use and possession of criminal property (contrary to s. 329 of the Proceeds of Crime Act 2002), when does PULCHER first commit the offence?

A When he takes possession of the gold bullion from ASTON.

B When he melts the gold bullion down.

C When he ships the gold abroad.

D When he receives the £50,000 from ASTON.

Question 14.22

CONWAY is contacted by MARLOW. MARLOW asks CONWAY to look after some jewellery for him for a few days as a favour to him; MARLOW tells CONWAY he has recently purchased the jewellery and is trying to sell it but does not want his wife to find out about his purchase as they have argued about this kind of business activity. CONWAY suspects that the jewellery may be stolen as he knows MARLOW has committed burglary offences in the past but he wants to help MARLOW so says 'Yes'.

Several hours later, MARLOW drops off the jewellery and CONWAY looks after it for a few days before MARLOW returns and takes it away. As it happens, CONWAY was right to be suspicious as the jewellery is stolen property.

Does CONWAY commit an offence of handling stolen goods contrary to s. 22 of the Theft Act 1968?

A No, because you must know or believe the property to be stolen to commit this offence.

B No, because he does not get paid for looking after the property in question.

C Yes, as suspecting that property is stolen is enough to prove this offence.

D Yes, and he would commit the offence at the moment he arranges to handle the stolen goods.

Question 14.23

MORGAN goes on holiday for two weeks. While MORGAN is away, and without the permission of MORGAN, FLOYD (MORGAN's next-door neighbour) moves the garden fence that separates their respective gardens 1 metre onto MORGAN's property, thus incorporating a strip of MORGAN's land onto his estate. FLOYD then digs up and removes an entire cultivated small cypress tree (including its roots) from the strip of MORGAN's land he has incorporated into his estate.

Has FLOYD committed an offence of theft (contrary to s. 1 of the Theft Act 1968) in these circumstances?

A Yes, but only in relation to the strip of land he incorporates into his estate.

B No, the offence of theft has not been committed by FLOYD because the land is not 'property' and the cypress tree was not taken for sale, reward or other commercial purpose.

C Yes, but only in relation to the cultivated cypress tree he removed from MORGAN's land.

D No, because there are no circumstances whatsoever whereby land can be stolen.

ANSWERS

Answer 14.1

Answer **A** — There are five key elements to the offence of theft. These are:

- dishonesty;
- appropriation;
- property;
- belonging to another;
- intention of permanently depriving.

So VENTHAM commits theft when she picks up the dress with the intention of permanently depriving the owner of it. She may well go on to commit a fraud offence but she meets all the elements of theft when she picks up the dress; answer D is therefore incorrect.

In *R v Gomez* [1993] AC 442, the House of Lords considered 'appropriation'; there may be an appropriation of the same property on more than one occasion. However, once property has been stolen (as opposed to merely appropriated), that same property cannot be stolen again by the same thief (*R v Atakpu* [1994] QB 69). So although the property was appropriated when the tag was changed and when it was picked up again, essentially theft cannot be committed the second or third time and answers B and C are therefore incorrect.

Crime, para. 1.14.2.4

Answer 14.2

Answer **C** — Burglary is dealt with by s. 9(1) of the Theft Act 1968 and the principles contained therein should be followed to determine when the offence is, or is not, committed.

Section 9(1)(a) burglary is committed where someone enters any building or part of a building as a trespasser and with intent to commit:

- stealing;
- inflicting grievous bodily harm;
- causing unlawful damage.

Section 9(1)(b) burglary is committed where someone having entered any building or part of a building as a trespasser:

- steals;
- inflicts, attempts to inflict grievous bodily harm.

Even though it is temporarily closed, BRUCE has entered part of the building he is not allowed in, and so he is a trespasser; answer D is therefore incorrect.

For both s. 9(1)(a) and (b), the offence is 'steal' which means theft, and with no intention of permanently depriving the owners of the watch there can be no theft which means no burglary; answers A and B are therefore incorrect.

Crime, para. 1.14.5

Answer 14.3

Answer **C** — Appropriation under s. 3 of the Theft Act 1968 is an assumption by a person of the rights of an owner and there is no requirement for a dishonest intention, making answer D incorrect. There have been a number of cases involving the swapping of price labels but after *R* v *Gomez* [1993] AC 442, the House of Lords concluded that the mere swapping of the price labels on goods amounted to an 'appropriation'; this eliminates answers A and B. This was the case regardless of any further intentions of the defendant.

Crime, para. 1.14.2.4

Answer 14.4

Answer **B** — Section 9 of the Theft Act 1968 states:

(1) A person is guilty of burglary if—
   (a) he enters any building or part of a building as a trespasser and with intent to commit any such offence as is mentioned in subsection (2) below; or
   (b) having entered any building or part of a building as a trespasser he steals or attempts to steal anything in the building or that part of it or inflicts or attempts to inflict on any person therein any grievous bodily harm.
(2) The offences referred to in subsection (1)(a) above are offences of stealing anything in the building or part of a building in question, of inflicting on any person therein any grievous bodily harm and of doing unlawful damage to the building or anything therein.

So a s. 9(1)(b) offence can only be committed after entry; answer A is therefore incorrect. BEYNON commits a s. 9(1)(a) offence when he enters intending GBH, but s. 9(1)(b) does not include criminal damage so he does not commit that; answers C and D are therefore incorrect.

Crime, paras 1.14.5.1, 1.14.5.5

Answer 14.5

Answer **C** — Section 9 of the Theft Act 1968 states:

(4) References in subsections (1) and (2) above to a building, ... and the reference in sub-section (3), above, to a building which is a dwelling, shall apply also to an inhabited vehicle or vessel, and shall apply to any such vehicle or vessel at times when the person having a habitation in it is not there as well as at times when he is.

The effect of s. 9(4) is to include inhabited vehicles and vessels (such as houseboats or motor homes) within the term. A canal boat that is not inhabited is not a building as whilst it may be capable of habitation, it is not being lived in; answers A and B are therefore incorrect.

What is important with a canal barge, then, is whether it is inhabited or not; if it is inhabited then it would be a building as per s. 9(4) even though at the time entry was made it was unoccupied; answer D is therefore incorrect.

Crime, para. 1.14.5.2

Answer 14.6

Answer **D** — Section 10 of the Theft Act 1968 states:

(1) A person is guilty of aggravated burglary if he commits any burglary and at the time has with him any firearm or imitation firearm, any weapon of offence, or any explo-sive; ...

An aggravated burglary is committed when a person commits an offence of burglary (either a s. 9(1)(a) or a s. 9(1)(b) offence) and at the time he has with him his WIFE.

W — Weapon of offence
I — Imitation firearm
F — Firearm
E — Explosive

So there are essentially two factors; a burglary committed and at the time it is com-mitted it is done with a WIFE.

So, who of the gang has committed burglary? Those who entered the building with the intention of stealing which is all the gang except BRITZ who remained outside the building. So BRITZ never commits burglary so he cannot commit aggra-vated burglary and as he was the one with a WIFE none of the gang, who committed burglary, committed aggravated burglary; answers A, B and C are therefore incorrect.

Crime, para. 1.14.6

Answer 14.7

Answer **C** — An offence under s. 12 is committed by a person who takes a vehicle without the owner's consent or other lawful authority, for his/her own or another's use.

The issue of consent was dealt with in the case of *R v Peart* [1970] 2 QB 672. The defendant was convicted of the offence after he falsely represented to the owner of a car that he needed it to drive from Bedlington to Alnwick to sign a contract. The owner let him have the vehicle, provided he returned it that day. As he had intended all along, Peart drove the car instead to Burnley in the evening.

The Court of Appeal subsequently quashed Peart's conviction by following the decision in *Whittaker v Campbell* [1984] QB 318, where it was held that there is no general principle of law that fraud vitiates consent.

Consequently, even if consent is obtained by fraud, it is still consent (making answer A incorrect). The case of *Peart* shows that even though the journey taken was different from the one agreed, an offence is still not committed (making answer B incorrect).

Lastly, the defence provided under s. 12(6) would apply where an offence has been committed. Since an offence has not been committed in these circumstances, the defence would not apply (which is why answer D is incorrect).

Crime, paras 1.14.7, 1.14.7.1

Answer 14.8

Answer **D** — First, a person must commit an offence under s. 12(1) of the Theft Act 1968 either by taking the vehicle or by being carried in it. Then, under s. 12A, it must be proved that at any time after the vehicle was taken (whether by him or another) and before it was recovered:

- it was driven dangerously on a road or public place; or
- owing to the driving of the vehicle, an accident occurred whereby injury was caused to any person; or
- owing to the driving of the vehicle, an accident occurred whereby damage was caused to any property other than the vehicle; or
- damage was caused to the vehicle.

The Act does not specify that the accident involving an injury to a person should occur on a road (making answer A incorrect).

All that the prosecution has to prove is that one of these circumstances occurred before the car was recovered (*Dawes v DPP* (1995) 1 Cr App R 65) (answer C is incorrect for this reason).

Answer B is incorrect because the offence may be committed by either the driver or the passenger, provided one of the circumstances applies.

Crime, paras 1.14.7, 1.14.8

Answer 14.9

Answer **D** — Quite simply, there can be no offence under s. 22 of the Theft Act 1968, unless goods have been stolen (answers A and B are therefore incorrect). Even though two of the participants have arranged to receive stolen goods, they will not commit the offence until the burglary takes place (answer C is therefore also incorrect).

If the plan ever does come to fruition, RENNIE, as the person stealing the goods, would not commit the offence. It is debatable whether ELLIOT would do so, if he assisted with the burglary, as he might be guilty of that offence.

Crime, para. 1.14.11

Answer 14.10

Answer **A** — For goods to be handled, they have to be stolen; if goods are not stolen, there is no handling. Whether they are so stolen is a question of fact for a jury or magistrate(s). There is no need to prove that the thief, blackmailer, etc. has been convicted of the primary offence before prosecuting the alleged handler, neither is it always necessary to identify who that person was; answers B, C and D are therefore incorrect.

However, care needs to be taken if a defendant is to be accused of handling goods stolen from a specific person or place. If that is the case, then ownership of the goods will become an integral part of the prosecution case and it will be necessary to provide evidence proving that aspect of the offence (*Iqbal* v *DPP* [2004] EWHC 2567 (Admin)).

Crime, paras 1.14.11, 1.14.11.1

Answer 14.11

Answer **C** — This is a typical question where police officers would think practically and decide, 'I would arrest those, where it was necessary to do so'. Avoid this approach and answer questions purely as points of law.

A person commits an offence under s. 3 of the Theft Act 1978 if, knowing that payment on the spot for goods supplied or services received is required, he/she dishonestly makes off without paying with intent to avoid payment.

In the scenario, even though the couple have made off without paying, there is no offence if they intend to defer payment to a later date (even though morally their actions may be regarded as wrong!). (Answer D is therefore incorrect.)

There is no requirement that the person practised some deception to prove the offence; simply making off with the required intent is enough (which is why answer B is incorrect).

The defence in answer A has been made up and does not exist.

Crime, para. 1.14.13

Answer 14.12

Answer **C** — A person commits an offence under s. 25 of the Theft Act 1968 when, not at his place of abode, he has with him any article for use in the course of or in connection with any burglary or theft.

The offence is designed as a preventative measure and therefore cannot be committed by a deed done in the past. The offence will be committed by a person who has an article with him/her for use by someone else (*R v Ellames* [1974] 1 WLR 1391).

Applying the Act to this scenario, GWYNN was not at his place of abode and had with him a credit card, which he intended EDDINGTON to use in the future in a cheat—this is neither theft nor burglary.

The question asks you specifically about s. 25 of the Theft Act 1968, not the Fraud Act 2006 (this would have been an offence in that statute). No offence under s. 25; answers A, B and D are therefore incorrect.

Crime, para. 1.14.10

Answer 14.13

Answer **D** — There is no such offence as 'attempted blackmail', making answer C incorrect. It is immaterial whether the menaces relate to action to be taken by the person making the demand, making answer B incorrect. 'Gain' for the purposes of blackmail includes a gain by keeping what one has, making answer A incorrect.

Crime, para. 1.14.4

Answer 14.14

Answer **C** — The person who commits this offence must know that the convey-ance has been taken without the consent of the owner or other lawful authority. If that person only 'suspects' that the conveyance has been taken, the offence is not committed; answers A and B are therefore incorrect. Further, the conveyance must actually move when the person drives it or allows themselves to be carried in or on it; answer D is therefore incorrect.

Crime, para. 1.14.7.6

Answer 14.15

Answer **B** — Generally, under ss. 327 to 329 of the Proceeds of Crime Act 2002, all offences of suspicion that money is criminal property suffice for the substantive offence to have been committed. However, in *R v Pace* [2014] EWCA Crim 186 the Court of Appeal rejected the argument that, on a charge of attempting to commit the offence under s. 327(1)(c), it would be sufficient for the prosecution to prove that D merely suspected the property in question to be criminal property. Therefore, for an attempt to commit the offence you need to prove more than just suspicion that the money was criminal property; answers C and D are therefore incorrect. For an attempt, you have to show knowledge, not just belief; answer A is therefore incorrect.

Crime, para. 1.14.14.4

Answer 14.16

Answer **A** — The points to prove for an offence of blackmail are:

- with a view to gain;
- for self or another; or
- with intent to cause loss to another;
- made an unwarranted demand with menaces.

Using a knife to threaten to kill someone is most certainly an unwarranted de-mand ('unwarranted demand' is defined as an unreasonable or unfair demand) and menacing! 'Menaces' is loosely delineated as a threat (including a veiled one) of any action detrimental or unpleasant to the person addressed. And the offence is complete at the time the demand is made, not when its desired consequences are brought about; answer B is therefore incorrect.

As the demand must be made with a view to the person's gain, has McIVOR actually 'gained'? The gain must be in money or other property and can be temporary or permanent. In a case not mentioned in the Manual, it was held that the drug was property and the injection involved 'gain' to the accused as he achieved pain relief. The fact that it was injected into him rather than being handed over did not mean that McIVOR did not gain that property; answer C is therefore incorrect. There does not have to be a loss, provided the demand is made with a view to gain; answer D is therefore incorrect.

Crime, para. 1.14.4.1

Answer 14.17

Answer **D** — CLIFF must know or believe the goods to be stolen and mere suspicion will not suffice, making answer A incorrect. To commit an offence of handling stolen goods, the retention, removal, disposal or realisation must be by or for the benefit of *another*. Retaining the car and then disposing of it is only done for the benefit of CLIFF so the offence is not made out, making answers B and C incorrect.

Crime, paras 1.14.11 to 1.14.11.5

Answer 14.18

Answer **C** — Under s. 2(1)(b) of the Theft Act 1968, a person's appropriation of property belonging to another is not to be regarded as dishonest if he/she appropriates the property in the belief that he/she would have the other's consent if the other knew of the appropriation and the circumstances of it. Therefore, the person appropriating the property must believe both elements, i.e. that the other person would have consented had he/she known of the appropriation and the circumstances of it. Answer D is therefore incorrect.

It is the belief of the person appropriating the property that is important, regardless of the belief of the owner. Therefore, even though RANKIN would state that he did not consent to the money being taken, if DOUGLAS can convince the court of these two elements, she may have a defence. Answer A is therefore incorrect. This includes occasions where the defendant had access to other funds, which could have been obtained by taking reasonable steps as this directly relates to the circumstances under which the defendant took the money, i.e. urgency in attending at the hospital; answer B is therefore incorrect.

Crime, para. 1.14.2.2

Answer 14.19

Answer **C** — One consequence of the decision of the House of Lords in *R v Preddy* [1996] AC 815 is that, where a person dishonestly obtains a money transfer from another, the sum thereby credited to the first person's account can no longer be categorised as stolen goods. This, indeed, was the view of the Law Commission when reviewing the impact of *Preddy*. Furthermore, even where a person, A, pays stolen bank notes directly into his/her account, the proceeds of a subsequent transfer from that account to an account held by another person B cannot be classed as stolen goods, because any credit balance thereby created in B's account is an entirely different chose ('thing in action') from the credit balance which previously represented the stolen money in A's account. B's credit balance admittedly represents the proceeds of A's original crime, but it has never done so in the hands of the original thief, and any argument that it does so in the hands of a handler of the stolen property (i.e. B) is circular, because that presupposes the very point it seeks to establish, namely that the funds in B's account are stolen goods! As they are not 'stolen goods' and therefore cannot be 'handled', answer D is incorrect.

Section 24A of the Theft Act 1968 addresses this problem in two ways.

First, s. 24A(2A) broadens the scope of s. 24A to cases in which the accused dishonestly retains a credit which he/she knows or correctly believes derives from an offence of:

(a) theft;
(b) blackmail;
(c) fraud (contrary to s. 1 of the Fraud Act 2006); or
(d) stolen goods.

If, for example, A pays stolen money into his account and transfers the funds from that account to an account owned by B, a wrongful credit has been made to B's account, and B may commit a s. 24A offence if he dishonestly retains it, knowing or believing it to be derived from one or other of those offences. In this scenario, this is exactly what happened and the s. 24A offence is complete only when the defendant dishonestly retained it; answers A and B are therefore incorrect.

Secondly s. 24A(8) provides that any money dishonestly withdrawn from an account to which a wrongful credit has been made can be classed once again as stolen goods.

It is curious that the proceeds of A's original theft can be classed as stolen goods when paid into A's own bank account, yet cease to be stolen goods when effectively 'transferred' to B's account, and yet revert to being stolen goods when dishonestly withdrawn as cash by B; but that is the law.

Any volunteers for a transfer to fraud investigation?

Crime, para. 1.14.12

Answer 14.20

Answer **D** — A robbery is committed *when a person steals* and immediately before or at the time of doing so, and in order to do so, uses force on any person or puts or seeks to put any person in fear of being then and there subjected to force. For the full offence to be committed, there must be a theft and until that takes place there is no robbery.

Crime, para. 1.14.3

Answer 14.21

Answer **A** — The offence under s. 329 is committed when a person acquires, uses or has possession of 'criminal property'. The gold bullion is most certainly criminal property so as soon as PULCHER takes possession of the gold bullion the offence is committed.

Crime, para. 1.14.14.6

Answer 14.22

Answer **A** — The offence under s. 22 of the Theft Act 1968 is committed when a person handles goods that they *know or believe* to have been stolen. Suspecting that the property is stolen would not be enough (which eliminates the 'Yes' responses at answers C and D). The person who commits the s. 22 offence does not have to gain anything from their actions (making answer B incorrect)—in fact, the retention, removal, disposal or realisation element of the offence must be done by or for the benefit of another (in this case MARLOW).

Crime, para. 1.14.11

Answer 14.23

Answer **C** — Answer A is incorrect as land itself cannot be stolen so if, for example, a homeowner goes on holiday and her neighbour moves a fence over a little to increase the size of his garden (and hence decrease the size of hers), this would not be regarded as theft. Answer D is incorrect as it states that there are no circumstances whatsoever whereby land can be stolen when that is not the case—for example, a trustee in charge of an estate or a person with a power of attorney who sells another's land for profit could commit theft. Taking a cultivated tree without permission amounts to theft (correct answer C). Answer B is incorrect as just because the cultivated cypress tree was not taken for sale, reward or other commercial purpose does not mean that the offence of theft has not been committed—the sale, reward or other commercial purpose only applies to wild plants, fruit, flowers and fungi growing wild.

Crime, para. 1.14.2.5

15 | Fraud

QUESTIONS

Question 15.1

THORP steals BING's wallet, which contains a store card for 'Callows Auto Parts' store in BING's name. THORP decides to use the store card to obtain a large quantity of car tools from the store for his own use. THORP goes into the store and puts £800 worth of car tools into his shopping trolley and takes them to the till. Intending to fool the cashier into thinking the card is his, THORP hands over BING's card in payment but does not say anything to the cashier. The cashier is not fooled by THORP and realises that the card does not belong to THORP as he has seen the real owner, BING, in the store on several previous occasions. However, the cashier is not at all concerned by THORP's behaviour and asks him to sign for the card payment which THORP does. THORP leaves the store with the car tools.

Considering the offence of fraud by false representation (contrary to s. 2 of the Fraud Act 2006), which of the following statements is correct?

A THORP has not committed the offence in these circumstances because he did not use any words to represent that the credit card belonged to him.

B The offence has not been committed because the cashier was not fooled into thinking that THORP was in fact BING.

C The offence has been committed. By handing the card to the cashier, THORP represents that he has authority to use it for that transaction. It does not matter that the cashier is not deceived or that words were not used.

D The offence has not been committed as fraud by false representation relates to a 'gain' for another and in these circumstances the gain is directly for the benefit of THORP.

Question 15.2

COXSEY is a career criminal who specialises in offences of fraud. He has a large amount of material at his disposal in order to commit these offences, which he keeps at various locations. The police raid COXSEY's home address and arrest him for fraud-related offences. In the searches that follow his arrest, the police find a 'phishing' kit in a bedroom at his home address (which COXSEY used last week to carry out an offence of fraud by false representation (contrary to s. 2 of the Fraud Act 2006)). In COXSEY's car, which was parked on the front drive of his home address, they find several blank credit cards (which COXSEY later states he was going to use to commit offences of fraud by false representation (contrary to s. 2 of the Fraud Act 2006)) and in a store room rented by COXSEY but several miles away from his home address, they find several hundred blank bank statements (which COXSEY states he was looking after for a friend who was going to use them to commit fraud-related offences).

In relation to which items does COXSEY commit the offence of possession or control of articles for use in frauds (contrary to s. 6 of the Fraud Act 2006)?

A The 'phishing' kit and the blank credit cards only.

B The blank credit cards only.

C The blank bank statements only.

D The blank credit cards and the blank bank statements only.

Question 15.3

RAMAGE is a member of a gym to which she took PASSARO. At the gym there was a new person working in reception. RAMAGE showed her membership card to the receptionist, saying, 'She's a member, too, but she forgot her card'. PASSARO was not a member but said nothing and was allowed entry, without paying the usual fee for guests. Both RAMAGE and PASSARO had agreed to do this before attending at the gym in order to secure free entry for PASSARO.

Who, if anyone, has committed an offence (under s. 2 of the Fraud Act 2006) of fraud by misrepresentation?

A Both have committed the offence in these circumstances.

B RAMAGE only as PASSARO made no representation that she was a member.

C PASSARO only as RAMAGE herself made no 'gain', whereas PASSARO gained entry to the gym for free.

D Neither, as no actual 'gain' was made by either of them as they received no money or property.

Question 15.4

PURDY is a solicitor who has a written contract with SORRELL to look after her property portfolio and the money that is earned from it, as SORRELL owns 30 houses and does not have the time to administer them herself. PURDY and SORRELL have an argument during which SORRELL insults PURDY. PURDY is extremely offended by SORRELL and to get revenge he does not tell SORRELL when several of her tenants fail to pay their rent. As a consequence of PURDY's inaction, SORRELL loses several thousand pounds in rent.

Would this constitute an offence under s. 3 of the Fraud Act 2006 (fraud by failing to disclose)?

A Yes, as PURDY would be under a legal duty to disclose the information to SORRELL.

B No, because the relationship between PURDY and SORRELL is not a fiduciary one.

C Yes, but only because the contract between PURDY and SORRELL was written.

D No, because PURDY acted in order to cause a loss to SORRELL rather than make a gain for himself.

Question 15.5

YOSHIMI was a sales representative and was given a company mobile phone. According to company rules, employees had to pay for private telephone calls. At the end of each month, YOSHIMI received a copy of the mobile phone bill and was required to highlight, to his company accounting department, any private calls he had made and pay for them. YOSHIMI knew that the accounting department was always busy and the bills were never examined closely. As a result, YOSHIMI regularly made international calls to family in America but never declared these as private calls and never paid for them.

Could YOSHIMI be found guilty of the offence of false accounting under s. 17 of the Theft Act 1968?

A No, an offence under this section cannot be committed by an omission alone; there must be an act done by the accused.

B Yes, provided it can be shown that YOSHIMI intended to permanently deprive the company of the money owed.

C Yes, an offence under this section may be committed by an omission alone.

D No, an offence under this section cannot be committed unless it is shown that documents were falsified, defaced or destroyed.

Question 15.6

CHANNING has made a card for a satellite TV system that allows him to watch all the channels for free. He boasts about this at work and several colleagues express a desire to also watch for free. CHANNING states he can do that and offers his colleagues the opportunity to buy the cards and takes a £10 deposit. He then makes the cards and supplies them to his colleagues.

At what point in time does Channing first commit an offence contrary to s. 7 of the Fraud Act 2006 of making and supplying articles for use in fraud?

A When he offers to supply his colleagues.

B When he accepts the money for making the cards.

C When he makes the cards.

D When he supplies the cards to his colleagues.

Question 15.7

ALBRIGHT, who is 15 years old, wishes to watch his local football team play at home in the FA Cup against West Ham United. However, the tickets are too expensive for him and he decides he will climb a fence to watch the game. He does so and enjoys the game; however, what he did not know was that for this special game anyone under 16 years of age was given free entry, on proof of age.

Which of the following is correct in relation to an offence under s. 11 of the Fraud Act 2006 (obtaining services dishonestly)?

A ALBRIGHT has committed an offence of obtaining services dishonestly as his intention was not to pay; the fact the game was free is irrelevant.

B ALBRIGHT has committed an offence of obtaining services dishonestly as he did not enter the ground properly, producing proof of age.

C ALBRIGHT has not obtained services dishonestly, the offence is not inchoate: it requires the actual obtaining of a service, and watching football is not such a service.

D ALBRIGHT has not obtained services dishonestly, whatever his intentions, as for his age the service was provided for free.

Question 15.8

NEWBURY works for a printing company and is responsible for marketing the company and securing new contracts. NEWBURY is working on obtaining a major contract that will provide the company with £10 million worth of business when he is approached by the owner of a rival firm. The owner of the rival firm tells NEWBURY that if he allows his company to win the battle for the printing contract then he will hire NEWBURY as the general manager and give him a pay rise worth £50K a year. NEWBURY agrees and as a result he fails to take up the chance of the contract, allowing the rival company to take it up at the expense of his current employer.

Considering offences under the Fraud Act 2006 only, what offence, if any, does NEWBURY commit?

A Fraud by false representation (contrary to s. 2 of the Fraud Act 2006).

B Fraud by failing to disclose information (contrary to s. 3 of the Fraud Act 2006).

C Fraud by abuse of position (contrary to s. 4 of the Fraud Act 2006).

D NEWBURY does not commit any offence in these circumstances.

Question 15.9

ASTBURY works for a credit card company. He is short of money and decides to supplement his income by selling a list of other people's credit card details that he has downloaded from the company computer onto a USB stick. He takes the USB stick to FOXLEY whom he knows commits offences of fraud and sells the USB stick to him. During the sale of the USB stick, ASTBURY offers to supply and sell FOXLEY 1,000 blank credit cards (even though he does not actually have possession of the cards). FOXLEY agrees to buy the cards and gives ASTBURY £500 for the USB stick and £500 for the blank credit cards.

With regard to the offence of making or supplying articles for use in frauds (contrary to s. 7 of the Fraud Act 2006), which of the following comments is true?

A ASTBURY commits the offence but only in respect of the USB stick containing lists of other people's credit card details.

B ASTBURY does not commit the offence as a USB stick containing other people's credit card details is not an 'article' and making an offer to supply requires the offender to be in possession of the article concerned.

C ASTBURY commits the offence but only in respect of the offer to supply the 1,000 credit cards to FOXLEY.

D ASTBURY commits the offence in respect of the USB stick and the offer to supply the 1,000 credit cards to FOXLEY.

Question 15.10

CHEESEMAN works for a leading commodities, financial futures and options broker. As such, she is privy to sensitive information although in work she cannot access any customer funds. Over the last month she has been transferring details of the broker's customer accounts from her work computer to her own laptop, with the intention of using the information to fraudulently transfer funds from their accounts to hers. She resigns from the brokers, and only when not employed by them does she try to transfer the money. Unfortunately for her, she is found out and arrested by the police prior to any transfer of funds to her own account.

In relation to s. 4 of the Fraud Act 2006 (fraud by abuse of position), at what point, if any, is the offence committed?

A When CHEESEMAN begins to transfer details to her own laptop.

B When CHEESEMAN accesses the information on her laptop with the intention of obtaining funds fraudulently.

C The offence cannot be committed as at the point when the transfer is arranged, CHEESEMAN is no longer in a position in which she was expected to safeguard, or not to act against, the financial interests of another person.

D The offence cannot be committed as CHEESEMAN was never in a position in which she was expected to safeguard, or not to act against, the financial interests of another person as she never had access to their funds in work.

Question 15.11

GIVENS is a plumber who visits a house to give a quote on a job. He returns home and writes a letter to the householder asking for a £500 deposit to be sent to him. At the time he sent the letter, GIVENS had no intentions of carrying out the work and only wished to take the householder's money. The householder receives the letter but does not send any money.

In relation to s. 2 of the Fraud Act 2006 (fraud by false representation), which of the following is correct?

A The offence has been committed, and it was committed when the letter was posted.

B The offence has been committed, and it was committed when the letter was received by the householder.

C An offence has not been committed as the householder did not send any money.

D An offence has not been committed, but an attempt to commit the offence has been.

ANSWERS

Answer 15.1

Answer **C** — The fact that THORP has not actually said anything in order to accomplish the offence makes no difference. The offence can be committed by a representation that is express or *implied* and is communicated by words or *conduct*. THORP's conduct would suffice, making answer A incorrect. Answer B is incorrect as whether the cashier was fooled by THORP is immaterial. What matters is that THORP makes a representation knowing that it is false, or might be. Answer D is incorrect as the 'gain' for this offence can be for the individual or another.

Crime, para. 1.15.3

Answer 15.2

Answer **D** — The offence of possession of articles for use in frauds relates to items that will be used in the *future* to commit such offences. This removes the 'phishing' kit from the equation as it was used last week to commit an offence and therefore answer A is incorrect. The offence is committed by having possession or *control* over items (covering both the blank credit cards and blank bank statements) not only for the defendant's own use but also for use by another to commit offences of fraud, which means that both the blank credit cards and blank bank statements would be covered, making answers B and C incorrect.

Crime, para. 1.15.7

Answer 15.3

Answer **A** — The elements of the offence under s. 2 of the Fraud Act 2006 are that the defendant:

- made
- a false representation
- dishonestly
- knowing that the representation was or might be untrue or misleading
- with intent to make a gain for himself or another, to cause loss to another or to expose another to risk of loss.

In the scenario, RAMAGE makes a false statement about her friend's membership status, with the intention to deceive, knowing the statement to be untrue. PASSARO said nothing. However, a representation may also be implied by conduct, or can be by omission. PASSARO failed to mention the fact that she was not a member and her actions in walking past the receptionist as if she were a member (albeit on her friend's word) would be a false representation; answer B is therefore incorrect. The dishonesty would stem from the agreement PASSARO had with RAMAGE to dupe the gym.

It's not just a gain that makes this offence out, it also includes 'loss'; that is, losing something that one might ordinarily have obtained, in this case the entry fee—answer D is therefore incorrect. So although RAMAGE made no gain, as she would have had free entry in any case, she is compliant in an act that causes a loss to the gym; answer C is therefore incorrect.

Crime, paras 1.15.3, 1.15.4

Answer 15.4

Answer **A** — A fiduciary relationship is one relating to the responsibility of looking after someone else's money in a correct way. Looking after SORRELL's property portfolio would be such a relationship, making answer B incorrect. The offence under s. 3 (fraud by failing to disclose information) is committed when a person has a legal duty to disclose information. Such a duty can arise from oral or written contracts, making answer C incorrect. Answer D is incorrect as the harm caused by failing to disclose such information is either to make a gain or cause a loss to another (see s. 3(b) of the Act).

Crime, para. 1.15.5

Answer 15.5

Answer **C** — Section 17 of the Theft Act 1968 creates *two* offences: destroying, defacing, falsifying, etc. accounts and documents (s. 17(1)(a)); and using false or misleading accounts or documents in furnishing information (s. 17(1)(b)). An offence under s. 17 can be committed by omission as well as by an act. Failing to make an entry in an accounts book, altering a till receipt or supplying an auditor with records that are incomplete may, if accompanied by the other ingredients, amount to an offence. In *R v Shama* [1990] 1 WLR 661, the Court of Appeal upheld the conviction of a telephone operator who had failed even to start filling out standard forms provided by his employer for the recording of international calls. He was held to have falsified the forms by leaving them unmarked; answers A and D are therefore incorrect.

Unlike the offence of theft, there is no requirement to prove an intention permanently to deprive—but there is a need to show dishonesty on behalf of the accused. Answer B is therefore incorrect.

Crime, para. 1.15.10

Answer 15.6

Answer **A** — The Fraud Act 2006, s. 7 states:

> (1) A person is guilty of an offence if he makes, adapts, supplies or offers to supply any article—
>   (a) knowing that it is designed or adapted for use in the course of or in connection with fraud, or
>   (b) intending it to be used to commit, or assist in the commission of, fraud.

This offence ensures that any activity in respect of the making, supplying, etc. of any 'article' for use in fraud offences is an offence. Making an 'offer to supply' would not require the defendant to be in possession of the 'article'. Examples of such behaviour include:

- a person makes a viewing card for a satellite TV system, enabling him/her to view all satellite channels for free;
- the same person then offers to sell similar cards to work colleagues although he/she has only made the one prototype card and does not actually have further cards to sell.

So the offence is first committed with the offer to supply; answers B, C and D are therefore incorrect.

Crime, para. 1.15.8

Answer 15.7

Answer **D** — Section 11 of the Fraud Act 2006 makes it an offence for any person, by any dishonest act, to obtain services for which payment is required, with intent to avoid payment. The person must know that the services are made available on the basis that they are chargeable, or that they might be. It is not possible to commit the offence by omission alone and it can be committed only where the dishonest act was done with the intent not to pay for the services as expected. This offence replaces the offence of obtaining services by deception in s. 1 of the Theft Act 1978, though the new offence contains no deception element.

The offence is not inchoate: it requires the actual obtaining of the service. For example, data or software may be made available on the Internet to a certain category of person who has paid for access rights to that service. A person dishonestly using false credit card details or other false personal information to obtain the service would be committing an offence under this clause. However, the section would also cover a situation where a person climbs over a wall and watches a football match without paying the entrance fee—such a person is not deceiving the provider of the service directly, but is obtaining a service which is provided on the basis that people will pay for it; answer C is therefore incorrect.

However, where services obtained are free, s. 11 cannot ever be charged, no matter the circumstances and intention of the defendant. In this scenario, the services are free for those under 16, therefore anyone within that age range could not commit the offence. Proof of age is a restriction placed by the football administrators not the law. For instance, if ALBRIGHT had attempted formal entry and had been turned away because he had no proof of age with him and had then climbed the fence, he would still not be guilty of an offence under s. 11 of the 2006 Act; answers A and B are therefore incorrect.

Crime, para. 1.15.9

Answer 15.8

Answer **C** — This is one of the examples provided in your Manual as to how an offence under s. 4 of the Fraud Act 2006 (fraud by abuse of position) may be committed. The crux of the offence is the abuse of a position of trust and while this may relate to the positive action of the defendant, it can also relate to omission.

Crime, para. 1.15.6

Answer 15.9

Answer **D** — Section 8 of the Fraud Act 2006 deals with the term 'article' and this will encompass programs or data held in electronic form (such as a USB stick containing other people's credit card details). Making and selling such an item would be caught by the offence, making answers B and C incorrect in the process. Making an offer to supply an article for use in frauds is similar to the concept of making an offer to supply a drug, i.e. it does not matter whether you actually have the goods; what matters is that you made the offer. This makes answer A incorrect.

Crime, para. 1.15.7

Answer 15.10

Answer **A** — The elements of the offence under s. 4 of the Fraud Act 2006 are that the defendant:

- occupies a position in which he was expected to safeguard, or not to act against, the financial interests of another person;
- abused that position;
- dishonestly;
- intending by that abuse to make a gain/cause a loss;
- the abuse may consist of an omission rather than an act.

This offence is committed when a person 'occupying a position' abuses it by transferring information that he/she intends to use in making a gain or causing a loss. Although when CHEESEMAN actually attempts to access another person's funds she is no longer 'occupying a position', the offence was complete when she transferred the information from the work computer to her home one; answers B and C are therefore incorrect.

Even though at work she cannot access funds, she is still, as an employee of the brokers, responsible for not acting against the financial interests of the broker; answer D is therefore incorrect.

Crime, para. 1.15.6

Answer 15.11

Answer **A** — Section 2(1) of the Fraud Act 2006 states:

   (1) A person is in breach of this section if he—
      (a) dishonestly makes a false representation, and
      (b) intends, by making the representation—
         (i)   to make a gain for himself or another, or
         (ii) to cause loss to another or to expose another to the risk of loss.
   (2) A representation is false if—
      (a) it is untrue or misleading, and
      (b) the person making it knows that it is, or might be, untrue or misleading.

(3) 'Representation' means any representation as to fact or law, including a representation as to the state of mind of—
   (a) the person making the representation, or
   (b) any other person.
(4) A representation may be express or implied ...

There has certainly been a false representation, give me £500 for doing nothing!

Deception offences under the Theft Acts 1968 and 1978 required the 'target' of the deception to be deceived by the words or conduct of the defendant; if this element were not present there would only be an attempted deception. The Fraud Act 2006 removes this requirement so that where a defendant makes a false representation knowing that it is false or might be, the offence of fraud is complete; answers C and D are therefore incorrect.

The offence is complete the moment the false representation is made. The representation need never be heard or communicated to the recipient and, if carried out by post, would be complete when the letter was posted (*Treacy* v *DPP* [1971] AC 537); answer B is therefore incorrect.

Crime, para. 1.15.4

16 | Criminal Damage

QUESTIONS

Question 16.1

DYKE has a long-standing disagreement with MONK over who owns a section of land that lies between their respective houses. One evening after DYKE has been drinking at his local pub, he decides to get revenge on MONK and walks up the drive of MONK's house intent on damaging MONK's property.

At what point does DYKE first commit an offence of criminal damage (contrary to s. 1(1) of the Criminal Damage Act 1971)?

A As DYKE enters the driveway he stamps on and destroys some flowers that are growing wild at the entrance to the drive.

B DYKE passes a garden shed owned by MONK and, although he knows it will easily be washed off, he smears the word 'Wanker' in mud across the shed.

C DYKE then picks up a large container of black paint and pours this over MONK's front lawn.

D DYKE then approaches a chicken coop and reaches inside. He picks up a chicken and breaks its legs.

Question 16.2

HATTON has been arrested for a motoring offence; his detention has been authorised and he has been placed in a cell while the officers make further inquiries. HATTON is disgusted by his arrest and therefore to cause trouble and reckless as to the consequences, he places the blanket provided in his cell down the toilet in the cell. HATTON then continually flushes the toilet. When the custody sergeant makes his first check on HATTON, the concrete floor of the cell is flooded and the blanket is soaking wet.

Considering the offence of criminal damage (contrary to s. 1(1) of the Criminal Damage Act 1971), does HATTON commit the offence?

A No, HATTON would not commit criminal damage in these circumstances as both the floor and the blanket could be dried out without any resulting damage to either.

B Yes, HATTON would commit criminal damage to the blanket, but not the floor as it could be dried out undamaged.

C No, HATTON would not commit criminal damage in these circumstances as there was no intention to damage property; it was just frustration at his circumstances.

D Yes, HATTON would be guilty of criminal damage to both the blanket and the floor.

Question 16.3

MAYHEW breaks off his engagement to CUTHBERT, who takes the news badly. CUTHBERT is desperate to rekindle the relationship and phones MAYHEW telling him that unless the two of them get back together, she will steal his car, set it alight and burn herself alive in it. CUTHBERT does not intend to carry out her threat but does intend for MAYHEW to believe her. Unknown to CUTHBERT, MAYHEW has sold his car and so does not actually fear that the threat will be carried out.

Which of the following statements is correct with regard to a threat to destroy or damage property under s. 2 of the Criminal Damage Act 1971?

A CUTHBERT is not guilty of the offence because MAYHEW has sold his car and therefore knows that the threat is incapable of being carried out.

B The offence is not committed because CUTHBERT has not threatened to destroy or damage her own property.

C The offence is not committed because CUTHBERT never intended to carry out her threat.

D CUTHBERT has committed the offence because her intention was to make MAYHEW fear that the threat would be carried out.

Question 16.4

FALLON is homeless and searching for somewhere to sleep for the night. He breaks into an abandoned detached house and, using some old furniture for fuel, sets a fire that quickly burns out of control, destroying part of the house. FALLON only escapes with his life because of the rapid attendance of the fire brigade. Because of the gap between the neighbouring houses, there is no likelihood that the fire will spread to any other buildings.

Would FALLON be liable for an offence under s. 1(2) of the Criminal Damage Act 1971 (aggravated criminal damage)?

A Yes, because of FALLON's actions he recklessly endangered his own life.

B No, because FALLON did not intend to endanger his own or any other person's life.

C Yes, what matters is the potential for damage and danger created by FALLON's conduct.

D No, because the fire brigade attended and because of the gap between the houses, there was no actual danger to life.

Question 16.5

SEARLE has a lighter in his pocket and is in his own back garden. He has been having an argument with his neighbour about a shed his neighbour has recently built. SEARLE has the lighter in case his neighbour continues to argue with him about the shed. His intention is that if there is another argument he will burn the shed down.

Has SEARLE committed the offence of having articles with intent to destroy or damage property (contrary to s. 3 of the Criminal Damage Act 1971)?

A Yes, as he has an article with intent to damage or destroy the shed and is in a position to do it.

B Yes, as he has an article for use and has a conditional intention to use it.

C No, he only has conditional intent to damage or destroy the shed.

D No, as this offence is only committed in public places.

Question 16.6

FRANCIS and PICKERING are members of an animal rights group. PICKERING applied for a job in a zoo, and they planned that if he was successful, he would damage customers' cars by placing sharp tacks under the tyres. FRANCIS bought ten packets of tacks at a DIY store the day before PICKERING's interview, intending to give them to him if he got the job.

Has either person committed an offence under s. 3 of the Criminal Damage Act 1971 (having articles with intent to damage property)?

A Only FRANCIS; he has control of the articles, intending that PICKERING should use them to cause damage.

B Neither person as FRANCIS does not intend to use the articles himself to cause criminal damage.

C Both people because of their joint intent that PICKERING should use the articles to cause damage.

D Neither person as the intent to commit damage is conditional on PICKERING being successful in his interview.

Question 16.7

DENNIS works in a butcher's shop. As a joke, on 1 April he came in early and sprinkled icing sugar on some meat on display. He then left a note for his boss, claiming to be from an animal rights group, saying they had sprinkled rat poison on the food. Unfortunately, before he was able to stop him, his boss threw the meat away.

Has DENNIS committed an offence under s. 38 of the Public Order Act 1986 (contamination of goods)?

A Yes, because he has caused economic loss to his employer.

B No, because he has not caused public alarm or anxiety.

C No, because he has not actually contaminated any goods.

D No, because he only intended his employer to treat it as a joke.

Question 16.8

HARDCASTLE assists his wife in her job as a warden of a block of flats for pensioners. HARDCASTLE's wife constantly complains about the poor condition of the fire alarm and worries that if it is not changed the pensioners' lives will be in danger and there might be a large amount of damage caused to the flats if there is a fire. To demonstrate to the owner of the flats that the fire alarm is defective and needs changing, HARDCASTLE sets fire to some bedding in one of the flats. Eventually, the fire alarm activates and the fire is put out. HARDCASTLE is arrested for arson.

Would HARDCASTLE be able to claim that he had a lawful excuse to commit criminal damage?

A Yes, because the damage was caused in order to protect the property.

B No, because what has been done by HARDCASTLE is not done in order to protect property.

C Yes, because the damage was caused in order to protect the lives of the pensioners.

D No, because the element of 'lawful excuse' does not apply to offences of arson.

Question 16.9

MANNIGER is sick to death of the behaviour of SMITH who is in the habit of parking his car outside MANNIGER's house and playing his music extremely loudly and late at night causing MANNIGER to lose sleep. One evening, MANNIGER has had enough and goes out on to the street and confronts SMITH who is sitting in the driving seat of his car with his girlfriend, INCE, sitting in the front passenger seat. MANNIGER states, 'If you don't stop playing that loud music, I'll follow you home and pour paint stripper all over this car!' MANNIGER intends SMITH to fear that his car will be damaged. SMITH is completely unconcerned by the threat and does not believe MANNIGER although INCE does believe the threat.

Does MANNIGER commit the offence of threats to destroy or damage property (contrary to s. 2 of the Criminal Damage Act 1971)?

A No, the offence has not been committed as this is a 'conditional' threat (if SMITH stops playing the music, the damage will not occur).

B Yes, the offence has been committed as MANNIGER intends SMITH to fear his or another's property will be damaged.

C No, the offence has not been committed as SMITH does not believe MANNIGER.

D Yes, the offence has been committed as INCE believes that MANNIGER will carry out the threat and damage SMITH's car.

ANSWERS

Answer 16.1

Answer **B** — Under s. 10 of the Criminal Damage Act 1971, flowers growing wild on any land would not be classed as property, making answer A incorrect. The items referred to in options B, C and D would all be classed as property; land can be subject to criminal damage along with wild creatures that are ordinarily kept in captivity or have been reduced into possession (the chickens). There is no requirement that criminal damage be associated with an economic loss. It has been held by the Divisional Court that graffiti smeared in mud, even though it is easily washed off, can amount to criminal damage (*Roe* v *Kingerlee* [1986] Crim LR 735). Therefore, the offence is first committed at point B.

Crime, para. 1.16.2.2

Answer 16.2

Answer **D** — A person commits an offence if they, without lawful excuse, destroy or damage any property belonging to another intending to destroy or damage any such property or being reckless as to whether any such property will be destroyed or damaged. The case of *R* v *Fiak* [2005] EWCA Crim 2381 has the same circumstances as this question. The reality was that the blanket could not be used until it had been dried and the flooded cell was out of action until the water had been cleared. Therefore, both had sustained damage for the purposes of the Act. Making D the correct answer.

Crime, para. 1.16.2.1

Answer 16.3

Answer **D** — The central element for the commission of this offence is that the defendant *intended* the complainant to fear that the threat would be carried out. That threat can be to destroy or damage property belonging to that or another person or to destroy or damage his/her own property in a way that will endanger the life of that other or a third person, making answer B incorrect. The fact that CUTHBERT never intended to carry out her threat or that the threat is incapable of being carried out makes no difference, making answers A and C incorrect.

Crime, para. 1.16.5

Answer 16.4

Answer **C** — The aggravated form of criminal damage can only be committed if the life endangered is someone else's other than the defendant's, making answers A and B incorrect. Answer B is further incorrect as the offence can be committed recklessly. Answer D is incorrect as it does not matter that there was no *actual* danger to life. What is relevant is the *potential danger* to life.

Crime, para. 1.16.3

Answer 16.5

Answer **B** — The Criminal Damage Act 1971, s. 3 states:

A person who has anything in his custody or under his control intending without lawful excuse to use it or cause or permit another to use it—
(a) to destroy or damage any property belonging to some other person; or
(b) to destroy or damage his own or the user's property in a way which he knows is likely to endanger the life of some other person;
shall be guilty of an offence.

The key element is intention. This time the required intention is that the 'thing' is used to cause criminal damage to another's property or to the defendant's own property in a way which the defendant knows is likely to endanger the life of another. Proximity to the target is irrelevant, however; answer A is therefore incorrect.

A conditional intent (an intent to use something to cause criminal damage if the need arises) will be enough (*R v Buckingham* (1976) 63 Cr App R 159); answer C is therefore incorrect.

It is not restricted to public places and answer D is therefore incorrect.

Crime, para. 1.16.6

Answer 16.6

Answer **A** — Section 3 of the Criminal Damage Act 1971 states:

A person who has anything in his custody or under his control, intending without lawful excuse to use it or cause or permit another to use it—
(a) to destroy or damage any property belonging to some other person; or
(b) to destroy or damage his own or the user's property in a way which he knows is likely to endanger the life of some other person;
shall be guilty of an offence.

Answer B is incorrect as a person may have control of articles which he/she intends to permit another to use. Answer C is incorrect as PICKERING did not have the articles in his custody or control at any time.

Answer D is incorrect because a conditional intention to use an article if given circumstances arise will amount to an offence (*R v Buckingham* (1976) 63 Cr App R 159).

Crime, para. 1.16.6

Answer 16.7

Answer **D** — Under s. 38 of the Public Order Act 1986, it is necessary to prove that a person contaminated or interfered with goods, or made it appear that goods had been contaminated or interfered with, or threatened or claimed to have done so.

However, the person must have done so with the intention of causing public alarm or anxiety, or of causing injury to members of the public consuming or using the goods, or of causing economic loss to any person by reason of the goods being shunned by members of the public, or of causing economic loss to any person by reason of steps taken to avoid such alarm or anxiety, injury or loss.

Therefore, even though DENNIS in the circumstances may have contaminated goods, and even caused economic loss, he did not do so with the required intention and cannot be guilty of this offence. Answer A is therefore incorrect.

Had DENNIS been proved to have had the required intent, answers B and C would still be incorrect because there is no need to prove that a person actually caused public alarm/anxiety, and the offence may be committed without actually contaminating goods.

Crime, para. 1.16.7

Answer 16.8

Answer **B** — Answer D is incorrect as the element of lawful excuse is contained within the s. 1(2) offence. Section 5(2) of the Criminal Damage Act 1971 gives the circumstances when a person may have a lawful excuse to damage or destroy property. This must involve an *immediate* need for the action taken in order to protect the property and also that the means adopted were reasonable having regard to the circumstances. In this question, HARDCASTLE's activities would not fall into either of the last two categories and the element of 'lawful excuse' would not be satisfied, making answers A and C incorrect (action taken in order to draw attention to a defective fire alarm and not done in order to protect property would not be a 'lawful excuse').

Crime, para. 1.16.2.6

Answer 16.9

Answer **B** — Section 2 of the Criminal Damage Act 1971 states that:

> A person who without lawful excuse makes to another a threat, intending that that other would fear it would be carried out,—
> (a) to destroy or damage any property belonging to that other or a third person; or
> (b) to destroy or damage his own property in a way which he knows is likely to endanger the life of that other or a third person;
> shall be guilty of an offence.

This is all about the intention of the offender and has nothing whatsoever to do with the 'victim' of the offence. So the fact that SMITH does not believe MANNIGER is immaterial (making answer C incorrect). 'Conditional' threats are relevant to offences of assault but not to threats to commit criminal damage, making answer A incorrect. Answer D is incorrect as the threat was made to SMITH and not INCE. The offence is committed by a person (MANNIGER) who without lawful excuse makes to another (SMITH) a threat, intending that *that* other (SMITH not INCE) will fear it will be carried out. So the offence is committed because MANNIGER made the threat to SMITH (regardless of what INCE believes/fears—correct answer B).

Crime, para. 1.16.5

Question Checklist

The following checklist is designed to help you keep track of your progress when answering the multiple-choice questions. If you fill this in after one attempt at each question, you will be able to check how many you have got right and which questions you need to revisit a second time. Also available online; to download visit www.blackstonespoliceservice.com.

	First attempt Correct (✔)	Second attempt Correct (✔)
1 *Mens Rea* (State of Mind)		
1.1		
1.2		
1.3		
1.4		
1.5		
1.6		
2 *Actus Reus* (Criminal Conduct)		
2.1		
2.2		
2.3		
2.4		
2.5		
2.6		

	First attempt Correct (✔)	Second attempt Correct (✔)
2.7		
2.8		
2.9		
2.10		
2.11		
2.12		
3 Incomplete Offences		
3.1		
3.2		
3.3		
3.4		
3.5		
3.6		
3.7		
3.8		

	First attempt Correct (✓)	Second attempt Correct (✓)
3.9		
3.10		
3.11		
3.12		
4 General Defences		
4.1		
4.2		
4.3		
4.4		
4.5		
4.6		
4.7		
4.8		
4.9		
4.10		
4.11		
4.12		
4.13		
5 Homicide		
5.1		
5.2		
5.3		
5.4		
5.5		

	First attempt Correct (✓)	Second attempt Correct (✓)
5.6		
5.7		
5.8		
5.9		
5.10		
6 Misuse of Drugs		
6.1		
6.2		
6.3		
6.4		
6.5		
6.6		
6.7		
6.8		
6.9		
6.10		
6.11		
6.12		
6.13		
6.14		
6.15		
6.16		
6.17		
6.18		
6.19		

	First attempt Correct (✓)	Second attempt Correct (✓)
7 Firearms and Gun Crime		
7.1		
7.2		
7.3		
7.4		
7.5		
7.6		
7.7		
7.8		
7.9		
7.10		
7.11		
7.12		
7.13		
7.14		
7.15		
8 Weapons		
8.1		
8.2		
8.3		
8.4		
8.5		
8.6		
8.7		

	First attempt Correct (✓)	Second attempt Correct (✓)
8.8		
8.9		
8.10		
9 Racially and Religiously Aggravated Offences		
9.1		
9.2		
9.3		
9.4		
9.5		
9.6		
10 Non-Fatal Offences Against the Person		
10.1		
10.2		
10.3		
10.4		
10.5		
10.6		
10.7		
10.8		
10.9		
10.10		
10.11		
10.12		
10.13		

	First attempt Correct (✔)	Second attempt Correct (✔)
11 Offences Involving the Deprivation of Liberty		
11.1		
11.2		
11.3		
11.4		
11.5		
11.6		
12 Sexual Offences		
12.1		
12.2		
12.3		
12.4		
12.5		
12.6		
12.7		
12.8		
12.9		
12.10		
12.11		
12.12		
12.13		
12.14		
12.15		
12.16		

	First attempt Correct (✔)	Second attempt Correct (✔)
12.17		
12.18		
12.19		
12.20		
12.21		
12.22		
12.23		
12.24		
12.25		
13 Child Protection		
13.1		
13.2		
13.3		
13.4		
13.5		
13.6		
13.7		
13.8		
13.9		
13.10		
13.11		
13.12		
13.13		

	First attempt Correct (✔)	Second attempt Correct (✔)
14 Theft and Related Offences		
14.1		
14.2		
14.3		
14.4		
14.5		
14.6		
14.7		
14.8		
14.9		
14.10		
14.11		
14.12		
14.13		
14.14		
14.15		
14.16		
14.17		
14.18		
14.19		
14.20		
14.21		
14.22		
14.23		

	First attempt Correct (✔)	Second attempt Correct (✔)
15 Fraud		
15.1		
15.2		
15.3		
15.4		
15.5		
15.6		
15.7		
15.8		
15.9		
15.10		
15.11		
16 Criminal Damage		
16.1		
16.2		
16.3		
16.4		
16.5		
16.6		
16.7		
16.8		
16.9		